Foreword

In the rapidly evolving world of programming languages, Java stands as a testament to versatility, robustness, and longevity. Since its inception in 1995, Java has continually evolved, adapting to modern development needs while maintaining backward compatibility—a rare feat in the technology landscape. Today, Java powers everything from enterprise applications and Android devices to financial systems and scientific computing platforms.

At Re-Wise Publishers, we recognize that learning Java is not merely about mastering syntax—it's about developing a mindset that values clean, maintainable, and efficient code. This book, *Java Programming Language Mastery in 1 week*, embodies our philosophy of practical, accessible, and comprehensive education.

Why This Book Is Different

The programming book market is saturated with Java titles, yet many either overwhelm with theory or oversimplify concepts to the point of limiting practical application. This guide charts a different course:

- **Practical-First Approach**: Every concept is accompanied by runnable code examples that you can experiment with immediately. We believe in learning by doing, not just reading.
- **Modern Java Focus**: While covering fundamental principles that have stood the test of time, this book embraces **Java 21** features like records, pattern matching, and enhanced switch expressions that make modern Java development more expressive and concise.
- **Progressive Learning Path**: The book follows a carefully structured journey from basic syntax to building complete applications, ensuring that each new concept builds upon a solid foundation of understanding.
- **Real-World Context**: Abstract concepts are grounded in practical scenarios and real-world applications, helping you understand not just how Java works, but why certain approaches are preferred.
- **Common Pitfalls and Solutions**: Programming is as much about avoiding mistakes as writing correct code. Throughout these pages, you'll find highlighted sections on common errors and misconceptions, saving you countless hours of debugging frustration.

How to Use This Book

Whether you're a complete newcomer to programming or transitioning from another language, this book accommodates your learning style.

The quizzes interspersed throughout chapters serve as checkpoints for your understanding. The mini-projects build incrementally, culminating in a complete application that demonstrates how individual concepts work together in a cohesive system.

By the time you reach the final chapter, "Building a Complete Java Application," you'll have all the tools needed to design, implement, and deploy Java programs that solve real-world problems.

A Note on Modern Development

Java has evolved significantly in recent years, embracing functional programming paradigms and offering more concise syntax options. This book introduces you to both traditional and modern approaches, ensuring you can read and maintain legacy code while leveraging the latest features for new development.

The brief introduction to essential tools like IntelliJ IDEA, Maven, Gradle, and JUnit provides a foundation for professional development practices that extend beyond pure code writing.

Our Promise

At Re-Wise Publishers, we promise that by the final page of this book, you will not only understand Java syntax but will have developed the problem-solving mindset essential for success in software development. You'll be equipped to continue your journey into specialized areas of Java development, whether that's web applications, Android development, or enterprise systems.

Programming is both a science and an art—may this book help you master the science while discovering the joy in crafting elegant solutions to complex problems.

Happy coding!

The Editorial Team
Re-Wise Publishers
May 2025

Table of Contents

Chapter 1: Getting Started with Java 21

1.1 Introduction to Java

Welcome to Java programming! In this chapter, we'll cover everything you need to know to get started with Java 21, the latest Long-Term Support (LTS) version of one of the world's most popular programming languages.

What is Java?

Java is a powerful, general-purpose programming language designed with a few key principles in mind:

- **Write Once, Run Anywhere**: Java code can run on any device that has a Java Virtual Machine (JVM), regardless of the underlying hardware or operating system.
- **Object-Oriented**: Java organizes code into "objects" that bundle data and functionality together.
- **Robust and Secure**: Java includes features like strong type checking, exception handling, and automatic memory management.
- **Platform-Independent**: Unlike languages like C++, Java code doesn't compile directly to machine code but to an intermediate "bytecode" that runs on the JVM.

Think of Java as a versatile toolkit that allows you to build everything from mobile apps to enterprise software, from web applications to data analysis tools.

Java development workflow

The Java development workflow represents the journey from writing code to executing a working program. It begins with developers creating source code (.java files) in an editor or IDE. This source code is then processed by the Java compiler (javac), which translates it into platform-independent bytecode (.class files). When execution is requested, the Java Virtual Machine (JVM) loads these bytecode files, performs just-in-time compilation to machine code, and runs the program while handling memory management and security. This compile-once-run-anywhere workflow embodies Java's core philosophy of platform independence, allowing developers to write code that can run on any device with a compatible JVM installed.

Java Development Workflow

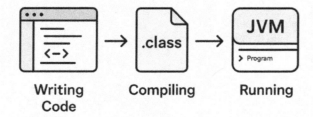

Writing Code   Compiling   Running

Before we install Java, let's understand three important components:

Component	Description	Analogy
JVM (Java Virtual Machine)	The runtime engine that executes Java bytecode	Like a translator that converts Java instructions into actions your computer understands
JRE (Java Runtime Environment)	Contains the JVM plus libraries needed to run Java applications	Like a theater with a stage (JVM) and props (libraries) needed for a performance
JDK (Java Development Kit)	Contains the JRE plus development tools like compiler, debugger, etc.	Like a complete workshop with tools (compiler) and materials (JRE) to build and run Java programs

As a developer, you'll need the JDK to write Java programs. Users who only want to run your Java application would only need the JRE.

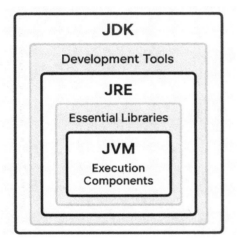

1.2 Installing Java 21 (Temurin OpenJDK)

Let's install the Temurin distribution of OpenJDK 21, which is free, open-source, and high-quality.

For Windows:

1. Visit the <u>Adoptium website</u>
2. Click "Download" and select the Windows package for Temurin JDK 21
3. Run the installer and follow the prompts
4. After installation, open Command Prompt and verify with:

```
java --version
```

For macOS:

1. Visit the <u>Adoptium website</u>

2. Download the macOS package for Temurin JDK 21
3. Run the installer and follow the prompts
4. Verify installation by opening Terminal and typing:

```
java --version
```

For Linux:

For Ubuntu/Debian:

```
sudo apt-get update
sudo apt-get install temurin-21-jdk
java --version
```

For other Linux distributions, check the Adoptium installation guides.

1.3 Setting Up Your Development Environment

While you could write Java code with a simple text editor, an Integrated Development Environment (IDE) makes coding much easier. Here are the top options:

IntelliJ IDEA

- Perfect for beginners and professionals
- Has a free Community Edition
- Download from JetBrains website

Visual Studio Code

- Lightweight and versatile
- Install the "Extension Pack for Java"
- Download from VS Code website

Eclipse

- Free and open-source
- Download from Eclipse website

For this guide, I recommend IntelliJ IDEA Community Edition for its beginner-friendly features and excellent Java support.

1.4 Your First Java Program

Let's create and run a simple Java program to make sure everything is set up correctly:

1. Open your IDE
2. Create a new Java project named "HelloJava"
3. Create a new Java class file named "HelloWorld.java"
4. Type the following code:

```
public class HelloWorld {
    public static void main(String[] args) {
        System.out.println("Hello, Java 21!");
    }
}
```

5. Run the program (usually by clicking the "Run" button or pressing Ctrl+Shift+F10 in IntelliJ)

If you see "Hello, Java 21!" printed in the output console, congratulations! You've successfully set up Java and run your first program.

Understanding the Code

Let's break down what each part of this simple program does:

- `public class HelloWorld { ... }`: Defines a class named HelloWorld. In Java, everything exists within classes.
- `public static void main(String[] args) { ... }`: This is the main method, the entry point of your program. When you run a Java program, execution starts here.
- `System.out.println("Hello, Java 21!");`: Prints the text "Hello, Java 21!" to the console.

1.5 Common Mistakes to Avoid

- **Incorrect Capitalization**: Java is case-sensitive. `System` works, but `system` will cause an error.
- **Missing Semicolons**: Almost every statement in Java ends with a semicolon (`;`).
- **Mismatched Braces**: Every opening brace `{` needs a matching closing brace `}`.

 Quiz: Test Your Understanding

1. Which component do you need to install to develop Java applications?
   - A) JVM
   - B) JRE
   - C) JDK
   - D) Java Compiler
2. What does the following code do?
3. `System.out.println("Java " + 2 + 1);`
   - A) Prints "Java 21"
   - B) Prints "Java 3"
   - C) Causes an error
   - D) Prints "3 Java"
4. In Java, where must the execution of a program begin?
   - A) Any method named "start"
   - B) The first line of code in the file
   - C) The main method

- o D) A method named "init"

1.7 What's Next?

In the next chapter, we'll dive into Java variables, data types, and basic operations - the fundamental building blocks for any Java program. You'll learn how to store and manipulate different kinds of data, and start building more complex programs.

 FAQ

Q: Why is Java platform-independent?

A: Java achieves platform independence through its "Write Once, Run Anywhere" philosophy. Java code is compiled into bytecode, which can run on any device with a Java Virtual Machine. The JVM acts as an interpreter between the bytecode and the underlying hardware/operating system.

Q: Do I need to pay for Java?

A: No, OpenJDK distributions like Temurin are completely free and open-source for both personal and commercial use.

Q: Is Java 21 the latest version of Java?

A: Java has a six-month release cycle, so newer versions may be available. However, Java 21 is an LTS (Long-Term Support) version, meaning it will receive updates and support for several years, making it ideal for learning.

Q: I've heard Java is verbose and difficult. Is that true?

A: Java can be more verbose than some modern languages, but this explicitness helps prevent errors and makes code more readable. Modern Java features have reduced verbosity while maintaining Java's core strengths.

Answers
1. C) JDK - The Java Development Kit includes everything needed to develop Java applications.
2. A) Prints "Java 21" - The + operator concatenates strings, so 2 and 1 are treated as strings, not numbers to be added.
3. C) The main method - Every Java application starts execution from the main method.

Chapter 2: Java Fundamentals - Variables, Data Types, and Operators

2.1 Introduction to Java Variables

In this chapter, we'll explore how Java stores and manipulates data - the foundation of any program you'll write. Think of variables as labeled containers that hold values your program can use and change.

2.2 Variables in Java

A variable is a named storage location in your computer's memory. In Java, every variable has:

- A name (identifier)
- A data type
- A value

Declaring Variables

Before using a variable in Java, you must declare it by specifying its type and name:

```
int age;  // Declares an integer variable named 'age'
```

Initializing Variables

Initializing means assigning an initial value to a variable:

```
int age = 25;  // Declares and initializes 'age' to 25
```

You can also declare first and initialize later:

```
String name;      // Declaration
name = "Maria";   // Initialization
```

Variable Naming Rules

When naming variables in Java:

- Names can contain letters, digits, underscores (_), and dollar signs ($)
- Names must begin with a letter, underscore, or dollar sign (not a digit)
- Names are case-sensitive (age and Age are different variables)
- Names cannot be Java keywords like class or int

9

- Use camelCase for variable names (start with lowercase, capitalize subsequent words)
- Choose descriptive names that explain the variable's purpose
- Avoid single-letter names except for temporary variables

```
// Good variable names
int userAge = 25;
double hourlyWage = 15.50;
boolean isActive = true;

// Avoid names like these
int a = 25;
double d = 15.50;
boolean b = true;
```

2.3 Data Types in Java

Java is a statically-typed language, meaning every variable must have a declared type that cannot change. Java has two categories of data types:

Primitive Data Types

Primitive types store simple values directly. Java has eight primitive data types:

Data Type	Description	Size	Example
byte	Very small integer	8 bits	byte smallNum = 127;
short	Small integer	16 bits	short mediumNum = 32000;
int	Integer (whole number)	32 bits	int population = 37500;
long	Large integer	64 bits	long worldPop = 8000000000L;
float	Single-precision floating point	32 bits	float price = 19.99f;
double	Double-precision floating point	64 bits	double precise = 19.99876;
char	Single character	16 bits	char grade = 'A';
boolean	True or false value	1 bit	boolean isValid = true;

Common Mistakes with Primitives:

- Forgetting the L suffix for long literals
- Forgetting the f suffix for float literals
- Confusing single quotes (for char) with double quotes (for String)

Reference Data Types

Reference types store references (memory addresses) to objects rather than the actual data. The most commonly used reference type is String:

```
String message = "Hello, Java!";
```

Other reference types include arrays, classes, and interfaces, which we'll explore in later chapters.

2.4 Using Modern Java: The `var` Keyword

Since Java 10, you can use the `var` keyword for local variable type inference:

```
// Instead of:
String greeting = "Hello";

// You can use:
var greeting = "Hello";   // Java infers that greeting is a String
```

The compiler determines the type based on the assigned value. This reduces verbosity while maintaining Java's type safety.

Best Practice: Use `var` when the type is obvious from the context or initialization, but use explicit types when clarity is needed.

2.5 Basic Operations in Java

Now that we can store data, let's learn how to manipulate it.

Arithmetic Operators

Operator	Description	Example
+	Addition	`int sum = 5 + 3;` // 8
-	Subtraction	`int diff = 5 - 3;` // 2
*	Multiplication	`int product = 5 * 3;` // 15
/	Division	`int quotient = 15 / 3;` // 5
%	Modulus (remainder)	`int remainder = 5 % 2;` // 1

Common Mistake: Integer division in Java truncates decimal values. To get a decimal result, at least one operand must be a floating-point type:

```
int x = 5;
int y = 2;
System.out.println(x / y);   // Outputs 2, not 2.5

// To get 2.5:
System.out.println((double)x / y);   // Outputs 2.5
```

Assignment Operators

Operator	Description	Example	Equivalent
=	Simple assignment	x = 5;	x = 5;
+=	Add and assign	x += 3;	x = x + 3;
-=	Subtract and assign	x -= 3;	x = x - 3;
*=	Multiply and assign	x *= 3;	x = x * 3;
/=	Divide and assign	x /= 3;	x = x / 3;
%=	Modulus and assign	x %= 3;	x = x % 3;

Increment and Decrement Operators

Operator	Description	Example
++	Increment by 1	x++; or ++x;
--	Decrement by 1	x--; or --x;

The position of these operators matters:

- ++x (prefix): Increments x first, then uses the value
- x++ (postfix): Uses the current value of x, then increments it

```
int a = 5;
int b = ++a;   // a is now 6, b is 6

int c = 5;
int d = c++;   // c is now 6, but d is 5 (old value of c)
```

Comparison Operators

Used to compare values, always resulting in a boolean value (true or false):

Operator	Description	Example
==	Equal to	x == y
!=	Not equal to	x != y
>	Greater than	x > y
<	Less than	x < y
>=	Greater than or equal to	x >= y
<=	Less than or equal to	x <= y

Critical Mistake Alert: When comparing objects (like String), the == operator checks if they refer to the same object in memory, not if they have the same content. For content comparison, use the .equals() method:

```
String str1 = "Hello";
String str2 = "Hello";
String str3 = new String("Hello");
```

12

```
System.out.println(str1 == str2);        // true (Java optimizes identical string
literals)
System.out.println(str1 == str3);        // false (different objects in memory)
System.out.println(str1.equals(str3));   // true (same content)
```

Logical Operators

Used to combine boolean expressions:

Operator	Description	Example
&&	Logical AND	(x > 5) && (y < 10)
|	Logical OR	(x > 5) || (y < 10)
!	Logical NOT	!(x > 5)

Short-Circuit Evaluation: In && expressions, if the first condition is false, the second won't be evaluated. In || expressions, if the first condition is true, the second won't be evaluated.

Working with Strings

Strings are sequences of characters and are among the most commonly used types in Java.

String Creation

```
// String literal
String name = "Alice";

// Using the String constructor
String name2 = new String("Bob");

// Empty string
String empty = "";
```

String Operations

```
String firstName = "John";
String lastName = "Doe";

// Concatenation using +
String fullName = firstName + " " + lastName;   // "John Doe"

// String length
int length = fullName.length();   // 8

// Getting a character at a specific position (zero-indexed)
char firstChar = firstName.charAt(0);   // 'J'

// Substring (from index 0 to 3, excluding 4)
String sub = firstName.substring(0, 4);   // "John"
```

13

```java
// Converting case
String upper = firstName.toUpperCase();   // "JOHN"
String lower = firstName.toLowerCase();   // "john"

// Checking if a string contains another string
boolean contains = fullName.contains("ohn");   // true

// Replacing parts of a string
String replaced = firstName.replace('J', 'T');   // "Tohn"

// Modern Java: String concatenation with formatted strings
String formatted = String.format("%s %s", firstName, lastName);   // "John Doe"

// Java 15 and later: Text blocks for multi-line strings
String html = """
            <html>
                <body>
                    <h1>Hello, Java!</h1>
                </body>
            </html>
            """;
```

Modern Java: Immutable Collections

Java 9 introduced convenient factory methods for creating immutable collections:

```java
// Create an immutable List
var names = List.of("Alice", "Bob", "Charlie");

// Create an immutable Set
var uniqueNames = Set.of("Alice", "Bob", "Charlie");

// Create an immutable Map
var ages = Map.of("Alice", 25, "Bob", 30, "Charlie", 35);
```

2.6 Type Conversion in Java

Sometimes you need to convert values from one type to another:

Implicit Conversion (Widening)

Java automatically converts a smaller type to a larger type:

```java
int intValue = 100;
long longValue = intValue;      // Automatically converts int to long
float floatValue = longValue;   // Automatically converts long to float
double doubleValue = floatValue;   // Automatically converts float to double
```

Explicit Conversion (Narrowing/Casting)

Converting a larger type to a smaller one requires explicit casting:

```java
double doubleValue = 9.78;
int intValue = (int) doubleValue;  // Explicitly cast double to int (9)
```

Warning: Casting can lose information (precision or magnitude).

Practical Example: Basic Calculator

Let's put everything together with a simple calculator program:

```java
public class SimpleCalculator {
    public static void main(String[] args) {
        // Declare and initialize variables
        double num1 = 10.5;
        double num2 = 5.0;

        // Perform calculations
        double sum = num1 + num2;
        double difference = num1 - num2;
        double product = num1 * num2;
        double quotient = num1 / num2;
        double remainder = num1 % num2;

        // Display results using string concatenation
        System.out.println("Number 1: " + num1);
        System.out.println("Number 2: " + num2);
        System.out.println("Sum: " + sum);
        System.out.println("Difference: " + difference);
        System.out.println("Product: " + product);
        System.out.println("Quotient: " + quotient);
        System.out.println("Remainder: " + remainder);

        // Using modern Java text block and formatted string (Java 15+)
        String output = """
                    Results with formatted output:
                    %s + %s = %s
                    %s - %s = %s
                    %s * %s = %s
                    %s / %s = %s
                    """.formatted(num1, num2, sum,
                            num1, num2, difference,
                            num1, num2, product,
                            num1, num2, quotient);

        System.out.println(output);
    }
}
```

2.7 Debugging Tips

When working with variables and operators, common issues include:

1. **Uninitialized Variables**: Always initialize variables before using them.
2. **Integer Division Truncation**: Use at least one floating-point number when you need decimal precision.
3. **Type Mismatch**: Ensure you're using compatible types in operations.
4. **String Comparison**: Use `.equals()` to compare String content, not `==`.

 Quiz: Test Your Understanding

1. What will be the output of the following code?

```
int x = 5;
int y = 2;
double z = x / y;
System.out.println(z);
```

A) 2.5
B) 2.0
C) 2
D) Error

2. Which statement correctly declares and initializes a character variable?

A) char letter = "A";
B) char letter = 'A';
C) Character letter = 'A';
D) char letter = A;

3. What's the value of `result` after executing the following code?

```
int a = 10;
int b = a++;
int c = ++a;
int result = b + c;
```

A) 20
B) 22
C) 23
D) 24

4. Which of the following is the correct way to create an immutable list in modern Java?

A) List<String> names = new ArrayList<>("Alice", "Bob");
B) List<String> names = Arrays.asList("Alice", "Bob");

16

C) List<String> names = List.of("Alice", "Bob");

D) var names = {"Alice", "Bob"};

What's Next?

In the next chapter, we'll explore control flow in Java - how to make decisions with if-else statements and switch expressions, and how to repeat code with loops. These tools will allow you to create more dynamic and responsive programs!

 FAQ

Q: When should I use primitive types vs. reference types?

A: Use primitive types (int, double, etc.) for simple values. They're more efficient. Use reference types when you need object behavior (methods) or when the concept is more complex than a single value.

Q: What's the difference between double and float?

A: Both store decimal numbers, but double has higher precision (15-17 significant digits) than float (6-7 digits). Use double unless you have specific memory constraints.

Q: Should I always use var instead of explicit types?

A: Not always. Use var when the type is obvious from the initialization. Use explicit types when clarity is more important or when the initialization doesn't clearly indicate the type.

Q: Why does my program show unexpected results with floating-point calculations?

A: Floating-point arithmetic in computers can lead to tiny precision errors. For financial calculations or when exact precision is needed, consider using BigDecimal (we'll cover this in a later chapter).

Answers:

1. 3) 2.0 - Integer division results in 2, which is then converted to a double (2.0) when assigned to z.

2. B) char letter = 'A'; - Character literals use single quotes in Java.
3. C) 23 - a starts at 10, a++ sets b to 10 and increments a to 11, ++a increments a to 12 and sets c to 12, so b + c = 10 + 12 = 22.
4. C) List<String> names = List.of("Alice", "Bob"); - This is the modern way to create immutable lists in Java 9+.

Chapter 3: Core Programming Constructs - Control Flow and Loops

3.1 Introduction to Control Flow

So far, our Java programs have executed line by line from top to bottom. But real-world programs need to make decisions and repeat actions. This is where control flow structures come in, allowing your code to:

1. Make decisions using conditional statements
2. Repeat code using loops
3. Jump to different parts of the program

Think of control flow as giving your program a brain to make decisions rather than blindly following instructions.

3.2 Conditional Statements

The if Statement

The if statement is the most basic decision-making structure. It executes a block of code only if a condition is true:

```java
int temperature = 28;

if (temperature > 25) {
    System.out.println("It's hot today!");
}
```

In this example, "It's hot today!" will only print if the temperature is greater than 25.

The if-else Statement

You can extend the if statement with an else clause that executes when the condition is false:

```java
int hour = 20;

if (hour < 12) {
    System.out.println("Good morning!");
} else {
```

19

```
    System.out.println("Good day!");
}
```

Since 20 is not less than 12, this code will print "Good day!".

The `if-else-if` Ladder

For multiple conditions, use the `if-else-if` ladder:

```
int score = 85;

if (score >= 90) {
    System.out.println("Grade: A");
} else if (score >= 80) {
    System.out.println("Grade: B");
} else if (score >= 70) {
    System.out.println("Grade: C");
} else if (score >= 60) {
    System.out.println("Grade: D");
} else {
    System.out.println("Grade: F");
}
```

This code will output "Grade: B" since 85 is between 80 and 90.

Nested `if` Statements

You can also place an `if` statement inside another `if` statement:

```
boolean isWeekend = true;
boolean isRaining = true;

if (isWeekend) {
    if (isRaining) {
        System.out.println("Stay home and read a book.");
    } else {
        System.out.println("Go for a hike!");
    }
} else {
    System.out.println("Go to work.");
}
```

This will print "Stay home and read a book." since both conditions are true.

Common Mistakes with Conditionals

1. **Using = instead of ==**: The = operator assigns values, while == compares them.

```
// WRONG
```

```
if (x = 5) { ... }  // This assigns 5 to x, doesn't check equality

// CORRECT
if (x == 5) { ... }  // This checks if x equals 5
```

2. **Forgetting curly braces**: Without braces, only the next statement is part of the conditional block.

```
// Potentially WRONG (depending on intention)
if (isRaining)
    System.out.println("Take an umbrella.");
    System.out.println("Wear  boots.");   // This  always  executes  regardless  of
isRaining

// CORRECT
if (isRaining) {
    System.out.println("Take an umbrella.");
    System.out.println("Wear boots.");   // This only executes if isRaining is true
}
```

3. **Complex conditions without parentheses**: Always use parentheses to make the order clear.

```
// UNCLEAR
if (a > b && c > d || e > f) { ... }

// CLEAR
if ((a > b && c > d) || e > f) { ... }
```

The switch Statement

The switch statement tests a variable against multiple values:

```
int day = 3;
String dayName;

switch (day) {
    case 1:
        dayName = "Monday";
        break;
    case 2:
        dayName = "Tuesday";
        break;
    case 3:
        dayName = "Wednesday";
        break;
    case 4:
        dayName = "Thursday";
        break;
    case 5:
        dayName = "Friday";
        break;
    case 6:
```

21

```
            dayName = "Saturday";
            break;
        case 7:
            dayName = "Sunday";
            break;
        default:
            dayName = "Invalid day";
            break;
}

System.out.println(dayName);   // Outputs "Wednesday"
```

The break statement is crucial – without it, execution "falls through" to the next case.

Modern Java: switch Expressions (Java 12+)

Java 12 introduced enhanced switch statements that can return values:

```
int day = 3;

String dayName = switch (day) {
    case 1 -> "Monday";
    case 2 -> "Tuesday";
    case 3 -> "Wednesday";
    case 4 -> "Thursday";
    case 5 -> "Friday";
    case 6 -> "Saturday";
    case 7 -> "Sunday";
    default -> "Invalid day";
};

System.out.println(dayName);   // Outputs "Wednesday"
```

Notice how this modern syntax:

- Uses arrow (->) instead of colons and break
- Returns a value directly
- Requires no break statements
- Is more concise and prevents fall-through errors

For multiple statements in a case, use a code block:

```
String dayType = switch (day) {
    case 1, 2, 3, 4, 5 -> {
        System.out.println("It's a weekday");
        yield "Weekday";  // The 'yield' keyword returns a value from a block
    }
    case 6, 7 -> {
        System.out.println("It's a weekend");
```

```
        yield "Weekend";
    }
    default -> "Invalid day";
};
```

3.3 Loops

Loops allow you to execute a block of code repeatedly. Java provides several types of loops.

The `for` Loop

The `for` loop is ideal when you know exactly how many times you want to execute a block of code:

```
// Print numbers from 1 to 5
for (int i = 1; i <= 5; i++) {
    System.out.println(i);
}
```

A `for` loop has three parts:

1. **Initialization**: `int i = 1;` (executed once at the beginning)
2. **Condition**: `i <= 5;` (checked before each iteration)
3. **Update**: `i++` (executed after each iteration)

Loop through an Array

Arrays (which we'll cover in depth later) can be easily traversed with a `for` loop:

```
String[] fruits = {"Apple", "Banana", "Cherry"};

for (int i = 0; i < fruits.length; i++) {
    System.out.println(fruits[i]);
}
```

The Enhanced `for` Loop (for-each)

Java provides a simpler way to iterate through arrays and collections:

```
String[] fruits = {"Apple", "Banana", "Cherry"};

for (String fruit : fruits) {
    System.out.println(fruit);
}
```

This is more readable but doesn't give you the index of the current element.

The `while` Loop

23

The `while` loop executes as long as a condition is true:

```
int count = 1;

while (count <= 5) {
    System.out.println(count);
    count++;
}
```

Use `while` loops when you don't know in advance how many iterations you need.

The do-while Loop

Similar to the `while` loop, but the condition is checked after the loop body executes, ensuring the body runs at least once:

```
int count = 1;

do {
    System.out.println(count);
    count++;
} while (count <= 5);
```

This will print numbers 1 through 5, just like the `while` loop example above.

Nested Loops

You can place loops inside other loops:

```
// Print a multiplication table for 1-5
for (int i = 1; i <= 5; i++) {
    for (int j = 1; j <= 5; j++) {
        System.out.printf("%d x %d = %d\n", i, j, i * j);
    }
    System.out.println("-----------");
}
```

Loop Control Statements

Java provides statements to alter the flow of loops:

The break Statement

The `break` statement exits the loop immediately:

```
for (int i = 1; i <= 10; i++) {
    if (i == 5) {
        break;  // Exit the loop when i reaches 5
```

```
    }
    System.out.println(i);
}
```

This will print numbers 1 through 4 only.

The continue Statement

The continue statement skips the current iteration and proceeds to the next one:

```
for (int i = 1; i <= 10; i++) {
    if (i % 2 == 0) {
        continue;   // Skip even numbers
    }
    System.out.println(i);
}
```

This will print only odd numbers: 1, 3, 5, 7, 9.

Common Loop Mistakes

1. **Infinite Loops**: Forgetting to update the loop variable or using an always-true condition.

```
// WRONG: Infinite loop
for (int i = 1; i >= 0; i++) {
    System.out.println(i);   // This will run forever (until int overflow)
}

// WRONG: Infinite loop
while (true) {
    // No break condition inside
}
```

2. **Off-by-one errors**: Starting or ending the loop at the wrong index.

```
// WRONG: If you want 1 to 10
for (int i = 0; i < 10; i++) {   // This gives 0 to 9
    System.out.println(i);
}

// CORRECT: For 1 to 10
for (int i = 1; i <= 10; i++) {
    System.out.println(i);
}
```

3. **Modifying loop variables inside the loop body**:

```
// WRONG: Unpredictable behavior
for (int i = 0; i < 10; i++) {
```

```
        System.out.println(i);
        i++;  // Skips values because i is also incremented in the for-loop expression
}
```

3.4 Practical Example: A Simple Menu System

Let's combine conditional statements and loops to create a menu-driven program:

```java
import java.util.Scanner;

public class MenuSystem {
    public static void main(String[] args) {
        Scanner scanner = new Scanner(System.in);
        boolean isRunning = true;

        while (isRunning) {
            // Display menu
            System.out.println("\n===== CALCULATOR MENU =====");
            System.out.println("1. Add two numbers");
            System.out.println("2. Subtract two numbers");
            System.out.println("3. Multiply two numbers");
            System.out.println("4. Divide two numbers");
            System.out.println("5. Exit");
            System.out.print("Enter your choice (1-5): ");

            // Get user choice
            int choice = scanner.nextInt();

            // Process the choice
            switch (choice) {
                case 1 -> {
                    System.out.print("Enter first number: ");
                    double num1 = scanner.nextDouble();
                    System.out.print("Enter second number: ");
                    double num2 = scanner.nextDouble();
                    System.out.printf("Result: %.2f + %.2f = %.2f\n", num1, num2,
num1 + num2);
                }
                case 2 -> {
                    System.out.print("Enter first number: ");
                    double num1 = scanner.nextDouble();
                    System.out.print("Enter second number: ");
                    double num2 = scanner.nextDouble();
                    System.out.printf("Result: %.2f - %.2f = %.2f\n", num1, num2,
num1 - num2);
                }
                case 3 -> {
                    System.out.print("Enter first number: ");
                    double num1 = scanner.nextDouble();
                    System.out.print("Enter second number: ");
                    double num2 = scanner.nextDouble();
```

```java
                    System.out.printf("Result: %.2f * %.2f = %.2f\n", num1, num2,
num1 * num2);
                }
                case 4 -> {
                    System.out.print("Enter first number: ");
                    double num1 = scanner.nextDouble();
                    System.out.print("Enter second number: ");
                    double num2 = scanner.nextDouble();
                    if (num2 == 0) {
                        System.out.println("Error: Cannot divide by zero");
                    } else {
                        System.out.printf("Result: %.2f / %.2f = %.2f\n", num1,
num2, num1 / num2);
                    }
                }
                case 5 -> {
                    System.out.println("Thank you for using the calculator!");
                    isRunning = false;  // Exit the loop
                }
                default -> System.out.println("Invalid choice. Please enter a number
between 1 and 5.");
            }
        }

        scanner.close();
    }
}
```

This program:

1. Uses a `while` loop to keep the program running until the user chooses to exit
2. Uses a `switch` expression (modern Java) to handle different menu options
3. Demonstrates input validation with the division case
4. Shows how to use `break` effectively (through setting the boolean flag)

3.5 Debugging Control Flow Issues

When working with control flow structures, these debugging tips can help:

1. **Use print statements to trace execution**: Add `System.out.println()` statements to see which branches of your code are being executed.
2. **Check boundary conditions**: Verify that your conditions handle edge cases correctly (empty collections, zero values, etc.).
3. **Watch for infinite loops**: If your program seems to freeze, you may have an infinite loop. Check your loop conditions and make sure your loop variables are being updated correctly.
4. **Use the debugger**: Most Java IDEs include a debugger that lets you set breakpoints and examine variables as your code executes. This is much more powerful than print statements for complex issues.

1. What will the following code print?

```java
int x = 10;
if (x > 5) {
    System.out.print("A");
    if (x > 15) {
        System.out.print("B");
    } else {
        System.out.print("C");
    }
} else {
    System.out.print("D");
}
```

   A) A

   B) AC

   C) AB

   D) D

2. How many times will "Hello" be printed in this code?

```java
for (int i = 0; i < 5; i++) {
    if (i % 2 == 0) {
        continue;
    }
    System.out.println("Hello");
}
```

   A) 5 times

   B) 3 times

   C) 2 times

   D) 0 times

3. What is the output of this code?

```java
int day = 3;
String result = switch(day) {
    case 1, 2, 3, 4, 5 -> "Weekday";
    case 6, 7 -> "Weekend";
    default -> "Invalid day";
};
System.out.println(result);
```

   A) 3

   B) Weekday

   C) Invalid day

D) Compilation error

4. What will be printed by this code?

```java
int i = 1;
while (i <= 5) {
    if (i == 3) {
        i++;
        continue;
    }
    System.out.print(i + " ");
    i++;
}
```

A) 1 2 3 4 5

B) 1 2 4 5

C) 1 2 3

D) 1 2 4

What's Next?

In the next chapter, we'll delve into methods and functions in Java. You'll learn how to organize your code into reusable blocks, pass parameters, return values, and leverage method overloading. Methods are crucial for making your code more modular, maintainable, and reusable.

 FAQ

Q: When should I use a `for` loop versus a `while` loop?

A: Use a `for` loop when you know in advance how many iterations you need. Use a `while` loop when the number of iterations depends on a condition that might change during execution.

Q: What's the difference between `break` and `continue`?

A: `break` exits the loop entirely, while `continue` skips the current iteration and moves to the next one.

Q: Can I use `switch` statements with String variables?

A: Yes, since Java 7, `switch` statements (and expressions) can use String variables as well as primitive types like int, char, and enum types.

Q: Are there any performance differences between different types of loops?

A: Generally, the performance differences are minimal and you should choose the loop type based on readability and the specific use case. For collections, the enhanced for-each loop is often preferred for simplicity.

Answers:

1. B) AC - x is greater than 5 but not greater than 15, so both A and C are printed.
2. C) 2 times - The continue statement skips the print for i values 0, 2, and 4, so "Hello" is printed only for i values 1 and 3.
3. B) Weekday - The switch expression returns "Weekday" for day values from 1 to 5.
4. B) 1 2 4 5 - When i equals 3, the loop skips the print statement and increments i to 4.

Chapter 4: Object-Oriented Programming Basics

4.1 Introduction to Object-Oriented Programming

So far, we've been writing code that follows a procedural approach, executing statements in sequence. Now we'll explore one of Java's most powerful features: object-oriented programming (OOP).

Object-oriented programming is a programming paradigm built around the concept of "objects" that contain both data (fields/attributes) and behaviors (methods). Java is designed from the ground up with OOP principles in mind.

Think of objects as real-world entities. For example, a car has:

- **Properties/Attributes**: color, model, engine size, current speed
- **Behaviors**: accelerate, brake, turn, honk

In Java, we use classes to define the blueprint for creating objects. Let's dive into how this works.

4.2 Classes and Objects

Creating a Class

A class is like a blueprint that defines what properties and behaviors an object will have.

For instance a cookie cutter creates objects that have a certain shape and size.

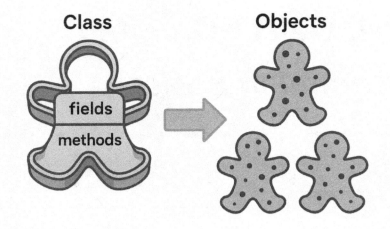

Class   **Objects**

Sample program with another analogy of a car:

```java
public class Car {
    // Fields (attributes/properties)
    String color;
    String model;
    int year;
    double currentSpeed;

    // Methods (behaviors)
    void accelerate(double amount) {
        currentSpeed += amount;
        System.out.println("Accelerating to " + currentSpeed + "
mph");
    }

    void brake(double amount) {
        currentSpeed = Math.max(0, currentSpeed - amount);
        System.out.println("Slowing down to " + currentSpeed + "
mph");
    }

    void honk() {
        System.out.println("Beep beep!");
    }
}
```

Creating Objects (Instances of a Class)

Once you have defined a class, you can create objects (instances) from it:

```
public class CarExample {
    public static void main(String[] args) {
        // Create two Car objects
        Car myCar = new Car();
        Car friendsCar = new Car();

        // Set attributes for myCar
        myCar.color = "Blue";
        myCar.model = "Tesla Model 3";
        myCar.year = 2023;
        myCar.currentSpeed = 0;

        // Set attributes for friendsCar
        friendsCar.color = "Red";
        friendsCar.model = "Toyota Prius";
        friendsCar.year = 2020;
        friendsCar.currentSpeed = 0;

        // Use behaviors
        System.out.println("My " + myCar.color + " " + myCar.model
+ " is starting to move.");
        myCar.accelerate(35.5);
        myCar.honk();
        myCar.brake(15.0);

        System.out.println("\nMy friend's " + friendsCar.color + "
" + friendsCar.model + " is also on the road.");
        friendsCar.accelerate(45.0);
        friendsCar.brake(20.0);
    }
}
```

When you run this program, you'll see how two different Car objects behave independently.

Object-Oriented Terminology

- **Class**: The blueprint or template that defines properties and behaviors
- **Object**: An instance of a class
- **Fields/Attributes/Properties**: Variables that store data inside a class
- **Methods**: Functions that define the behaviors of a class
- **Instance**: Another term for an object created from a class

4.3 Constructors

Constructors are special methods that initialize new objects. They have the same name as the class and don't specify a return type.

Default Constructor

If you don't define any constructors, Java provides a default constructor that takes no arguments and initializes fields to their default values:

```
Car myCar = new Car();  // Using the default constructor
```

Custom Constructors

You can define your own constructors to initialize objects with specific values:

```java
public class Car {
    String color;
    String model;
    int year;
    double currentSpeed;

    // Constructor
    public Car(String carColor, String carModel, int carYear) {
        color = carColor;
        model = carModel;
        year = carYear;
        currentSpeed = 0;  // Starting speed is always 0
    }

    // Methods remain the same
    void accelerate(double amount) {
        currentSpeed += amount;
        System.out.println("Accelerating to " + currentSpeed + " mph");
    }

    void brake(double amount) {
        currentSpeed = Math.max(0, currentSpeed - amount);
        System.out.println("Slowing down to " + currentSpeed + " mph");
    }

    void honk() {
        System.out.println("Beep beep!");
    }
}
```

Now we can create cars with initial values:

```java
// Create cars using our constructor
Car myCar = new Car("Blue", "Tesla Model 3", 2023);
Car friendsCar = new Car("Red", "Toyota Prius", 2020);
```

You can provide multiple constructors to initialize objects in different ways:

```java
public class Car {
    String color;
    String model;
    int year;
    double currentSpeed;

    // Constructor with all parameters
    public Car(String color, String model, int year, double startSpeed) {
        this.color = color;        // Note the use of "this" to distinguish
        this.model = model;        // between parameters and class fields
        this.year = year;          // that have the same name
        this.currentSpeed = startSpeed;
    }

    // Constructor with default speed of 0
    public Car(String color, String model, int year) {
        this.color = color;
        this.model = model;
        this.year = year;
        this.currentSpeed = 0;
    }

    // No-argument constructor with default values
    public Car() {
        this.color = "Unknown";
        this.model = "Generic";
        this.year = 2023;
        this.currentSpeed = 0;
    }

    // Methods remain the same
    void accelerate(double amount) {
        currentSpeed += amount;
        System.out.println("Accelerating to " + currentSpeed + " mph");
    }

    void brake(double amount) {
        currentSpeed = Math.max(0, currentSpeed - amount);
        System.out.println("Slowing down to " + currentSpeed + " mph");
    }

    void honk() {
        System.out.println("Beep beep!");
    }
}
```

The this Keyword

The `this` keyword refers to the current object. It's often used to distinguish between class fields and parameters with the same name, as shown in the constructors above.

Constructor Chaining with `this()`

You can call one constructor from another using `this()`:

```java
public class Car {
    String color;
    String model;
    int year;
    double currentSpeed;

    // Primary constructor
    public Car(String color, String model, int year, double startSpeed) {
        this.color = color;
        this.model = model;
        this.year = year;
        this.currentSpeed = startSpeed;
    }

    // Constructor that calls the primary constructor
    public Car(String color, String model, int year) {
        this(color, model, year, 0);  // Calls the constructor with 4 parameters
    }

    // No-argument constructor that calls another constructor
    public Car() {
        this("Unknown", "Generic", 2023);  // Calls the constructor with 3 parameters
    }

    // Methods remain the same
    void accelerate(double amount) {
        currentSpeed += amount;
        System.out.println("Accelerating to " + currentSpeed + " mph");
    }

    void brake(double amount) {
        currentSpeed = Math.max(0, currentSpeed - amount);
        System.out.println("Slowing down to " + currentSpeed + " mph");
    }

    void honk() {
        System.out.println("Beep beep!");
    }
}
```

Constructor chaining helps reduce code duplication and makes your code more maintainable.

4.4 Encapsulation and Access Modifiers

Encapsulation is one of the four fundamental OOP concepts (along with inheritance, polymorphism, and abstraction). It refers to bundling data and methods that operate on that data within a single unit (class) and restricting access to some of the object's components.

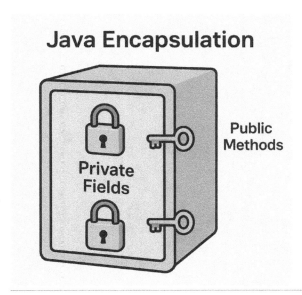

The above image shows how a class acts as a container with private fields protected inside and public methods as interfaces to access those fields. It uses a secure box metaphor with locks that only open via specific keys (methods).

Access Modifiers

Java provides four access modifiers to control the visibility of classes, methods, and fields:

Modifier	Class	Package	Subclass	World
public	Yes	Yes	Yes	Yes
protected	Yes	Yes	Yes	No
default (no modifier)	Yes	Yes	No	No
private	Yes	No	No	No

Encapsulation with Private Fields and Public Methods

A best practice in Java is to make fields private and provide public methods to access and modify them (getters and setters):

```java
public class Car {
    // Private fields (encapsulated)
    private String color;
    private String model;
    private int year;
    private double currentSpeed;
```

```java
// Public constructors
public Car(String color, String model, int year) {
    this.color = color;
    this.model = model;
    this.year = year;
    this.currentSpeed = 0;
}

// Getter methods
public String getColor() {
    return color;
}

public String getModel() {
    return model;
}

public int getYear() {
    return year;
}

public double getCurrentSpeed() {
    return currentSpeed;
}

// Setter methods
public void setColor(String color) {
    this.color = color;
}

public void setModel(String model) {
    this.model = model;
}

public void setYear(int year) {
    if (year > 1885) { // First automobile was invented in 1885
        this.year = year;
    } else {
        System.out.println("Invalid year provided.");
    }
}

// No setter for currentSpeed - it can only be changed through accelerate/brake

// Behavior methods
public void accelerate(double amount) {
    if (amount > 0) {
        currentSpeed += amount;
        System.out.println("Accelerating to " + currentSpeed + " mph");
    }
}
```

```java
    public void brake(double amount) {
        if (amount > 0) {
            currentSpeed = Math.max(0, currentSpeed - amount);
            System.out.println("Slowing down to " + currentSpeed + " mph");
        }
    }

    public void honk() {
        System.out.println("Beep beep!");
    }
}
```

Benefits of Encapsulation

1. **Data Hiding**: Internal state of objects is protected from direct external modification
2. **Validation**: You can validate input before setting field values
3. **Flexibility**: You can change the internal implementation without affecting code that uses your class
4. **Read-Only or Write-Only**: You can make fields read-only or write-only as needed

Using the Encapsulated Class

```java
public class EncapsulationExample {
    public static void main(String[] args) {
        Car myCar = new Car("Blue", "Tesla Model 3", 2023);

        // Access using getters
        System.out.println("My car details:");
        System.out.println("Color: " + myCar.getColor());
        System.out.println("Model: " + myCar.getModel());
        System.out.println("Year: " + myCar.getYear());
        System.out.println("Current Speed: " + myCar.getCurrentSpeed() + " mph");

        // Modify using setters
        myCar.setColor("Midnight Blue");

        // Invalid year - validation prevents the change
        myCar.setYear(1800);

        // Try to set a negative year
        myCar.setYear(2024);

        // Check the changes
        System.out.println("\nAfter modifications:");
        System.out.println("Color: " + myCar.getColor());
        System.out.println("Year: " + myCar.getYear());

        // Use methods that modify the speed
        myCar.accelerate(60);
        myCar.brake(25);
    }
}
```

39

In Java, members (fields and methods) can belong to either the class itself or instances of the class.

Instance Members

Instance members belong to individual objects of the class. Each object has its own copy of instance fields and can call instance methods.

```java
public class Car {
    // Instance fields - each Car object has its own copies
    private String color;
    private double currentSpeed;

    // Instance method - operates on a specific Car object
    public void accelerate(double amount) {
        currentSpeed += amount;
    }
}
```

Static (Class) Members

Static members belong to the class itself, not to individual objects. All instances of the class share the same static fields and methods.

```java
public class Car {
    // Instance fields - each Car object has its own copies
    private String color;
    private double currentSpeed;

    // Static field - shared across all Car objects
    private static int totalCarsCreated = 0;

    // Constructor that increments the static counter
    public Car(String color) {
        this.color = color;
        this.currentSpeed = 0;
        totalCarsCreated++;  // Increment the static counter
    }

    // Static method to get the total number of cars created
    public static int getTotalCarsCreated() {
        return totalCarsCreated;
    }

    // Instance method
    public void accelerate(double amount) {
        currentSpeed += amount;
    }
```

```
}
```

Using static members:

```
public class StaticExample {
    public static void main(String[] args) {
        // Access static method directly through class name
        System.out.println("Total cars before: " + Car.getTotalCarsCreated());

        // Create car objects
        Car car1 = new Car("Red");
        Car car2 = new Car("Blue");
        Car car3 = new Car("Green");

        // Access static method again
        System.out.println("Total cars after: " + Car.getTotalCarsCreated());

        // You can also access static members through objects, but this is not
recommended
        System.out.println("Total    cars    (through    car1):    "    +
car1.getTotalCarsCreated());
    }
}
```

When to Use Static Members

- Use static fields for properties shared by all instances of a class
- Use static methods for operations that don't depend on instance state
- Common examples include counters, utility methods, and constants

```
public class MathUtils {
    // Static constant
    public static final double PI = 3.14159265359;

    // Static utility method
    public static double calculateCircleArea(double radius) {
        return PI * radius * radius;
    }

    // Static utility method
    public static double calculateCircleCircumference(double radius) {
        return 2 * PI * radius;
    }
}
```

You can use these without creating an instance of MathUtils:

```
double area = MathUtils.calculateCircleArea(5);
double circumference = MathUtils.calculateCircleCircumference(5);
System.out.println("PI value: " + MathUtils.PI);
```

Common Mistakes with Static and Instance Members

1. **Accessing instance variables from static methods:**

```java
public class Mistake {
    private int x = 10;

    // WRONG: Static method trying to access instance field
    public static void printX() {
        System.out.println(x);   // Compilation error
    }
}
```

2. **Using `this` in static methods:**

```java
public class Mistake {
    // WRONG: 'this' refers to an instance, but there is no instance in static
context
    public static void printMessage() {
        System.out.println(this.toString());   // Compilation error
    }
}
```

3. **Creating utility classes with instance methods:**

```java
// BETTER: All methods are static since they don't depend on instance state
public class MathUtils {
    public static double square(double x) {
        return x * x;
    }
}

// WORSE: Forces unnecessary object creation for utility methods
public class MathUtils {
    public double square(double x) {
        return x * x;
    }
}
```

4.6 Modern Java Features for Classes

Records (Java 16+)

Records are a compact way to declare classes that are primarily used to store data (like DTOs - Data Transfer Objects):

```java
// Traditional class with boilerplate code
public class Person {
    private final String name;
    private final int age;

    public Person(String name, int age) {
```

42

```java
        this.name = name;
        this.age = age;
    }

    public String getName() { return name; }
    public int getAge() { return age; }

    @Override
    public boolean equals(Object o) {
        if (this == o) return true;
        if (o == null || getClass() != o.getClass()) return false;
        Person person = (Person) o;
        return age == person.age && Objects.equals(name, person.name);
    }

    @Override
    public int hashCode() {
        return Objects.hash(name, age);
    }

    @Override
    public String toString() {
        return "Person{name='" + name + "', age=" + age + "}";
    }
}

// Equivalent record definition (Java 16+)
public record Person(String name, int age) {
    // All boilerplate code above is generated automatically!
}
```

Records automatically generate:

- Constructor
- Accessor methods (like `name()` and `age()` instead of `getName()` and `getAge()`)
- `equals()`, `hashCode()`, and `toString()`

Records are immutable by default (all fields are `final`).

Using a Record

```java
public class RecordExample {
    public static void main(String[] args) {
        Person person = new Person("Alice", 30);

        // Access fields using accessor methods
        System.out.println("Name: " + person.name());
        System.out.println("Age: " + person.age());

        // toString() is automatically implemented
        System.out.println(person);
```

43

```
        // equals() is automatically implemented
        Person person2 = new Person("Alice", 30);
        System.out.println("Are equal? " + person.equals(person2));
    }
}
```

Custom methods in Records

You can add custom methods to records:

```
public record Person(String name, int age) {
    // Custom method
    public boolean isAdult() {
        return age >= 18;
    }

    // Custom constructor that validates input
    public Person {
        if (age < 0) {
            throw new IllegalArgumentException("Age cannot be negative");
        }
    }
}
```

Records are perfect for simple data-carrying classes but remember they have limitations:

- All fields are final (immutable)
- Records cannot extend other classes
- Records cannot be extended by other classes

4.7 Practical Example: Building a Bank Account System

Let's bring all these concepts together with a practical example of a bank account system:

```
public class BankAccount {
    // Static (class) field to keep track of all accounts
    private static int totalAccounts = 0;

    // Instance fields
    private String accountNumber;
    private String ownerName;
    private double balance;
    private boolean active;

    // Constructor
    public BankAccount(String ownerName, double initialDeposit) {
        this.accountNumber = generateAccountNumber();
        this.ownerName = ownerName;
        this.balance = Math.max(0, initialDeposit);
```

44

```java
        this.active = true;
        totalAccounts++;
    }

    // Private helper method to generate account numbers
    private String generateAccountNumber() {
        return "ACCT-" + (1000 + totalAccounts);
    }

    // Static method to get total account count
    public static int getTotalAccounts() {
        return totalAccounts;
    }

    // Instance methods
    public void deposit(double amount) {
        if (!active) {
            System.out.println("Cannot deposit to inactive account.");
            return;
        }

        if (amount <= 0) {
            System.out.println("Deposit amount must be positive.");
            return;
        }

        balance += amount;
        System.out.printf("Deposited $%.2f. New balance: $%.2f\n", amount, balance);
    }

    public void withdraw(double amount) {
        if (!active) {
            System.out.println("Cannot withdraw from inactive account.");
            return;
        }

        if (amount <= 0) {
            System.out.println("Withdrawal amount must be positive.");
            return;
        }

        if (amount > balance) {
            System.out.println("Insufficient funds.");
            return;
        }

        balance -= amount;
        System.out.printf("Withdrew $%.2f. New balance: $%.2f\n", amount, balance);
    }

    public void closeAccount() {
        if (balance > 0) {
```

```java
            System.out.printf("Returning remaining balance of $%.2f to customer.\n",
balance);
        }
        active = false;
        balance = 0;
        System.out.println("Account closed.");
    }

    // Getters
    public String getAccountNumber() {
        return accountNumber;
    }

    public String getOwnerName() {
        return ownerName;
    }

    public double getBalance() {
        return balance;
    }

    public boolean isActive() {
        return active;
    }

    // No setter for accountNumber (shouldn't change)
    // No setter for balance (should only change via deposit/withdraw)

    // Setters
    public void setOwnerName(String ownerName) {
        this.ownerName = ownerName;
    }

    // toString method for better printing
    @Override
    public String toString() {
        return String.format("Account %s - Owner: %s, Balance: $%.2f, Status: %s",
                accountNumber, ownerName, balance, active ? "Active" : "Inactive");
    }
}
```

Now let's use our bank account class:

```java
public class BankDemo {
    public static void main(String[] args) {
        System.out.println("Creating bank accounts...");
        System.out.println("Total accounts: " + BankAccount.getTotalAccounts());

        // Create accounts
        BankAccount aliceAccount = new BankAccount("Alice Johnson", 1000);
        BankAccount bobAccount = new BankAccount("Bob Williams", 500);

        System.out.println("Total accounts: " + BankAccount.getTotalAccounts());
```

46

```java
        // Display initial states
        System.out.println("\nInitial account states:");
        System.out.println(aliceAccount);
        System.out.println(bobAccount);

        // Perform some transactions
        System.out.println("\nPerforming transactions...");
        aliceAccount.deposit(250);
        bobAccount.withdraw(100);

        // Try some invalid operations
        aliceAccount.withdraw(2000);   // More than balance
        bobAccount.deposit(-50);       // Negative amount

        // Update an account owner name
        bobAccount.setOwnerName("Robert Williams");

        // Display updated states
        System.out.println("\nUpdated account states:");
        System.out.println(aliceAccount);
        System.out.println(bobAccount);

        // Close an account
        System.out.println("\nClosing Bob's account...");
        bobAccount.closeAccount();

        // Try operations on closed account
        bobAccount.deposit(100);
        bobAccount.withdraw(50);

        // Final states
        System.out.println("\nFinal account states:");
        System.out.println(aliceAccount);
        System.out.println(bobAccount);
    }
}
```

 Quiz: Test Your Understanding

---

1. **What does the following code print?**

```java
public class Counter {
    private static int count = 0;

    public Counter() {
        count++;
```

```java
    public static int getCount() {
        return count;
    }
}

public class Main {
    public static void main(String[] args) {
        Counter c1 = new Counter();
        Counter c2 = new Counter();
        Counter c3 = new Counter();
        System.out.println(Counter.getCount());
    }
}
```

A) 0

B) 1

C) 3

D) Compilation error

2. Which access modifier makes a field visible only within its own class?

A) public

B) protected

C) private

D) default

3. What is the output of this code?

```java
public class Test {
    private String name;

    public Test() {
        this("Unknown");
        System.out.print("A");
    }

    public Test(String name) {
        this.name = name;
        System.out.print("B");
    }

    public static void main(String[] args) {
        Test test = new Test();
    }
}
```

A) A

B) B

C) BA

D) AB

4. Which of the following is true about Java records?

A) Records can extend other classes
B) Record fields can be modified after creation
C) Records automatically generate equals, hashCode, and toString methods
D) Records were introduced in Java 8

4.9 What's Next?

In the next chapter, we'll explore inheritance and polymorphism - powerful OOP concepts that allow you to create hierarchies of classes, reuse code, and make your programs more flexible and extensible.

 FAQ

Q: When should I make a field or method static?

A: Make a field static when it should be shared across all instances of a class (like a counter or configuration value). Make a method static when it doesn't depend on instance state and operates solely on its parameters or other static fields.

Q: What's the difference between encapsulation and information hiding?

A: Encapsulation is the practice of bundling data and methods together, while information hiding is the principle of restricting access to certain components. Encapsulation is a mechanism for achieving information hiding.

Q: Should I always provide getters and setters for all fields?

A: Not necessarily. Provide getters for values that should be readable and setters for values that should be modifiable. Some fields might need only getters (read-only) or only setters (write-only), and some might need neither.

Q: When should I use records instead of regular classes?

A: Use records when you need simple data carrier classes with immutable fields. They're perfect for DTOs, value objects, or any situation where you mainly need to store and transport data rather than define complex behaviors.

Answers:

1. C) 3 - The static count variable is shared by all instances and incremented three times.
2. C) private - Private members are only accessible within the class that defines them.
3. C) BA - The constructor calls another constructor using this("Unknown"), which prints B first, then continues with the original constructor and prints A.
4. C) Records automatically generate equals, hashCode, and toString methods - Records provide automatic implementations of these methods based on the record's components.

Chapter 5: Inheritance and Polymorphism

5.1 Introduction to Inheritance

Inheritance is one of the fundamental concepts in object-oriented programming that allows us to create new classes based on existing ones. Think of inheritance like a family tree: children inherit traits from their parents while adding their own unique characteristics.

What is Inheritance?

Inheritance is a mechanism where a new class (called the **subclass** or **child class**) inherits properties and behaviors (fields and methods) from an existing class (called the **superclass** or **parent class**).

Java Inheritance

```
         Parent class
   void method1() {
   void method2() { }
              │ extends
   ┌──────────┼──────────┐
   ▼          ▼          ▼
Child class  Child class  Child class
void        void         void
method1()   method3()    method3()
{ }         {            {
void        extends →    void
method2()   { }          method2()
{ }                      {
```

Real-world Analogy

Think of inheritance like vehicle models. A "Vehicle" class might define basic properties like having wheels and the ability to move. Then, more specific vehicles like "Car" and "Bicycle" inherit these general properties while adding their own unique features.

Benefits of Inheritance

1. **Code Reusability**: Reuse fields and methods of existing classes
2. **Extensibility**: Extend functionality of existing classes without modifying them

51

3. **Hierarchical Classification**: Organize classes in a logical hierarchy
4. **Method Overriding**: Change or enhance behavior of superclass methods

Inheritance Syntax in Java

```java
// Superclass (parent class)
public class Vehicle {
    // fields and methods
}


// Subclass (child class) extends the superclass
public class Car extends Vehicle {
    // additional fields and methods
    // plus inherited fields and methods from Vehicle
}
```

5.2 Creating Parent and Child Classes

Let's create a practical example of inheritance:

```java
// Parent class
public class Vehicle {
    // Protected fields can be accessed by subclasses
    protected String brand;
    protected String model;
    protected int year;

    // Constructor
    public Vehicle(String brand, String model, int year) {
        this.brand = brand;
        this.model = model;
        this.year = year;
    }

    // Method
    public void displayInfo() {
        System.out.println("Vehicle: " + year + " " + brand + " " + model);
    }

    public void start() {
        System.out.println("The vehicle is starting...");
    }
}

// Child class
public class Car extends Vehicle {
    // Additional field for Car
    private int numDoors;

    // Constructor
    public Car(String brand, String model, int year, int numDoors) {
```

```java
        // Call the parent constructor using super()
        super(brand, model, year);
        this.numDoors = numDoors;
    }

    // Additional method specific to Car
    public void honk() {
        System.out.println("Beep beep!");
    }
}
```

Let's see how we can use these classes:

```java
public class InheritanceDemo {
    public static void main(String[] args) {
        // Create a Vehicle object
        Vehicle vehicle = new Vehicle("Generic", "Transport", 2023);
        vehicle.displayInfo(); // Output: Vehicle: 2023 Generic Transport
        vehicle.start();       // Output: The vehicle is starting...

        // Create a Car object
        Car car = new Car("Toyota", "Corolla", 2023, 4);
        car.displayInfo();       // Output: Vehicle: 2023 Toyota Corolla (inherited
method)
        car.start();             // Output: The vehicle is starting... (inherited
method)
        car.honk();              // Output: Beep beep! (Car's own method)
    }
}
```

Important Points About Inheritance

- A subclass inherits all **public** and **protected** members (fields, methods, nested classes) from its superclass
- **Private** members are not inherited
- Constructors are not inherited, but the parent constructor can be called using `super()`
- In Java, a class can only extend one class (single inheritance for classes)
- All Java classes inherit from `Object` class implicitly if no other superclass is specified

5.3 The `super` Keyword

The `super` keyword refers to the parent class and is used to:

1. Call the parent class constructor
2. Access parent class methods
3. Access parent class fields

Calling Parent Constructor

```java
public class ElectricCar extends Car {
    private int batteryCapacity;
```

53

```java
    public ElectricCar(String brand, String model, int year, int numDoors, int
batteryCapacity) {
        // Call parent constructor first
        super(brand, model, year, numDoors);
        this.batteryCapacity = batteryCapacity;
    }
}
```

Accessing Parent Methods

```java
public class Car extends Vehicle {
    // ...

    // Override the displayInfo method
    @Override
    public void displayInfo() {
        // Call the parent's displayInfo method
        super.displayInfo();
        // Add more information specific to Car
        System.out.println("Number of doors: " + numDoors);
    }
}
```

Common Mistakes with super

- **Forgetting to call super constructor**: If the parent class doesn't have a no-argument constructor, you must explicitly call a parent constructor using `super()`
- **Using super after statements**: The call to `super()` must be the first statement in a constructor
- **Using super in a static context**: The `super` keyword cannot be used in static methods

5.4 Method Overriding

Method overriding allows a subclass to provide a specific implementation of a method that is already defined in its superclass.

Rules for Method Overriding

1. The method in the subclass must have the same name as in the superclass
2. The method must have the same parameter list
3. The return type must be the same or a subtype of the return type declared in the superclass
4. The access level cannot be more restrictive than the overridden method
5. The method cannot throw new or broader checked exceptions

Method Overriding Example

```java
// Parent class
public class Vehicle {
    // ...

    public void start() {
        System.out.println("The vehicle is starting...");
```

54

```
        }
}

// Child class
public class Car extends Vehicle {
    // ...

    // Override the start method
    @Override
    public void start() {
        System.out.println("Insert key, turn ignition, and press gas pedal");
    }
}

// Another child class
public class ElectricCar extends Car {
    // ...

    // Override the start method again
    @Override
    public void start() {
        System.out.println("Press the start button");
    }
}
```

Usage example:

```
public class OverridingDemo {
    public static void main(String[] args) {
        Vehicle vehicle = new Vehicle();
        Car car = new Car("Toyota", "Corolla", 2023, 4);
        ElectricCar tesla = new ElectricCar("Tesla", "Model 3", 2023, 4, 75);

        // Each object uses its own implementation of start()
        vehicle.start(); // Output: The vehicle is starting...
        car.start();     // Output: Insert key, turn ignition, and press gas pedal
        tesla.start();   // Output: Press the start button
    }
}
```

The @Override Annotation

The @Override annotation is not required, but it's a good practice to use it when overriding methods because:

1. It clearly communicates your intent to override a method
2. It helps prevent errors - if the method doesn't actually override a superclass method, the compiler will generate an error

5.5 Polymorphism

Polymorphism means "many forms" and is one of the most powerful features of OOP. It allows objects of different classes to be treated as objects of a common superclass.

Types of Polymorphism

1. **Compile-time Polymorphism** (Method Overloading): Multiple methods with the same name but different parameters
2. **Runtime Polymorphism** (Method Overriding): Objects determining which method implementation to use at runtime

Runtime Polymorphism Example

```java
public class PolymorphismDemo {
    public static void main(String[] args) {
        // Create an array of Vehicle references
        Vehicle[] vehicles = new Vehicle[3];

        // Assign different types of vehicles to the array
        vehicles[0] = new Vehicle("Generic", "Transport", 2023);
        vehicles[1] = new Car("Toyota", "Corolla", 2023, 4);
        vehicles[2] = new ElectricCar("Tesla", "Model 3", 2023, 4, 75);

        // Polymorphic behavior - the appropriate start() method is called
        // based on the actual object type, not the reference type
        for (Vehicle v : vehicles) {
            System.out.print(v.getClass().getSimpleName() + ": ");
            v.start();
        }
    }
}
```

Output:

```
Vehicle: The vehicle is starting...
Car: Insert key, turn ignition, and press gas pedal
ElectricCar: Press the start button
```

Real-world Application of Polymorphism

Polymorphism is extremely useful in creating flexible and extensible applications:

```java
// A method that works with any Vehicle type
public void performMaintenance(Vehicle vehicle) {
    System.out.println("Performing maintenance on:");
    vehicle.displayInfo();

    // The correct implementation will be called based on the actual object type
    vehicle.start();

    // Special handling for specific vehicle types
    if (vehicle instanceof Car car) {
```

56

```java
    // Using pattern matching for instanceof (Java 16+)
    car.honk();
    }
}
```

5.6 Abstract Classes

An abstract class is a class that cannot be instantiated directly and is designed to be subclassed. It can contain both abstract methods (methods without implementation) and concrete methods (methods with implementation).

Why Use Abstract Classes?

1. To provide a common interface while forcing subclasses to provide implementations for certain methods
2. To share code among closely related classes
3. To define a template for a group of subclasses

Abstract Class Example

```java
// Abstract class
public abstract class Shape {
    // Fields
    protected String color;

    // Constructor
    public Shape(String color) {
        this.color = color;
    }

    // Concrete method
    public String getColor() {
        return color;
    }

    // Abstract methods (no implementation)
    public abstract double calculateArea();
    public abstract double calculatePerimeter();
}

// Concrete subclass
public class Circle extends Shape {
    private double radius;

    public Circle(String color, double radius) {
        super(color);
        this.radius = radius;
    }

    // Implement abstract methods
    @Override
    public double calculateArea() {
```

57

```java
            return Math.PI * radius * radius;
        }

        @Override
        public double calculatePerimeter() {
            return 2 * Math.PI * radius;
        }
    }

// Another concrete subclass
public class Rectangle extends Shape {
    private double length;
    private double width;

    public Rectangle(String color, double length, double width) {
        super(color);
        this.length = length;
        this.width = width;
    }

    @Override
    public double calculateArea() {
        return length * width;
    }

    @Override
    public double calculatePerimeter() {
        return 2 * (length + width);
    }
}
```

Usage:

```java
public class AbstractClassDemo {
    public static void main(String[] args) {
        // Shape shape = new Shape("Red"); // Error: Cannot instantiate abstract
class

        Shape circle = new Circle("Red", 5.0);
        Shape rectangle = new Rectangle("Blue", 4.0, 6.0);

        System.out.println("Circle area: " + circle.calculateArea());
        System.out.println("Rectangle area: " + rectangle.calculateArea());

        // Polymorphism with abstract classes
        printShapeInfo(circle);
        printShapeInfo(rectangle);
    }

    public static void printShapeInfo(Shape shape) {
        System.out.println("Shape type: " + shape.getClass().getSimpleName());
```

```
        System.out.println("Color: " + shape.getColor());
        System.out.println("Area: " + shape.calculateArea());
        System.out.println("Perimeter: " + shape.calculatePerimeter());
        System.out.println();
    }
}
```

Key Points About Abstract Classes

- Cannot be instantiated directly
- May contain abstract methods (methods without implementation)
- May also contain concrete methods (methods with implementation)
- Subclasses must implement all abstract methods unless the subclass is also abstract
- Can have constructors, fields, and normal methods

5.7 Interfaces

An interface is a completely abstract type that defines a contract of methods and constants. Classes implement interfaces to guarantee they provide specific functionality.

Why Use Interfaces?

1. To define a common behavior that can be implemented by unrelated classes
2. To achieve multiple inheritance of type (a class can implement multiple interfaces)
3. To separate what needs to be done from how it's done

Interface Basics

```java
// Define an interface
public interface Drivable {
    // Constants (implicitly public, static, and final)
    int MAX_SPEED = 120;

    // Abstract methods (implicitly public and abstract)
    void accelerate(int speed);
    void brake();

    // Default method (introduced in Java 8)
    default void honk() {
        System.out.println("Beep!");
    }

    // Static method (introduced in Java 8)
    static boolean isSpeedLegal(int speed) {
        return speed <= MAX_SPEED;
    }
}

// Implementing the interface
public class SportsCar implements Drivable {
    private int currentSpeed = 0;
```

59

```java
    @Override
    public void accelerate(int speed) {
        currentSpeed += speed;
        System.out.println("Sports car accelerating to " + currentSpeed + " km/h");
    }

    @Override
    public void brake() {
        currentSpeed = 0;
        System.out.println("Sports car coming to a complete stop");
    }

    // We can also override the default method
    @Override
    public void honk() {
        System.out.println("Sports car honks loudly!");
    }
}
```

Multiple Interface Implementation

Unlike classes, a class can implement multiple interfaces:

```java
// Another interface
public interface Chargeable {
    void charge();
    int getBatteryLevel();
}

// Class implementing multiple interfaces
public class ElectricSportsCar extends Vehicle implements Drivable, Chargeable {
    private int batteryLevel = 0;
    private int currentSpeed = 0;

    public ElectricSportsCar(String brand, String model, int year) {
        super(brand, model, year);
    }

    // Implementing Drivable methods
    @Override
    public void accelerate(int speed) {
        if (batteryLevel > 0) {
            currentSpeed += speed;
            batteryLevel -= speed / 10;
            System.out.println("Electric car accelerating to " + currentSpeed + "
km/h");
        } else {
            System.out.println("Cannot accelerate - battery is empty");
        }
    }
```

```java
    @Override
    public void brake() {
        currentSpeed = 0;
        System.out.println("Electric car stopped");
    }

    // Implementing Chargeable methods
    @Override
    public void charge() {
        batteryLevel = 100;
        System.out.println("Battery fully charged");
    }

    @Override
    public int getBatteryLevel() {
        return batteryLevel;
    }
}
```

Interface vs. Abstract Class

Feature	Interface	Abstract Class
Multiple inheritance	A class can implement multiple interfaces	A class can extend only one abstract class
State	Cannot have state (instance variables) except for constants	Can have state (instance variables)
Constructor	Cannot have constructors	Can have constructors
Method implementation	Can have default and static methods (Java 8+)	Can have concrete methods
Access modifiers	All methods are implicitly public	Can have methods with any access modifier
Purpose	Define a contract of behavior	Define a template for subclasses

5.8 Interface Default Methods (Java 8+)

Starting with Java 8, interfaces can have default methods with implementation. This allows adding new methods to interfaces without breaking existing implementations.

```java
public interface Playable {
    void play();

    // Default method with implementation
    default void pause() {
        System.out.println("Paused playback");
    }
```

```java
    default void stop() {
        System.out.println("Stopped playback");
    }
}

public class MusicPlayer implements Playable {
    @Override
    public void play() {
        System.out.println("Playing music");
    }

    // No need to implement pause() and stop() as they have default implementations
}
```

Interface Static Methods (Java 8+)

Interfaces can also have static methods, which belong to the interface itself rather than to objects that implement the interface:

```java
public interface MathOperations {
    // Static method
    static int add(int a, int b) {
        return a + b;
    }

    static int subtract(int a, int b) {
        return a - b;
    }
}

// Usage
public class MathDemo {
    public static void main(String[] args) {
        // Call static interface methods directly
        System.out.println(MathOperations.add(5, 3));      // Output: 8
        System.out.println(MathOperations.subtract(5, 3)); // Output: 2
    }
}
```

5.9 Interface Private Methods (Java 9+)

Starting with Java 9, interfaces can have private methods to help organize code within the interface:

```java
public interface Logger {
    default void logInfo(String message) {
        log(message, "INFO");
    }

    default void logError(String message) {
        log(message, "ERROR");
    }
```

```
    // Private helper method - only accessible within the interface
    private void log(String message, String level) {
        System.out.println(level + ": " + message);
    }
}
```

5.10 Common Inheritance & Polymorphism Patterns

1. Template Method Pattern

Abstract classes often implement the Template Method pattern, where a method in the parent class calls abstract methods that are implemented by subclasses:

```
public abstract class DataProcessor {
    // Template method
    public final void processData() {
        readData();
        processData();
        saveResults();
    }

    // Abstract methods to be implemented by subclasses
    protected abstract void readData();
    protected abstract void processData();
    protected abstract void saveResults();
}
```

2. Strategy Pattern Using Interfaces

Interfaces are perfect for implementing the Strategy pattern, which enables selecting an algorithm at runtime:

```
// Strategy interface
public interface SortingStrategy {
    void sort(int[] array);
}

// Concrete strategies
public class BubbleSort implements SortingStrategy {
    @Override
    public void sort(int[] array) {
        System.out.println("Sorting using bubble sort");
        // Bubble sort implementation
    }
}

public class QuickSort implements SortingStrategy {
    @Override
    public void sort(int[] array) {
```

```java
        System.out.println("Sorting using quick sort");
        // Quick sort implementation
    }
}

// Context class
public class Sorter {
    private SortingStrategy strategy;

    public void setStrategy(SortingStrategy strategy) {
        this.strategy = strategy;
    }

    public void sortArray(int[] array) {
        strategy.sort(array);
    }
}
```

5.11 Common Mistakes and Best Practices

Common Mistakes

1. **Overextending inheritance hierarchies**: Creating too deep hierarchies makes code harder to understand and maintain
2. **Using inheritance for code reuse only**: Use composition instead if there's no true "is-a" relationship
3. **Forgetting to call super constructor**: If parent has no default constructor, you must explicitly call another constructor
4. **Improper method overriding**: Mistakes in method signature or access modifiers
5. **Confusing overriding and overloading**: Overriding replaces a method, overloading adds a new one

Best Practices

1. **Favor composition over inheritance**: When possible, use object composition rather than inheritance
2. **Design for inheritance or prohibit it**: Either design your class carefully for extension or declare it final
3. **Program to interfaces, not implementations**: Depend on abstractions rather than concrete classes
4. **Use the Liskov Substitution Principle**: Subtypes should be substitutable for their base types
5. **Keep interfaces small and focused**: Create many small interfaces rather than a few large ones
6. **Use abstract classes for "is-a" relationships with common behavior**
7. **Use interfaces for cross-cutting behaviors**: When behavior needs to be applied to otherwise unrelated classes

 Quiz: Test Your Understanding

1. What keyword is used to define a subclass in Java?
   - a) `implements`
   - b) `extends`

- o c) `inherits`
- o d) `subclass`

2. Which of the following is NOT inherited from a superclass?
    - o a) Protected methods
    - o b) Public fields
    - o c) Constructors
    - o d) Public methods

3. What is the output of the following code?

```java
class Animal {
    public void makeSound() {
        System.out.println("Animal makes a sound");
    }
}

class Dog extends Animal {
    @Override
    public void makeSound() {
        System.out.println("Dog barks");
    }
}

public class Main {
    public static void main(String[] args) {
        Animal myPet = new Dog();
        myPet.makeSound();
    }
}
```

- a) "Animal makes a sound"
- b) "Dog barks"
- c) Compilation error
- d) Runtime error

4. Which statement about abstract classes is false?
    - o a) Abstract classes can have constructors
    - o b) Abstract classes can be instantiated directly
    - o c) Abstract classes can have both abstract and non-abstract methods
    - o d) A class can extend only one abstract class

5. How many interfaces can a class implement in Java?
    - o a) Only one
    - o b) Two at most
    - o c) Multiple interfaces
    - o d) None if it already extends a class

 FAQ

65

Q1: What's the difference between "extends" and "implements"?

A: `extends` is used to inherit from a class (either concrete or abstract), while `implements` is used to implement an interface. A class can extend only one class but can implement multiple interfaces.

Q2: Can I prevent a method from being overridden?

A: Yes, you can use the `final` keyword to prevent a method from being overridden:

```
public final void methodName() {
    // Method implementation
}
```

Q3: Can an interface extend another interface?

A: Yes, an interface can extend one or more other interfaces using the `extends` keyword:

```
public interface AdvancedDrivable extends Drivable {
    void activateTurbo();
}
```

Q4: What is the "diamond problem" in inheritance?

A: The diamond problem occurs in multiple inheritance when a class inherits from two classes that both inherit from a common base class. Java avoids this problem by not allowing multiple inheritance of classes, only of interfaces.

Q5: What happens if a class implements two interfaces with the same default method?

A: This creates an ambiguity, and the class must override the default method to resolve it:

```
public interface A {
    default void show() {
        System.out.println("A");
    }
}

public interface B {
    default void show() {
        System.out.println("B");
    }
}

public class C implements A, B {
    // Must override show() to resolve the conflict
    @Override
    public void show() {
        // Can call either implementation if needed
```

```
        A.super.show();
        // or
        B.super.show();
        // or provide a completely new implementation
    }
}
```

Exercise: Build a Simple Banking System Using Inheritance and Polymorphism

Design a simple banking system with the following requirements:

1. Create an abstract `Account` class with:
   - Account number, balance, and owner name
   - Abstract method `calculateInterest()`
   - Concrete methods `deposit()` and `withdraw()`
2. Create subclasses:
   - `SavingsAccount` with higher interest rate but withdrawal limitations
   - `CheckingAccount` with lower interest rate but no withdrawal limitations
   - `FixedDepositAccount` with highest interest rate but fixed term
3. Create an interface `Transferable` with methods:
   - `transferTo(Account destination, double amount)`
   - `canTransfer(double amount)`
4. Make appropriate accounts implement the `Transferable` interface
5. Create a test class to demonstrate polymorphism by creating different account types and processing them uniformly

Answers to Quiz:

1. b) extends
2. c) Constructors
3. b) "Dog barks"
4. b) Abstract classes can be instantiated directly
5. c) Multiple interfaces

Chapter 6: Exception Handling

6.1 Introduction to Exceptions

When you're writing Java programs, things don't always go as planned. Files might be missing, network connections could drop, or users might enter invalid data. Exception handling is how Java deals with these unexpected situations gracefully.

What Are Exceptions?

An **exception** is an event that disrupts the normal flow of a program's instructions. When an error occurs, Java creates an exception object and "throws" it.

Real-world Analogy

Think of exceptions like fire alarms in a building. When something goes wrong (smoke is detected), the alarm (exception) is triggered. The building (your program) has a predefined evacuation plan (exception handler) to deal with the emergency in an orderly way rather than panicking.

Why Exception Handling Is Important

1. **Separation of error-handling code**: Keep the main logic separate from error-handling code
2. **Proper resource cleanup**: Ensure resources like files and network connections are closed properly
3. **Graceful error recovery**: Provide meaningful messages to users instead of crashing
4. **Propagating errors**: Pass exceptions up the call stack to be handled at the appropriate level

The Exception Hierarchy

In Java, all exceptions are subclasses of the `java.lang.Throwable` class. There are two main categories:
1. **Checked Exceptions** (Subclasses of `Exception` excluding `RuntimeException`)
   - Must be either caught or declared in the method signature
   - Represent recoverable conditions
   - Examples: IOException, SQLException
2. Unchecked Exceptions
   - Do not need to be explicitly caught or declared
   - Include:
     - **Runtime Exceptions** (Subclasses of `RuntimeException`)
       - Represent programming errors
       - Examples: NullPointerException, ArrayIndexOutOfBoundsException
     - **Errors** (Subclasses of `Error`)
       - Represent serious system problems
       - Examples: OutOfMemoryError, StackOverflowError

Here's a simplified view of the exception hierarchy:

Throwable

├── Error (unchecked)

```
|   ┝── CutOfMemoryError
|   ┝── StackOverflowError
|   └── ...
└── Exception
    ┝── RuntimeException (unchecked)
    |   ┝── NullPointerException
    |   ┝── ArithmeticException
    |   ┝── IndexOutOfBoundsException
    |   └── ...
    └── Checked Exceptions
        ┝── IOException
        ┝── SQLException
        └── ...
```

6.2 The try-catch Block

The fundamental mechanism for handling exceptions in Java is the `try-catch` block.

Basic Syntax

```java
try {
    // Code that might throw an exception
} catch (ExceptionType1 e1) {
    // Handler for ExceptionType1
} catch (ExceptionType2 e2) {
    // Handler for ExceptionType2
} finally {
    // Code that always executes, whether an exception occurred or not
}
```

Simple Example

```java
public class DivisionExample {
    public static void main(String[] args) {
        try {
            int result = divideNumbers(10, 0);
            System.out.println("Result: " + result);
        } catch (ArithmeticException e) {
            System.out.println("Error: Cannot divide by zero!");
            System.out.println("Exception message: " + e.getMessage());
        }

        System.out.println("Program continues execution...");
    }

    public static int divideNumbers(int dividend, int divisor) {
```

69

```
        return dividend / divisor; // This will throw ArithmeticException if divisor is 0
    }
}
```

Output:

Error: Cannot divide by zero!
Exception message: / by zero
Program continues execution...

Multiple catch Blocks

You can have multiple catch blocks to handle different types of exceptions:

```
public class MultipleExceptionExample {
  public static void main(String[] args) {
    try {
      int[] numbers = {1, 2, 3};
      int result = 10 / numbers[5]; // This line has two potential exceptions
    } catch (ArithmeticException e) {
      System.out.println("Arithmetic error: " + e.getMessage());
    } catch (ArrayIndexOutOfBoundsException e) {
      System.out.println("Array index error: " + e.getMessage());
      System.out.println("Valid indices are 0-" + (numbers.length - 1));
    }

    System.out.println("Program continues execution...");
  }
}
```

Output:

Array index error: Index 5 out of bounds for length 3
Valid indices are 0-2
Program continues execution...

The finally Block

The `finally` block contains code that always executes, whether an exception occurs or not:

```
public class FinallyExample {
  public static void main(String[] args) {
    FileReader reader = null;

    try {
      reader = new FileReader("file.txt");
      // Read operations on the file...
    } catch (FileNotFoundException e) {
      System.out.println("File not found: " + e.getMessage());
```

70

```java
    } finally {
        // This runs regardless of whether an exception occurred
        System.out.println("Executing finally block");

        // Close the resource if it was opened
        if (reader != null) {
            try {
                reader.close();
            } catch (IOException e) {
                System.out.println("Error closing file: " + e.getMessage());
            }
        }
    }

    System.out.println("Program continues execution...");
  }
}
```

Common Mistakes with try-catch

1. **Catching Exception too broadly**: Avoid catching the generic `Exception` class when you could catch specific exceptions
2. **Empty catch blocks**: Never leave catch blocks empty; at least log the exception
3. **Returning from a finally block**: This will override the return value from the try or catch block
4. **Not closing resources properly**: Always close resources (files, connections, etc.) in finally blocks or use try-with-resources

6.3 Catching Multiple Exceptions (Java 7+)

Starting with Java 7, you can catch multiple exception types in a single catch block:

```java
public class MultiCatchExample {
    public static void main(String[] args) {
        try {
            String input = args[0];
            int value = Integer.parseInt(input);
            int result = 100 / value;
            System.out.println("Result: " + result);
        } catch (ArrayIndexOutOfBoundsException | NumberFormatException e) {
            System.out.println("Input error: " + e.getClass().getSimpleName());
            System.out.println("Please provide a valid integer argument");
        } catch (ArithmeticException e) {
            System.out.println("Arithmetic error: " + e.getMessage());
        }
    }
}
```

Rules for multi-catch:
- Exception types must not have a subtype relationship
- The catch parameter (e) is effectively final (cannot be modified)

6.4 The try-with-resources Statement (Java 7+)

Before Java 7, ensuring resources were closed properly was verbose and error-prone. The try-with-resources statement simplifies this:

Before Java 7

```java
public class OldResourceHandling {
  public static void main(String[] args) {
    BufferedReader reader = null;
    try {
      reader = new BufferedReader(new FileReader("file.txt"));
      String line = reader.readLine();
      System.out.println(line);
    } catch (IOException e) {
      System.out.println("Error reading file: " + e.getMessage());
    } finally {
      if (reader != null) {
        try {
          reader.close();
        } catch (IOException e) {
          System.out.println("Error closing reader: " + e.getMessage());
        }
      }
    }
  }
}
```

With try-with-resources (Java 7+)

```java
public class TryWithResourcesExample {
  public static void main(String[] args) {
    // Resources declared here are automatically closed when the block completes
    try (BufferedReader reader = new BufferedReader(new FileReader("file.txt"))) {
      String line = reader.readLine();
      System.out.println(line);
    } catch (IOException e) {
      System.out.println("Error: " + e.getMessage());
    }
    // No finally block needed for closing resources!
  }
}
```

72

Multiple Resources

You can manage multiple resources in a single try-with-resources statement:

```java
public class MultipleResourcesExample {
  public static void main(String[] args) {
    try (
      FileInputStream input = new FileInputStream("input.txt");
      FileOutputStream output = new FileOutputStream("output.txt")
    ) {
      // Read from input and write to output
      byte[] buffer = new byte[1024];
      int bytesRead;
      while ((bytesRead = input.read(buffer)) != -1) {
        output.write(buffer, 0, bytesRead);
      }
      System.out.println("File copied successfully");
    } catch (IOException e) {
      System.out.println("Error during file operations: " + e.getMessage());
    }
    // Both input and output are automatically closed
  }
}
```

Creating Your Own Resources

Any class that implements the `AutoCloseable` or `Closeable` interface can be used with try-with-resources:

```java
public class CustomResource implements AutoCloseable {
  private String name;

  public CustomResource(String name) {
    this.name = name;
    System.out.println("Resource '" + name + "' opened");
  }

  public void doOperation() {
    System.out.println("Resource '" + name + "' performing operation");
  }

  @Override
  public void close() throws Exception {
    System.out.println("Resource '" + name + "' closed");
  }
}
```

```java
public class CustomResourceExample {
    public static void main(String[] args) {
        try (CustomResource resource = new CustomResource("MyResource")) {
            resource.doOperation();
        } catch (Exception e) {
            System.out.println("Error: " + e.getMessage());
        }
    }
}
```

Output:

Resource 'MyResource' opened

Resource 'MyResource' performing operation

Resource 'MyResource' closed

6.5 Throwing Exceptions

Sometimes you need to throw exceptions yourself when exceptional conditions occur in your code.

The throw Statement

```java
public class ThrowExample {
    public static void main(String[] args) {
        try {
            validateAge(15);
            System.out.println("Age is valid");
        } catch (IllegalArgumentException e) {
            System.out.println("Validation error: " + e.getMessage());
        }
    }

    public static void validateAge(int age) {
        if (age < 18) {
            throw new IllegalArgumentException("Age must be 18 or older");
        }
    }
}
```

Output:

Validation error: Age must be 18 or older

Using the throws Clause

When a method can throw a checked exception, you must either:

1. Handle it with try-catch, or
2. Declare it with the `throws` clause

```java
public class ThrowsExample {
    // This method declares that it might throw an IOException
```

74

```java
public static void readFile(String filename) throws IOException {
    BufferedReader reader = new BufferedReader(new FileReader(filename));
    String line = reader.readLine();
    System.out.println("First line: " + line);
    reader.close();
}

public static void main(String[] args) {
    try {
        readFile("nonexistent.txt");
    } catch (IOException e) {
        System.out.println("Error reading file: " + e.getMessage());
    }
}
}
```

Re-throwing Exceptions

Sometimes you want to catch an exception, do something with it, and then rethrow it:

```java
public void processFile(String filename) throws IOException {
    try {
        // File operations
        BufferedReader reader = new BufferedReader(new FileReader(filename));
        //..
    } catch (IOException e) {
        System.out.println("Logging the error: " + e.getMessage());

        // Rethrow the exception
        throw e;
    }
}
```

Exception Chaining

You can wrap one exception in another to provide more context:

```java
public void processData(String filename) throws DataProcessingException {
    try {
        // File operations that might throw IOException
        BufferedReader reader = new BufferedReader(new FileReader(filename));
        // ...
    } catch (IOException e) {
        // Wrap the original exception in a custom exception
        throw new DataProcessingException("Error while processing " + filename, e);
    }
}
```

75

```
// Custom exception class
public class DataProcessingException extends Exception {
    public DataProcessingException(String message, Throwable cause) {
        super(message, cause);
    }
}
```

6.6 Creating Custom Exceptions

For domain-specific errors, you can create your own exception classes.

When to Create Custom Exceptions

- To provide more meaningful exception types for your application's domain
- To include additional information relevant to your application
- To distinguish between different error cases in your code

Creating a Basic Custom Exception

```
// Checked custom exception
public class InsufficientFundsException extends Exception {
    private double balance;
    private double withdrawalAmount;

    public InsufficientFundsException(String message, double balance, double withdrawalAmount) {
        super(message);
        this.balance = balance;
        this.withdrawalAmount = withdrawalAmount;
    }

    public double getBalance() {
        return balance;
    }

    public double getWithdrawalAmount() {
        return withdrawalAmount;
    }

    public double getDeficit() {
        return withdrawalAmount - balance;
    }
}
```

Using Custom Exceptions

```
public class BankAccount {
```

```java
    private String accountNumber;
    private double balance;

    public BankAccount(String accountNumber, double initialBalance) {
        this.accountNumber = accountNumber;
        this.balance = initialBalance;
    }

    public void withdraw(double amount) throws InsufficientFundsException {
        if (amount <= 0) {
            throw new IllegalArgumentException("Withdrawal amount must be positive");
        }

        if (amount > balance) {
            throw new InsufficientFundsException(
                "Not enough funds for withdrawal",
                balance,
                amount
            );
        }

        balance -= amount;
        System.out.println("Withdrew " + amount + ". New balance: " + balance);
    }

    public double getBalance() {
        return balance;
    }
}

public class BankDemo {
    public static void main(String[] args) {
        BankAccount account = new BankAccount("123456", 1000);

        try {
            account.withdraw(500);  // Works fine
            account.withdraw(700);  // Will throw exception
        } catch (InsufficientFundsException e) {
            System.out.println("Error: " + e.getMessage());
            System.out.println("Current balance: " + e.getBalance());
            System.out.println("Attempted withdrawal: " + e.getWithdrawalAmount());
            System.out.println("You need " + e.getDeficit() + " more to complete this transaction");
        }
    }
}
```

```
}
```

Output:

Withdrew 500.0. New balance: 500.0
Error: Not enough funds for withdrawal
Current balance: 500.0
Attempted withdrawal: 700.0
You need 200.0 more to complete this transaction

Checked vs. Unchecked Custom Exceptions

- **Checked Exceptions** (extend `Exception`): For recoverable conditions that the caller should be aware of

```
public class FileFormatException extends Exception {
  public FileFormatException(String message) {
    super(message);
  }
}
```

- **Unchecked Exceptions** (extend `RuntimeException`): For programming errors that shouldn't occur

```
public class InvalidUserStateException extends RuntimeException {
  public InvalidUserStateException(String message) {
    super(message);
  }
}
```

6.7 Exception Handling Best Practices

1. Only Catch Exceptions You Can Handle

Catch exceptions only if you can do something meaningful with them:

```
// Good: Specific exception handling
try {
  int value = Integer.parseInt(userInput);
} catch (NumberFormatException e) {
  System.out.println("Please enter a valid number");
}
```

```
// Bad: Generic exception catching without proper handling
try {
  // Complex operations
} catch (Exception e) {
  // Swallowing the exception without proper handling
  System.out.println("An error occurred");
}
```

2. Don't Swallow Exceptions

Never leave catch blocks empty or simply print the exception without proper handling:

```java
// Bad: Swallowing the exception
try {
    readFile("data.txt");
} catch (IOException e) {
    // Empty catch block is dangerous!
}

// Better. At least log the exception
try {
    readFile("data.txt");
} catch (IOException e) {
    System.err.println("Error reading file: " + e.getMessage());
    e.printStackTrace();
}
```

3. Close Resources Properly

Always close resources, preferably using try-with-resources:

```java
// Good: Using try-with-resources
try (FileInputStream fis = new FileInputStream("file.txt")) {
    // Use the resource
} catch (IOException e) {
    // Handle exception
}
```

4. Throw Exceptions Early, Catch Them Late

Validate parameters at the beginning of methods and let exceptions propagate to where they can be meaningfully handled:

```java
// Good: Early validation
public void processUser(User user) {
    if (user == null) {
        throw new IllegalArgumentException("User cannot be null");
    }

    // Rest of method knowing user is non-null
}
```

5. Include Informative Error Messages

Make your exception messages descriptive:

```java
// Bad
throw new IllegalArgumentException("Invalid input");

// Good: More descriptive
```

```
throw new IllegalArgumentException("User age must be between 18 and 120, got: " + age);
```

6. Use Exception Hierarchy to Your Advantage

Structure your exceptions in a hierarchy to allow for different levels of exception handling:

```java
// Base exception for all database errors
public class DatabaseException extends Exception {
    public DatabaseException(String message) {
        super(message);
    }

    public DatabaseException(String message, Throwable cause) {
        super(message, cause);
    }
}

// More specific exceptions
public class ConnectionException extends DatabaseException {
    public ConnectionException(String message) {
        super(message);
    }
}

public class QueryException extends DatabaseException {
    public QueryException(String message) {
        super(message);
    }
}
```

Now clients can choose the appropriate level of granularity:

```java
try {
    database.executeQuery(query);
} catch (ConnectionException e) {
    // Handle connection issues
} catch (QueryException e) {
    // Handle query syntax issues
} catch (DatabaseException e) {
    // Handle any other database issues
}
```

7. Document Exceptions

Always document the exceptions your methods can throw:

```java
/**
 * Transfers money between accounts.
 *
```

```
 * @param fromAccount The source account
 * @param toAccount The destination account
 * @param amount The amount to transfer
 * @throws InsufficientFundsException If the source account doesn't have enough money
 * @throws AccountNotFoundException If either account doesn't exist
 */
public void transferMoney(String fromAccount, String toAccount, double amount)
        throws InsufficientFundsException, AccountNotFoundException {
    // Method implementation
}
```

6.8 Common Java Exceptions

RuntimeExceptions (Unchecked)

1. NullPointerException
    - Thrown when you try to use a null reference where an object is required

```
String str = null;
int length = str.length(); // NullPointerException
```

2. ArrayIndexOutOfBoundsException
    - Thrown when you try to access an array element with an invalid index

```
int[] numbers = {1, 2, 3};
int value = numbers[3]; // ArrayIndexOutOfBoundsException
```

3. NumberFormatException
    - Thrown when an attempt is made to convert a string to a numeric type, but the string doesn't have the appropriate format

```
int number = Integer.parseInt("abc"); // NumberFormatException
```

4. ArithmeticException
    - Thrown when an exceptional arithmetic condition occurs

```
int result = 10 / 0; // ArithmeticException
```

5. ClassCastException
    - Thrown when an attempt is made to cast an object to a subclass of which it is not an instance

```
Object obj = "Hello";
Integer number = (Integer) obj; // ClassCastException
```

Checked Exceptions

1. IOException
    - Thrown when an I/O operation fails

```
try {
    FileReader file = new FileReader("nonexistent.txt");
} catch (FileNotFoundException e) {
    // FileNotFoundException is a subclass of IOException
    System.out.println("File not found: " + e.getMessage());
}
```

2. SQLException

o   Thrown when a database access error occurs

```java
try {
  Connection conn = DriverManager.getConnection("invalid_url");
} catch (SQLException e) {
  System.out.println("Database error: " + e.getMessage());
}
```

3. ParseException
o   Thrown when parsing operations fail

```java
try {
  SimpleDateFormat format = new SimpleDateFormat("yyyy-MM-dd");
  Date date = format.parse("2023/01/01"); // Wrong format
} catch (ParseException e) {
  System.out.println("Date parsing error: " + e.getMessage());
}
```

6.9 Debugging Exceptions

Using Stack Traces

A stack trace shows the execution path that led to the exception:

```
java.lang.NullPointerException: Cannot invoke "String.length()" because "str" is null
  at com.example.ExceptionDemo.processString(ExceptionDemo.java:15)
  at com.example.ExceptionDemo.main(ExceptionDemo.java:7)
```

Reading stack traces from top to bottom:
1. The top line shows the exception type and message
2. Subsequent lines show the call stack, with the most recent call at the top
3. Each line shows the class, method, and line number where the exception occurred

Printing Stack Traces

```java
try {
// Code that might throw an exception
} catch (Exception e) {
  e.printStackTrace(); // Prints the stack trace to System.err

  // Or get the stack trace as a string
  StringWriter sw = new StringWriter();
  PrintWriter pw = new PrintWriter(sw);
  e.printStackTrace(pw);
  String stackTraceString = sw.toString();

  // Or get the stack trace as an array
  StackTraceElement[] stackElements = e.getStackTrace();
  for (StackTraceElement element : stackElements) {
    System.out.println(element.getClassName() + "." +
            element.getMethodName() + " at line " +
            element.getLineNumber());
```

```
    }
}
```

Getting the Root Cause

For nested exceptions, you might want to find the root cause:

```java
public Throwable getRootCause(Throwable throwable) {
  Throwable cause = throwable.getCause();
  if (cause == null) {
    return throwable;
  }
  return getRootCause(cause);
}
```

6.10 Modern Exception Handling (Java 10+)

Using var with Exceptions (Java 10+)

The `var` keyword can be used with exception handling:

```java
try {
  // Some code that might throw an exception
} catch (var e) { // Type is inferred as Exception
  System.out.println("Exception: " + e.getMessage());
}
```

Helpful NullPointerExceptions (Java 14+)

Starting with Java 14, NullPointerExceptions include more helpful messages:

```java
// Before Java 14
Person person = null;
System.out.println(person.getName()); // NullPointerException

// Output: java.lang.NullPointerException

// With Java 14+
Person person = null;
System.out.println(person.getName()); // More helpful NullPointerException

// Output: java.lang.NullPointerException: Cannot invoke "Person.getName()" because "person" is null
```

 Quiz: Test Your Understanding

1. Which statement is true about checked exceptions?
   - a) They must be caught or declared in the method signature
   - b) They are subclasses of RuntimeException
   - c) They represent unrecoverable errors
   - d) They are automatically handled by JVM
2. What is the output of the following code?

83

```java
public class ExceptionQuiz {
    public static void main(String[] args) {
        try {
            System.out.print("A");
            riskyMethod();
            System.out.print("B");
        } catch (Exception e) {
            System.out.print("C");
        } finally {
            System.out.print("D");
        }
    }

    public static void riskyMethod() {
        throw new NullPointerException();
    }
}
```

- a) ABCD
- b) ACD
- c) ABD
- d) AD

3. Which of the following is NOT a benefit of try-with-resources?
    - a) Automatic resource closing
    - b) Cleaner code with less boilerplate
    - c) Handling of suppressed exceptions
    - d) Ability to catch unchecked exceptions without declaring them

4. What happens if an exception is thrown in a finally block?
    - a) It's ignored because finally blocks cannot throw exceptions
    - b) It overrides any exception from the try or catch block
    - c) It's added to a list of suppressed exceptions
    - d) The program terminates immediately

5. Which of the following is a checked exception?
    - a) NullPointerException
    - b) ArithmeticException
    - c) IOException
    - d) IllegalArgumentException

 FAQ

Q1: When should I use checked vs. unchecked exceptions?

A: Use checked exceptions for recoverable conditions that the caller should be aware of and handle (like file not found). Use unchecked exceptions (RuntimeExceptions) for programming errors that shouldn't happen if the code is correct (like null pointer dereference or illegal argument).

Q2: Is it bad practice to catch Exception?

A: Generally, yes. Catching the generic Exception class can hide bugs and make debugging difficult. It's better to catch specific exceptions that you know how to handle. However, there are valid use cases for catching Exception, such as at application boundaries or in top-level error handlers.

Q3: What's the difference between throw and throws?

A: `throw` is used to actually throw an exception in code (e.g., `throw new IOException()`), while `throws` is used in method signatures to declare that the method might throw certain exceptions (e.g., `public void readFile() throws IOException`).

Q4: Can I use multiple catch blocks with try-with-resources?

A: Yes, try-with-resources can be combined with catch and finally blocks:

```
try (Resource resource = new Resource()) {
  // Use resource
} catch (Exception e) {
  // Handle exception
} finally {
  // Additional cleanup
}
```

Q5: Should I create my own exceptions or use existing ones?

A: Create custom exceptions when they provide meaningful, domain-specific information. Use standard exceptions when they accurately represent the error condition. For example, use `IllegalArgumentException` for invalid parameters rather than creating `InvalidParameterException`.

Exercise: Build a Simple File Processing Application with Exception Handling

Create a file processing application that reads student records from a CSV file and processes them. The application should:

1. Use proper exception handling techniques
2. Handle various error scenarios:
    - File not found
    - File format problems
    - Data validation issues
3. Use custom exceptions for domain-specific errors
4. Implement try-with-resources for file handling
5. Provide useful error messages

Here's a starting point:

```
public class StudentRecordProcessor {
  public static void main(String[] args) {
    try {
      processStudentRecords("students.csv");
    } catch (FileNotFoundException e) {
      System.out.println("Error: Student file not found");
      System.out.println("Please ensure 'students.csv' exists in the application directory");
    } catch (Exception e) {
      System.out.println("An unexpected error occurred: " + e.getMessage());
    }
```

```
}

public static void processStudentRecords(String filename) throws FileNotFoundException {
    // TODO: Implement file processing with proper exception handling
    // 1. Open the file using try-with-resources
    // 2. Read and validate each line
    // 3. Process valid records
    // 4. Create custom exceptions for validation errors
}
}
```

Answers to Quiz:
1. a) They must be caught or declared in the method signature
2. b) ACD
3. d) Ability to catch unchecked exceptions without declaring them
4. b) It overrides any exception from the try or catch block
5. c) IOException

Chapter 7: Java Collections Framework

7.1 Introduction to Collections

The Java Collections Framework is a unified architecture for representing and manipulating collections of objects. It contains interfaces, implementations, and algorithms that allow you to store, retrieve, process, and manipulate groups of objects efficiently.

Why Collections Matter

Imagine you need to store a list of student names, track unique visitors to a website, or maintain key-value pairs like user IDs and passwords. Instead of creating custom data structures for each purpose, Java provides a rich set of collection classes that handle these common scenarios.

```
// Without collections (using arrays)
String[] studentNames = new String[100]; // Fixed size
int studentCount = 0;

// With collections
List<String> studentNames = new ArrayList<>(); // Dynamic size
```

Collections Framework Hierarchy

The Java Collections Framework is organized around a set of interfaces with multiple implementations:

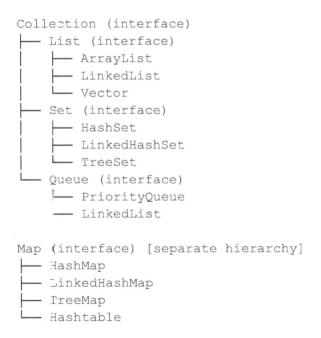

```
Collection (interface)
├── List (interface)
│   ├── ArrayList
│   ├── LinkedList
│   └── Vector
├── Set (interface)
│   ├── HashSet
│   ├── LinkedHashSet
│   └── TreeSet
└── Queue (interface)
    ├── PriorityQueue
    └── LinkedList

Map (interface) [separate hierarchy]
├── HashMap
├── LinkedHashMap
├── TreeMap
└── Hashtable
```

A `List` is an ordered collection that allows duplicate elements. You can access elements by their index (position).

ArrayList: Dynamic Array Implementation

`ArrayList` is the most commonly used List implementation. It's backed by a resizable array.

```java
import java.util.ArrayList;
import java.util.List;

public class ArrayListExample {
    public static void main(String[] args) {
        // Creating an ArrayList
        List<String> fruits = new ArrayList<>();

        // Adding elements
        fruits.add("Apple");
        fruits.add("Banana");
        fruits.add("Orange");
        fruits.add("Apple");   // Duplicates allowed!

        // Accessing elements by index
        System.out.println("First fruit: " + fruits.get(0));

        // Size of the list
        System.out.println("Number of fruits: " + fruits.size());

        // Iterating through elements
        System.out.println("All fruits:");
        for (String fruit : fruits) {
            System.out.println("- " + fruit);
        }

        // Modern way to create an immutable list (Java 9+)
        List<String> vegetables = List.of("Carrot", "Broccoli", "Spinach");
        //      vegetables.add("Potato");      // This      will      throw
UnsupportedOperationException!

        // Checking if an element exists
        System.out.println("Contains Banana? " + fruits.contains("Banana"));

        // Removing elements
        fruits.remove("Apple");   // Removes first occurrence
        System.out.println("After removing Apple: " + fruits);

        // Removing by index
        fruits.remove(0);
        System.out.println("After removing index 0: " + fruits);
```

```
        }
}
```

LinkedList: Doubly-Linked List Implementation

LinkedList implements both List and Queue interfaces. It's backed by a doubly-linked list.

```java
import java.util.LinkedList;
import java.util.List;

public class LinkedListExample {
    public static void main(String[] args) {
        LinkedList<String> names = new LinkedList<>();

        // Adding elements
        names.add("Alex");
        names.add("Barbara");
        names.add("Carlos");

        // LinkedList specific operations
        names.addFirst("Zoe");   // Add to the beginning
        names.addLast("David");  // Add to the end

        System.out.println("Names: " + names);

        // Queue-like operations
        String first = names.removeFirst(); // Removes and returns first element
        String last = names.removeLast();    // Removes and returns last element

        System.out.println("Removed first: " + first);
        System.out.println("Removed last: " + last);
        System.out.println("After removals: " + names);
    }
}
```

When to Use Each List Type

- Use ArrayList when:
    o You need frequent access to elements by index
    o You mostly add/remove elements at the end
    o You need fast iteration
- Use LinkedList when:
    o You frequently add/remove elements from the beginning or middle
    o You need queue or stack functionality
    o Memory overhead isn't a concern

7.3 Sets: Collections of Unique Elements

A Set is a collection that does not allow duplicate elements.

89

HashSet uses a hash table for storage, providing constant-time performance for basic operations.

```java
import java.util.HashSet;
import java.util.Set;

public class HashSetExample {
    public static void main(String[] args) {
        // Creating a HashSet
        Set<String> uniqueColors = new HashSet<>();

        // Adding elements
        uniqueColors.add("Red");
        uniqueColors.add("Green");
        uniqueColors.add("Blue");
        uniqueColors.add("Red");   // Duplicate - will be ignored

        System.out.println("Unique colors: " + uniqueColors);
        System.out.println("Count: " + uniqueColors.size());

        // Testing for existence
        System.out.println("Contains Yellow? " + uniqueColors.contains("Yellow"));

        // Modern way to create an immutable set (Java 9+)
        Set<String> primaryColors = Set.of("Red", "Blue", "Yellow");

        // Finding common elements (intersection)
        Set<String> commonColors = new HashSet<>(uniqueColors);
        commonColors.retainAll(primaryColors);
        System.out.println("Common colors: " + commonColors);

        // Removing an element
        uniqueColors.remove("Green");
        System.out.println("After removing Green: " + uniqueColors);
    }
}
```

TreeSet: Sorted Set

TreeSet stores elements in sorted order.

```java
import java.util.TreeSet;
import java.util.Set;

public class TreeSetExample {
    public static void main(String[] args) {
        // Creating a TreeSet
        TreeSet<String> sortedNames = new TreeSet<>();
```

```
        // Adding elements (will be automatically sorted)
        sortedNames.add("Zack");
        sortedNames.add("Eve");
        sortedNames.add("Adam");
        sortedNames.add("Bob");

        System.out.println("Sorted names: " + sortedNames);

        // TreeSet specific navigation methods
        System.out.println("First: " + sortedNames.first());
        System.out.println("Last: " + sortedNames.last());
        System.out.println("Higher than Bob: " + sortedNames.higher("Bob"));
        System.out.println("Lower than Eve: " + sortedNames.lower("Eve"));

        // Subset operations
        Set<String> subSet = sortedNames.subSet("Adam", "Eve");
        System.out.println("Subset between Adam and Eve: " + subSet);
    }
}
```

LinkedHashSet: Order of Insertion

LinkedHashSet maintains insertion order while still providing set functionality.

```
import java.util.LinkedHashSet;
import java.util.Set;

public class LinkedHashSetExample {
    public static void main(String[] args) {
        // Creating a LinkedHashSet
        Set<String> orderedSet = new LinkedHashSet<>();

        // Adding elements (order will be preserved)
        orderedSet.add("First");
        orderedSet.add("Second");
        orderedSet.add("Third");
        orderedSet.add("First");   // Duplicate - will be ignored

        // Elements are iterated in insertion order
        System.out.println("Ordered set (insertion order): " + orderedSet);
    }
}
```

When to Use Each Set Type

- Use HashSet when:
    - You need the fastest performance
    - Order doesn't matter
- Use TreeSet when:
    - You need elements in sorted order

91

- o You need to find ranges of elements
- Use `LinkedHashSet` when:
  - o You need to maintain insertion order
  - o You still want set functionality (no duplicates)

7.4 Maps: Key-Value Collections

A `Map` is a collection that maps keys to values, with no duplicate keys allowed.

HashMap: Fast, Unordered Map

`HashMap` provides constant-time performance for basic operations.

```java
import java.util.HashMap;
import java.util.Map;

public class HashMapExample {
    public static void main(String[] args) {
        // Creating a HashMap
        Map<String, Integer> ageMap = new HashMap<>();

        // Adding key-value pairs
        ageMap.put("Alice", 25);
        ageMap.put("Bob", 30);
        ageMap.put("Charlie", 35);

        // Accessing values by key
        System.out.println("Bob's age: " + ageMap.get("Bob"));

        // Default value if key not found
        System.out.println("David's age: " + ageMap.getOrDefault("David", 0));

        // Checking if a key exists
        if (ageMap.containsKey("Alice")) {
            System.out.println("We know Alice's age");
        }

        // Updating a value
        ageMap.put("Alice", 26);   // Overwrites the previous value
        System.out.println("Alice's updated age: " + ageMap.get("Alice"));

        // Modern way to create an immutable map (Java 9+)
        Map<String, String> capitalCities = Map.of(
            "USA", "Washington DC",
            "UK", "London",
            "France", "Paris"
        );

        // Size of the map
        System.out.println("Number of entries: " + ageMap.size());
```

```java
        // Iterating through a map
        System.out.println("\nAll people and their ages:");
        for (Map.Entry<String, Integer> entry : ageMap.entrySet()) {
            System.out.println(entry.getKey() + " is " + entry.getValue() + " years
old");
        }

        // Modern iteration (Java 8+)
        System.out.println("\nUsing forEach:");
        ageMap.forEach((name, age) -> System.out.println(name + " is " + age + "
years old"));

        // Getting all keys
        System.out.println("\nAll names: " + ageMap.keySet());

        // Getting all values
        System.out.println("All ages: " + ageMap.values());

        // Removing an entry
        ageMap.remove("Charlie");
        System.out.println("\nAfter removing Charlie: " + ageMap);
    }
}
```

TreeMap: Sorted Map

TreeMap stores entries in key-sorted order.

```java
import java.util.TreeMap;
import java.util.Map;

public class TreeMapExample {
    public static void main(String[] args) {
        // Creating a TreeMap (keys will be sorted)
        TreeMap<String, Double> grades = new TreeMap<>();

        // Adding key-value pairs
        grades.put("John", 3.8);
        grades.put("Alice", 4.0);
        grades.put("Bob", 3.6);
        grades.put("Zack", 3.2);

        // Entries are sorted by keys
        System.out.println("Sorted grades: " + grades);

        // TreeMap specific navigation methods
        System.out.println("First student: " + grades.firstKey());
        System.out.println("Last student: " + grades.lastKey());
        System.out.println("Students before John: " + grades.headMap("John"));
        System.out.println("Students after John: " + grades.tailMap("John"));
```

```
        }
}
```

LinkedHashMap: Order of Insertion

LinkedHashMap **maintains insertion order of keys.**

```java
import java.util.LinkedHashMap;

import java.util.Map;


public class LinkedHashMapExample {

    public static void main(String[] args) {

        // Creating a LinkedHashMap

        Map<String, String> userPreferences = new LinkedHashMap<>();


        // Adding entries (order will be preserved)

        userPreferences.put("theme", "dark");

        userPreferences.put("language", "en");

        userPreferences.put("notifications", "on");


        // Entries are iterated in insertion order
        System.out.println("User preferences (in order set): " +
userPreferences);
    }
}
```

When to Use Each Map Type

- Use HashMap **when:**
    - You need the fastest access
    - Order doesn't matter
- Use TreeMap **when:**
    - You need entries sorted by key
    - You need to find ranges of entries
- Use LinkedHashMap **when:**
    - You need to maintain insertion order
    - You want predictable iteration order

7.5 Queue and Deque: FIFO and More

Queues represent collections designed for holding elements prior to processing.

Queue Implementation: LinkedList

`LinkedList` can be used as a queue.

```java
import java.util.LinkedList;
import java.util.Queue;

public class QueueExample {
    public static void main(String[] args) {
        // Creating a Queue using LinkedList implementation
        Queue<String> queue = new LinkedList<>();

        // Adding elements to the queue
        queue.offer("First");
        queue.offer("Second");
        queue.offer("Third");

        System.out.println("Queue: " + queue);

        // Peek at the head of queue without removing
        System.out.println("Head of queue: " + queue.peek());

        // Remove and return the head of queue
        String removed = queue.poll();
        System.out.println("Removed: " + removed);
        System.out.println("Queue after removal: " + queue);

        // Add another element
        queue.offer("Fourth");
        System.out.println("After adding Fourth: " + queue);
    }
}
```

PriorityQueue: Ordering by Priority

`PriorityQueue` orders elements according to their natural ordering or a provided comparator.

```java
import java.util.PriorityQueue;
import java.util.Queue;

public class PriorityQueueExample {
    public static void main(String[] args) {
        // Creating a PriorityQueue (min heap by default)
        Queue<Integer> priorityQueue = new PriorityQueue<>();

        // Adding elements
        priorityQueue.offer(5);
        priorityQueue.offer(1);
```

```java
        priorityQueue.offer(3);
        priorityQueue.offer(2);

        System.out.println("PriorityQueue: " + priorityQueue);

        // Elements are dequeued in priority order (lowest first by default)
        while (!priorityQueue.isEmpty()) {
            System.out.println("Polling: " + priorityQueue.poll());
        }

        // Custom priority with a Comparator (max heap)
        Queue<Integer> reversePriorityQueue = new PriorityQueue<>((a, b) -> b - a);

        reversePriorityQueue.offer(5);
        reversePriorityQueue.offer(1);
        reversePriorityQueue.offer(3);
        reversePriorityQueue.offer(2);

        System.out.println("\nMax priority queue:");
        while (!reversePriorityQueue.isEmpty()) {
            System.out.println("Polling: " + reversePriorityQueue.poll());
        }
    }
}
```

Deque: Double-Ended Queue

Deque (pronounced "deck") is a double-ended queue that supports element insertion and removal at both ends.

```java
import java.util.ArrayDeque;
import java.util.Deque;

public class DequeExample {
    public static void main(String[] args) {
        // Creating a Deque
        Deque<String> deque = new ArrayDeque<>();

        // Adding elements to both ends
        deque.addFirst("First");
        deque.addLast("Last");
        deque.offerFirst("Very First");
        deque.offerLast("Very Last");

        System.out.println("Deque: " + deque);

        // Peeking at both ends
        System.out.println("First element: " + deque.peekFirst());
        System.out.println("Last element: " + deque.peekLast());

        // Removing from both ends
```

```java
        System.out.println("Removed first: " + deque.pollFirst());
        System.out.println("Removed last: " + deque.pollLast());

        System.out.println("Deque after removals: " + deque);

        // Using Deque as a stack (LIFO)
        Deque<String> stack = new ArrayDeque<>();

        stack.push("Bottom");      // Adds to front
        stack.push("Middle");
        stack.push("Top");

        System.out.println("\nStack: " + stack);
        System.out.println("Popped: " + stack.pop());   // Removes from front
        System.out.println("Stack after pop: " + stack);
    }
}
```

7.6 Utility Classes: Collections and Arrays

Java provides utility classes with static methods for working with collections.

Collections Class

The Collections class provides algorithms for collections, such as sorting and searching.

```java
import java.util.*;

public class CollectionsUtilityExample {
    public static void main(String[] args) {
        // Creating a list
        List<Integer> numbers = new ArrayList<>(List.of(5, 2, 8, 1, 9, 3));
        System.out.println("Original list: " + numbers);

        // Sorting
        Collections.sort(numbers);
        System.out.println("Sorted list: " + numbers);

        // Binary search (works on sorted lists)
        int index = Collections.binarySearch(numbers, 8);
        System.out.println("Index of 8: " + index);

        // Reversing
        Collections.reverse(numbers);
        System.out.println("Reversed list: " + numbers);

        // Shuffling
        Collections.shuffle(numbers);
        System.out.println("Shuffled list: " + numbers);
```

```java
        // Finding min and max
        System.out.println("Min value: " + Collections.min(numbers));
        System.out.println("Max value: " + Collections.max(numbers));

        // Frequency of an element
        System.out.println("Frequency of 3: " + Collections.frequency(numbers, 3));

        // Immutable collections
        List<String> immutableList = Collections.unmodifiableList(
            new ArrayList<>(List.of("One", "Two", "Three"))
        );

        try {
            immutableList.add("Four"); // Will throw exception
        } catch (UnsupportedOperationException e) {
            System.out.println("Cannot modify an unmodifiable list!");
        }
    }
}
```

Arrays Class

The `Arrays` class provides utility methods for arrays.

```java
import java.util.Arrays;
import java.util.List;

public class ArraysUtilityExample {
    public static void main(String[] args) {
        // Creating an array
        int[] numbers = {5, 2, 8, 1, 9, 3};
        System.out.println("Original array: " + Arrays.toString(numbers));

        // Sorting
        Arrays.sort(numbers);
        System.out.println("Sorted array: " + Arrays.toString(numbers));

        // Binary search
        int index = Arrays.binarySearch(numbers, 8);
        System.out.println("Index of 8: " + index);

        // Filling an array
        int[] filledArray = new int[5];
        Arrays.fill(filledArray, 7);
        System.out.println("Filled array: " + Arrays.toString(filledArray));

        // Comparing arrays
        int[] array1 = {1, 2, 3};
        int[] array2 = {1, 2, 3};
        int[] array3 = {1, 2, 4};
```

```java
        System.out.println("array1    equals    array2:    "    +    Arrays.equals(array1,
array2));
        System.out.println("array1    equals    array3:    "    +    Arrays.equals(array1,
array3));

        // Converting array to list
        String[] fruits = {"Apple", "Banana", "Orange"};
        List<String> fruitList = Arrays.asList(fruits);
        System.out.println("Fruit list: " + fruitList);

        // Note: The List returned by Arrays.asList is fixed-size
        // fruitList.add("Mango"); // Will throw UnsupportedOperationException

        // To get a modifiable list:
        List<String> modifiableFruitList = new ArrayList<>(Arrays.asList(fruits));
        modifiableFruitList.add("Mango");
        System.out.println("Modifiable fruit list: " + modifiableFruitList);
    }
}
```

7.7 Working with Collections Effectively

Iterating Through Collections

There are multiple ways to iterate through collections in Java:

```java
import java.util.*;

public class CollectionIterationExample {
    public static void main(String[] args) {
        List<String> fruits = new ArrayList<>(List.of("Apple", "Banana", "Orange",
"Mango"));

        System.out.println("Using enhanced for loop:");
        for (String fruit : fruits) {
            System.out.println("- " + fruit);
        }

        System.out.println("\nUsing iterator:");
        Iterator<String> iterator = fruits.iterator();
        while (iterator.hasNext()) {
            String fruit = iterator.next();
            System.out.println("- " + fruit);
        }

        System.out.println("\nUsing forEach (Java 8+):");
        fruits.forEach(fruit -> System.out.println("- " + fruit));

        // Using iterator to remove elements while iterating
        List<Integer> numbers = new ArrayList<>(List.of(1, 2, 3, 4, 5, 6));
```

```java
        Iterator<Integer> numIterator = numbers.iterator();
        while (numIterator.hasNext()) {
            Integer num = numIterator.next();
            if (num % 2 == 0) {
                numIterator.remove(); // Safe way to remove during iteration
            }
        }

        System.out.println("\nAfter removing even numbers: " + numbers);

        // WRONG WAY to remove elements during iteration
        List<Integer> moreNumbers = new ArrayList<>(List.of(1, 2, 3, 4, 5, 6));

        try {
            for (Integer num : moreNumbers) {
                if (num % 2 == 0) {
                    moreNumbers.remove(num);         //         Will        throw
ConcurrentModificationException
                }
            }
        } catch (ConcurrentModificationException e) {
            System.out.println("\nConcurrentModificationException   caught!   Don't
modify a collection while iterating with for-each loop!");
        }
    }
}
```

Type Safety with Generics

Generics provide type safety for collections.

```java
import java.util.*;

public class GenericCollectionsExample {
    public static void main(String[] args) {
        // With generics (type-safe)
        List<String> safeList = new ArrayList<>();
        safeList.add("Hello");
        // safeList.add(123); // Compile error! Type safety in action

        String firstItem = safeList.get(0); // No casting needed
        System.out.println("First item: " + firstItem);

        // Without generics (before Java 5) - don't do this in modern code!
        List unsafeList = new ArrayList();
        unsafeList.add("Hello");
        unsafeList.add(123); // No compile error, but can cause runtime issues

        // Need explicit casting
        String firstUnsafe = (String) unsafeList.get(0);
        try {
```

```java
            String secondUnsafe = (String) unsafeList.get(1); // ClassCastException!
        } catch (ClassCastException e) {
            System.out.println("ClassCastException caught! Can't cast Integer to String");
        }
    }
}
```

Common Pitfalls and Best Practices

```java
import java.util.*;

public class CollectionsPitfallsExample {
    public static void main(String[] args) {
        // Pitfall #1: Using == instead of equals() for content comparison
        ArrayList<String> list1 = new ArrayList<>(List.of("a", "b", "c"));
        ArrayList<String> list2 = new ArrayList<>(List.of("a", "b", "c"));

        System.out.println("list1 == list2: " + (list1 == list2)); // False, different objects
        System.out.println("list1.equals(list2): " + list1.equals(list2)); // True, same content

        // Pitfall #2: Forgetting that Collections.sort() modifies the original list
        List<Integer> numbers = new ArrayList<>(List.of(5, 3, 1, 4, 2));
        Collections.sort(numbers);
        System.out.println("Sorted numbers (original list modified): " + numbers);

        // Pitfall #3: Using wrong Map method (put vs. putIfAbsent)
        Map<String, String> settings = new HashMap<>();
        settings.put("theme", "light");
        settings.put("theme", "dark"); // Overwrites without warning
        System.out.println("Theme setting after put: " + settings.get("theme"));

        settings.putIfAbsent("theme", "light"); // Won't change existing value
        System.out.println("Theme setting after putIfAbsent: " + settings.get("theme"));

        settings.putIfAbsent("language", "en"); // New key-value pair is added
        System.out.println("Language setting: " + settings.get("language"));

        // Pitfall #4: Not considering thread safety
        // Standard collections are not thread-safe by default
        List<String> threadSafeList = Collections.synchronizedList(new ArrayList<>());
        // Now threadSafeList can be safely used by multiple threads

        // Pitfall #5: Misunderstanding collection views
        Map<String, Integer> scores = new HashMap<>();
        scores.put("Alice", 95);
        scores.put("Bob", 87);
        scores.put("Charlie", 92);
```

```java
        // keySet() returns a view, not a separate collection
        Set<String> names = scores.keySet();
        names.remove("Bob"); // This also removes Bob from the original map!

        System.out.println("Scores after removing Bob from keySet view: " + scores);
    }
}
```

7.8 Modern Collection Operations (Java 8+)

Java 8 introduced Stream API for processing collections in a functional style.

```java
import java.util.*;
import java.util.stream.Collectors;

public class ModernCollectionsExample {
    public static void main(String[] args) {
        List<String> names = List.of("Alice", "Bob", "Charlie", "David", "Eve", "Frank");

        // Filtering
        List<String> namesStartingWithA = names.stream()
                .filter(name -> name.startsWith("A"))
                .collect(Collectors.toList());
        System.out.println("Names starting with A: " + namesStartingWithA);

        // Mapping (transform elements)
        List<String> upperCaseNames = names.stream()
                .map(String::toUpperCase)
                .collect(Collectors.toList());
        System.out.println("Uppercase names: " + upperCaseNames);

        // Sorting
        List<String> sortedNames = names.stream()
                .sorted()
                .collect(Collectors.toList());
        System.out.println("Sorted names: " + sortedNames);

        // Sorting with custom comparator
        List<String> sortedByLength = names.stream()
                .sorted(Comparator.comparing(String::length))
                .collect(Collectors.toList());
        System.out.println("Names sorted by length: " + sortedByLength);

        // Collecting results into different collections
        Set<String> namesSet = names.stream()
                .collect(Collectors.toSet());
        System.out.println("Names as set: " + namesSet);

        // Joining elements
```

```java
        String joinedNames = names.stream()
                .collect(Collectors.joining(", "));
        System.out.println("Joined names: " + joinedNames);

        // Numeric operations
        List<Integer> numbers = List.of(1, 2, 3, 4, 5, 6, 7, 8, 9, 10);

        // Sum
        int sum = numbers.stream()
                .mapToInt(Integer::intValue)
                .sum();
        System.out.println("Sum: " + sum);

        // Average
        double average = numbers.stream()
                .mapToInt(Integer::intValue)
                .average()
                .orElse(0);
        System.out.println("Average: " + average);

        // Min/Max
        int max = numbers.stream()
                .mapToInt(Integer::intValue)
                .max()
                .orElse(0);
        System.out.println("Max: " + max);

        // Grouping
        Map<Character, List<String>> namesByFirstLetter = names.stream()
                .collect(Collectors.groupingBy(name -> name.charAt(0)));
        System.out.println("Names grouped by first letter: " + namesByFirstLetter);
    }
}
```

7.9 Practice Exercises

Exercise 1: Shopping Cart Implementation

Create a simple shopping cart using collections.

```java
import java.util.*;

class Product {
    private String name;
    private double price;

    public Product(String name, double price) {
        this.name = name;
        this.price = price;
    }
```

```java
    public String getName() {
        return name;
    }

    public double getPrice() {
        return price;
    }

    @Override
    public String toString() {
        return name + " ($" + price + ")";
    }

    @Override
    public boolean equals(Object o) {
        if (this == o) return true;
        if (o == null || getClass() != o.getClass()) return false;
        Product product = (Product) o;
        return Double.compare(product.price, price) == 0 && Objects.equals(name,
product.name);
    }

    @Override
    public int hashCode() {
        return Objects.hash(name, price);
    }
}

class ShoppingCart {
    private Map<Product, Integer> items = new HashMap<>();

    public void addProduct(Product product, int quantity) {
        items.put(product, items.getOrDefault(product, 0) + quantity);
    }

    public void removeProduct(Product product) {
        items.remove(product);
    }

    public void updateQuantity(Product product, int quantity) {
        if (items.containsKey(product)) {
            items.put(product, quantity);
        }
    }

    public double getTotalPrice() {
        double total = 0;
        for (Map.Entry<Product, Integer> entry : items.entrySet()) {
            total += entry.getKey().getPrice() * entry.getValue();
        }
        return total;
    }
```

```java
    public void displayCart() {
        System.out.println("Shopping Cart Contents:");
        if (items.isEmpty()) {
            System.out.println("  Cart is empty");
            return;
        }

        for (Map.Entry<Product, Integer> entry : items.entrySet()) {
            System.out.printf("  %s - Quantity: %d - Subtotal: $%.2f%n",
                entry.getKey(),
                entry.getValue(),
                entry.getKey().getPrice() * entry.getValue());
        }
        System.out.printf("Total: $%.2f%n", getTotalPrice());
    }
}

public class ShoppingCartExample {
    public static void main(String[] args) {
        // Create some products
        Product laptop = new Product("Laptop", 999.99);
        Product headphones = new Product("Headphones", 59.99);
        Product mouse = new Product("Mouse", 24.99);

        // Create and use a shopping cart
        ShoppingCart cart = new ShoppingCart();

        // Add products
        cart.addProduct(laptop, 1);
        cart.addProduct(headphones, 2);
        cart.addProduct(mouse, 1);

        // Display initial cart
        cart.displayCart();

        // Update quantity
        cart.updateQuantity(headphones, 3);
        System.out.println("\nAfter updating headphones quantity:");
        cart.displayCart();

        // Remove a product
        cart.removeProduct(mouse);
        System.out.println("\nAfter removing mouse:");
        cart.displayCart();
    }
}
```

Exercise 2: Frequency Counter

Create a program that counts the frequency of words in a text.

```java
import java.util.*;

public class WordFrequencyCounter {
    public static void main(String[] args) {
        String text = "Java collections framework is powerful. Java collections include " +
                      "Lists, Sets, and Maps. The Java collections framework provides " +
                      "data structures and algorithms to store and manipulate groups of objects.";

        // Convert to lowercase and split by non-word characters
        String[] words = text.toLowerCase().split("\\W+");

        // Count word frequency
        Map<String, Integer> wordFrequency = new HashMap<>();

        for (String word : words) {
            if (!word.isEmpty()) { // Skip empty strings
                wordFrequency.put(word, wordFrequency.getOrDefault(word, 0) + 1);
            }
        }

        // Sort by frequency (highest first)
        List<Map.Entry<String, Integer>> sortedEntries = new ArrayList<>(wordFrequency.entrySet());
        sortedEntries.sort((e1, e2) -> e2.getValue().compareTo(e1.getValue()));

        // Display results
        System.out.println("Word Frequency (sorted by count):");
        for (Map.Entry<String, Integer> entry : sortedEntries) {
            System.out.printf("%-15s : %d%n", entry.getKey(), entry.getValue());
        }

        // Find the most common word
        if (!sortedEntries.isEmpty()) {
            Map.Entry<String, Integer> mostCommon = sortedEntries.get(0);
            System.out.printf("%nMost common word: \"%s\" (appears %d times)%n",
                mostCommon.getKey(), mostCommon.getValue());
        }
    }
}
```

Exercise 3: Student Records System

Build a small student records system using collections.

```java
import java.util.*;
```

```java
class Student {
    private int id;
    private String name;
    private List<String> courses;
    private Map<String, Integer> grades;

    public Student(int id, String name) {
        this.id = id;
        this.name = name;
        this.courses = new ArrayList<>();
        this.grades = new HashMap<>();
    }

    public int getId() {
        return id;
    }

    public String getName() {
        return name;
    }

    public void enrollCourse(String course) {
        courses.add(course);
    }

    public void assignGrade(String course, int grade) {
        if (courses.contains(course)) {
            grades.put(course, grade);
        } else {
            System.out.println("Error: Student not enrolled in " + course);
        }
    }

    public double getGPA() {
        if (grades.isEmpty()) {
            return 0.0;
        }

        int sum = 0;
        for (int grade : grades.values()) {
            sum += grade;
        }
        return (double) sum / grades.size();
    }

    public void printRecord() {
        System.out.println("Student ID: " + id);
        System.out.println("Name: " + name);
        System.out.println("Courses: " + courses);
        System.out.println("Grades: " + grades);
```

```java
            System.out.printf("GPA: %.2f%n", getGPA());
        }

        @Override
        public boolean equals(Object o) {
            if (this == o) return true;
            if (o == null || getClass() != o.getClass()) return false;
            Student student = (Student) o;
            return id == student.id;
        }

        @Override
        public int hashCode() {
            return Objects.hash(id);
        }
    }

class StudentRegistry {
    private Map<Integer, Student> students;

    public StudentRegistry() {
        students = new HashMap<>();
    }

    public void addStudent(Student student) {
        students.put(student.getId(), student);
    }

    public Student getStudent(int id) {
        return students.get(id);
    }

    public List<Student> getAllStudents() {
        return new ArrayList<>(students.values());
    }

    public List<Student> getStudentsSortedByGPA() {
        List<Student> studentList = getAllStudents();
        studentList.sort(Comparator.comparing(Student::getGPA).reversed());
        return studentList;
    }

    public void displayAllStudents() {
        if (students.isEmpty()) {
            System.out.println("No students registered.");
            return;
        }

        for (Student student : students.values()) {
            student.printRecord();
            System.out.println();
```

```java
        }
    }
}

public class StudentRecordsExample {
    public static void main(String[] args) {
        // Create registry
        StudentRegistry registry = new StudentRegistry();

        // Add students
        Student alice = new Student(1001, "Alice Smith");
        Student bob = new Student(1002, "Bob Johnson");
        Student charlie = new Student(1003, "Charlie Brown");

        registry.addStudent(alice);
        registry.addStudent(bob);
        registry.addStudent(charlie);

        // Enroll students in courses
        alice.enrollCourse("Java Programming");
        alice.enrollCourse("Database Systems");
        alice.enrollCourse("Web Development");

        bob.enrollCourse("Java Programming");
        bob.enrollCourse("Database Systems");
        bob.enrollCourse("Mobile Development");

        charlie.enrollCourse("Java Programming");
        charlie.enrollCourse("Web Development");
        charlie.enrollCourse("Network Security");

        // Assign grades
        alice.assignGrade("Java Programming", 95);
        alice.assignGrade("Database Systems", 88);
        alice.assignGrade("Web Development", 92);

        bob.assignGrade("Java Programming", 82);
        bob.assignGrade("Database Systems", 90);
        bob.assignGrade("Mobile Development", 85);

        charlie.assignGrade("Java Programming", 78);
        charlie.assignGrade("Web Development", 80);
        charlie.assignGrade("Network Security", 88);

        // Display all students
        System.out.println("All Student Records:");
        registry.displayAllStudents();

        // Get and display students sorted by GPA
        System.out.println("Students by GPA (highest first):");
        List<Student> sortedStudents = registry.getStudentsSortedByGPA();
```

```java
        for (Student student : sortedStudents) {
            System.out.printf("%s     -     GPA:     %.2f%n",     student.getName(),
student.getGPA());
        }
    }
}
```

 Quiz: Test Your Collections Knowledge

Quiz 1: Basic Collections

1. Which collection type would you use to store unique elements in sorted order?
   a) ArrayList
   b) LinkedList
   c) HashSet
   d) TreeSet

2. Which collection allows you to access elements by key?
   a) ArrayList
   b) LinkedList
   c) HashMap
   d) TreeSet

3. What is the output of the following code?
```java
List<String> names = new ArrayList<>();
names.add("Alice");
names.add("Bob");
names.add("Alice");
Set<String> uniqueNames = new HashSet<>(names);
System.out.println(uniqueNames.size());
```

a) 1 b) 2 c) 3 d) 4

4. Which collection would be most efficient for frequent insertions and deletions at both ends? a) ArrayList
   b) LinkedList c) HashSet d) TreeSet
5. Which method is used to get an immutable list in Java 9+? a) List.create() b) List.of() c) List.immutable()
   d) Collections.immutableList()

Quiz 2: Advanced Collections

1. Which collection is not thread-safe by default? a) Vector b) Hashtable c) ArrayList d) ConcurrentHashMap
2. What is the output of the following code?

```java
Map<String, Integer> map = new HashMap<>();
map.put("one", 1);
map.put("two", 2);
map.put("one", 3);
System.out.println(map.size() + " " + map.get("one"));
```

   a) 2 1 b) 2 3 c) 3 3 d) 3 1

3. Which statement about LinkedHashMap is true? a) It maintains insertion order b) It sorts entries by key c) It's thread-safe d) It's more memory efficient than HashMap
4. Consider the following Java code:

```java
List<String> list = new ArrayList<>();
list.add("A");
list.add("B");
list.add("C");
list.add(1, "D");
list.remove(2);
System.out.println(list);
```

   What is the output? a) [A, D, C] b) [A, B, C] c) [A, D, B] d) [A, B, D]

5. Which method would you use to convert a collection to a thread-safe collection? a) Collections.threadSafe() b) Collections.synchronizedCollection() c) collection.makeThreadSafe() d) new ThreadSafeCollection()

Quiz 3: Collection Operations

1. What is the time complexity of contains() operation in HashSet? a) O(1) b) O(log n) c) O(n) d) O(n log n)
2. Which statement about Collections.sort() is true? a) It returns a new sorted list b) It sorts the list in-place c) It only works with primitive types d) It sorts in descending order by default
3. What will be the output of the following code?

```java
Set<Integer> set1 = new HashSet<>(Arrays.asList(1, 2, 3, 4));
Set<Integer> set2 = new HashSet<>(Arrays.asList(3, 4, 5, 6));
set1.retainAll(set2);
System.out.println(set1);
```

   a) [1, 2, 3, 4] b) [3, 4, 5, 6] c) [3, 4] d) [1, 2, 5, 6]

4. Which of the following won't compile? a) `Map<String, Integer> map = new HashMap<>();` b) `Map<String, int> map = new HashMap<>();` c) `Map<String, List<Integer>> map = new HashMap<>();` d) `Map<String, String[]> map = new HashMap<>();`

5. What is the output of the following code?

```
PriorityQueue<Integer> pq = new PriorityQueue<>();
pq.offer(5);
pq.offer(1);
pq.offer(3);
System.out.print(pq.poll() + " ");
System.out.print(pq.poll() + " ");
System.out.print(pq.poll());
```

a) 5 1 3 b) 1 3 5 c) 5 3 1 d) 3 1 5

Answer Key

Quiz 1:

1. d) TreeSet
2. c) HashMap
3. b) 2
4. b) LinkedList
5. b) List.of()

Quiz 2:

1. c) ArrayList
2. b) 2 3
3. a) It maintains insertion order
4. a) [A, D, C]
5. b) Collections.synchronizedCollection()

Quiz 3:

1. a) O(1)
2. b) It sorts the list in-place
3. c) [3, 4]
4. b) `Map<String, int> map = new HashMap<>();`
5. b) 1 3 5

7.10 Summary

In this chapter, we've explored the Java Collections Framework and learned:

1. **Collection Types**: Lists, Sets, Maps, Queues, and Deques, each with specific use cases.
2. **List Implementations**:
   o `ArrayList`: Fast random access, slower insertions/deletions
   o `LinkedList`: Fast insertions/deletions, slower random access
3. **Set Implementations**:
   o `HashSet`: Fast operations, unordered
   o `TreeSet`: Sorted order, slower operations
   o `LinkedHashSet`: Maintains insertion order
4. **Map Implementations**:
   o `HashMap`: Fast operations, unordered
   o `TreeMap`: Sorted by key
   o `LinkedHashMap`: Maintains insertion order
5. **Queue and Deque**:
   o `LinkedList`: Can be used as a queue
   o `PriorityQueue`: Elements ordered by priority
   o `ArrayDeque`: Efficient implementation of a deque
6. **Utility Classes**:
   o `Collections`: Contains methods for sorting, searching, and synchronizing collections
   o `Arrays`: Contains methods for working with arrays
7. **Common Operations**:
   o Adding/removing elements
   o Searching
   o Iterating
   o Sorting
8. **Modern Techniques**:
   o Stream API for functional-style operations
   o Immutable collections with `List.of()`, `Set.of()`, and `Map.of()`

Remember these key points:

- Choose the right collection type for your specific needs
- Use generics for type safety
- Consider thread safety if needed
- Watch for common pitfalls like `==` vs `.equals()`
- Use the power of the Collections utility class for common operations

The Java Collections Framework provides a rich set of interfaces and implementations to handle almost any data structure need in your applications. Understanding these tools is essential for writing efficient and maintainable Java code.

7.11   Further Reading

- Java Documentation - Collections Framework, Java Tutorials - Collections, Java Generics and Collections by Maurice Naftalin and Philip Wadler.

Chapter 8: File I/O and Text Processing in Java

Introduction

File input/output (I/O) operations are fundamental in programming, allowing applications to persistently store and retrieve data. Java provides robust APIs for working with files and processing text. This chapter covers how to perform file operations, use streams for efficient I/O, and process text data effectively.

8.1 Understanding File I/O Concepts

What is File I/O?

File I/O refers to reading data from and writing data to files on your computer's storage. Java provides several APIs for file operations:

- **Java I/O API (`java.io`)**: The traditional API for file operations
- **Java NIO.2 (`java.nio.file`)**: The modern API introduced in Java 7 with improved features

File Paths and Representation

In Java, files are represented by different classes depending on the API:

- **`java.io.File`**: The traditional class for representing files and directories
- **`java.nio.file.Path`**: The modern interface for representing file paths

```
// Using java.io.File
File traditionalFile = new File("example.txt");

// Using java.nio.file.Path
Path modernPath = Path.of("example.txt");
// Or alternatively:
Path anotherPath = Paths.get("example.txt");
```

Common File Operations

Java allows you to perform various operations on files:

- Creating files and directories
- Checking if files exist
- Reading and writing data
- Moving, copying, and deleting files

114

- Getting file metadata (size, creation time, etc.)

8.2 Reading and Writing Files (Java NIO.2)

Reading Files

Java NIO.2 provides several convenient methods for reading files:

```java
import java.nio.file.Files;
import java.nio.file.Path;
import java.io.IOException;
import java.util.List;

public class FileReadingExample {
    public static void main(String[] args) {
        try {
            // Read all lines into a List
            Path path = Path.of("example.txt");
            List<String> lines = Files.readAllLines(path);

            // Print each line
            for (String line : lines) {
                System.out.println(line);
            }

            // Alternatively, read the entire file as a String
            String content = Files.readString(path);
            System.out.println("File content: " + content);

        } catch (IOException e) {
            System.err.println("Error reading file: " + e.getMessage());
        }
    }
}
```

Writing Files

Writing to files is equally straightforward:

```java
import java.nio.file.Files;
import java.nio.file.Path;
import java.io.IOException;
import java.util.List;

public class FileWritingExample {
    public static void main(String[] args) {
        try {
            Path path = Path.of("output.txt");

            // Write a single string to a file
```

```java
            Files.writeString(path, "Hello, Java File I/O!");

            // Write multiple lines to a file
            List<String> lines = List.of(
                "First line",
                "Second line",
                "Third line"
            );
            Files.write(path, lines);

        } catch (IOException e) {
            System.err.println("Error writing to file: " + e.getMessage());
        }
    }
}
```

Common File Operations with NIO.2

```java
import java.nio.file.Files;
import java.nio.file.Path;
import java.nio.file.StandardCopyOption;
import java.io.IOException;

public class FileOperationsExample {
    public static void main(String[] args) {
        try {
            Path source = Path.of("source.txt");
            Path target = Path.of("target.txt");
            Path directory = Path.of("new_directory");

            // Check if a file exists
            boolean exists = Files.exists(source);
            System.out.println("File exists: " + exists);

            // Create a new file
            if (!Files.exists(source)) {
                Files.createFile(source);
                System.out.println("Created new file: " + source);
            }

            // Create a directory
            Files.createDirectories(directory);
            System.out.println("Created directory: " + directory);

            // Copy a file
            Files.copy(source, target, StandardCopyOption.REPLACE_EXISTING);
            System.out.println("Copied file from " + source + " to " + target);

            // Delete a file
            Files.deleteIfExists(target);
            System.out.println("Deleted file: " + target);
```

```
            // Get file size
            long size = Files.size(source);
            System.out.println("File size: " + size + " bytes");

        } catch (IOException e) {
            System.err.println("Error    performing    file    operations:    "    +
e.getMessage());
        }
    }
}
```

8.3 Working with Streams

Introduction to Streams

Streams provide a way to read and write data sequentially. Java offers two main types of streams:

1. **Byte Streams**: For working with binary data (e.g., images, audio files)
2. **Character Streams**: For working with text data

Byte Streams

The base classes for byte streams are InputStream and OutputStream:

```java
import java.io.FileInputStream;
import java.io.FileOutputStream;
import java.io.IOException;

public class ByteStreamExample {
    public static void main(String[] args) {
        try (FileInputStream in = new FileInputStream("input.dat");
            FileOutputStream out = new FileOutputStream("output.dat")) {

            // Create a buffer for reading data
            byte[] buffer = new byte[1024];
            int bytesRead;

            // Read data in chunks and write to the output file
            while ((bytesRead = in.read(buffer)) != -1) {
                out.write(buffer, 0, bytesRead);
            }

            System.out.println("File copied successfully!");

        } catch (IOException e) {
            System.err.println("Error processing file: " + e.getMessage());
        }
    }
}
```

The base classes for character streams are Reader and Writer:

```java
import java.io.FileReader;
import java.io.FileWriter;
import java.io.IOException;

public class CharacterStreamExample {
    public static void main(String[] args) {
        try (FileReader reader = new FileReader("input.txt");
             FileWriter writer = new FileWriter("output.txt")) {

            // Create a buffer for reading data
            char[] buffer = new char[1024];
            int charsRead;

            // Read data in chunks and write to the output file
            while ((charsRead = reader.read(buffer)) != -1) {
                writer.write(buffer, 0, charsRead);
            }

            System.out.println("File copied successfully!");

        } catch (IOException e) {
            System.err.println("Error processing file: " + e.getMessage());
        }
    }
}
```

Buffered Streams

Buffered streams improve performance by reducing the number of I/O operations:

```java
import java.io.BufferedReader;
import java.io.BufferedWriter;
import java.io.FileReader;
import java.io.FileWriter;
import java.io.IOException;

public class BufferedStreamExample {
    public static void main(String[] args) {
        try    (BufferedReader    reader    =    new    BufferedReader(new
FileReader("input.txt"));
            BufferedWriter    writer    =    new    BufferedWriter(new
FileWriter("output.txt"))) {

            String line;
            // Read line by line and write to output
            while ((line = reader.readLine()) != null) {
```

```java
            writer.write(line);
            writer.newLine(); // Add a line separator
        }

        System.out.println("File copied successfully!");

    } catch (IOException e) {
        System.err.println("Error processing file: " + e.getMessage());
    }
  }
}
```

8.4 Text Processing

Reading and Parsing Text

Java provides several ways to process text:

```java
import java.io.BufferedReader;
import java.io.FileReader;
import java.io.IOException;

public class TextProcessingExample {
    public static void main(String[] args) {
        try (BufferedReader reader = new BufferedReader(new FileReader("data.txt")))
{
            String line;
            int lineCount = 0;
            int wordCount = 0;
            int charCount = 0;

            while ((line = reader.readLine()) != null) {
                lineCount++;
                charCount += line.length();

                // Count words by splitting on whitespace
                String[] words = line.split("\\s+");
                wordCount += words.length;
            }

            System.out.println("File statistics:");
            System.out.println("Lines: " + lineCount);
            System.out.println("Words: " + wordCount);
            System.out.println("Characters: " + charCount);

        } catch (IOException e) {
            System.err.println("Error processing file: " + e.getMessage());
        }
    }
}
```

119

Java provides powerful string manipulation capabilities:

```java
public class StringManipulationExample {
    public static void main(String[] args) {
        String text = "Java programming is fun and powerful!";

        // String operations
        System.out.println("Original text: " + text);
        System.out.println("Length: " + text.length());
        System.out.println("Uppercase: " + text.toUpperCase());
        System.out.println("Lowercase: " + text.toLowerCase());

        // Searching
        System.out.println("Contains 'fun': " + text.contains("fun"));
        System.out.println("Index of 'fun': " + text.indexOf("fun"));

        // Substring
        System.out.println("Substring (5-16): " + text.substring(5, 16));

        // Replace
        System.out.println("Replace: " + text.replace("fun", "exciting"));

        // Split
        String[] words = text.split(" ");
        System.out.println("Word count: " + words.length);

        // Join
        String joined = String.join("-", words);
        System.out.println("Joined with hyphens: " + joined);
    }
}
```

Regular Expressions

Regular expressions are powerful for text pattern matching:

```java
import java.util.regex.Matcher;
import java.util.regex.Pattern;

public class RegexExample {
    public static void main(String[] args) {
        String text = "Contact us at info@example.com or support@java.com";

        // Define a pattern for email addresses
        Pattern pattern = Pattern.compile("[a-zA-Z0-9._%+-]+@[a-zA-Z0-9.-]+\\.[a-zA-Z]{2,}");
        Matcher matcher = pattern.matcher(text);
```

```java
        // Find all matches
        System.out.println("Email addresses found:");
        while (matcher.find()) {
            System.out.println(matcher.group());
        }

        // Replace all email addresses with "[EMAIL]"
        String redacted = text.replaceAll("[a-zA-Z0-9._%+-]+@[a-zA-Z0-9.-]+\\.[a-zA-Z]{2,}", "[EMAIL]");
        System.out.println("Redacted text: " + redacted);
    }
}
```

8.5 Working with CSV and JSON Files

CSV Files

CSV (Comma-Separated Values) files are common for data exchange:

```java
import java.io.BufferedReader;
import java.io.FileReader;
import java.io.IOException;
import java.util.ArrayList;
import java.util.List;

class Person {
    private String name;
    private int age;
    private String email;

    public Person(String name, int age, String email) {
        this.name = name;
        this.age = age;
        this.email = email;
    }

    @Override
    public String toString() {
        return "Person{name='" + name + "', age=" + age + ", email='" + email + "'}";
    }
}

public class CSVProcessingExample {
    public static void main(String[] args) {
        List<Person> people = new ArrayList<>();

        try (BufferedReader reader = new BufferedReader(new FileReader("people.csv"))) {
            // Skip header if present
            String header = reader.readLine();
```

```java
            String line;
            while ((line = reader.readLine()) != null) {
                // Split the line on commas
                String[] data = line.split(",");
                if (data.length >= 3) {
                    String name = data[0].trim();
                    int age = Integer.parseInt(data[1].trim());
                    String email = data[2].trim();

                    people.add(new Person(name, age, email));
                }
            }

            // Print all people
            System.out.println("Loaded " + people.size() + " people from CSV:");
            for (Person person : people) {
                System.out.println(person);
            }

        } catch (IOException e) {
            System.err.println("Error reading CSV file: " + e.getMessage());
        } catch (NumberFormatException e) {
            System.err.println("Error parsing number: " + e.getMessage());
        }
    }
}
```

JSON Files

JSON (JavaScript Object Notation) is a popular data format. Java doesn't have built-in JSON support, but libraries like Jackson or Gson can be used:

```java
// Using Jackson library (you would need to add this dependency)
import com.fasterxml.jackson.databind.ObjectMapper;
import java.io.File;
import java.io.IOException;
import java.util.Arrays;
import java.util.List;

class User {
    private String name;
    private int age;
    private String[] hobbies;

    // Default constructor needed for Jackson
    public User() {}

    public User(String name, int age, String[] hobbies) {
        this.name = name;
        this.age = age;
        this.hobbies = hobbies;
```

```java
    }

    // Getters and setters
    public String getName() { return name; }
    public void setName(String name) { this.name = name; }

    public int getAge() { return age; }
    public void setAge(int age) { this.age = age; }

    public String[] getHobbies() { return hobbies; }
    public void setHobbies(String[] hobbies) { this.hobbies = hobbies; }

    @Override
    public String toString() {
        return "User{name='" + name + "', age=" + age +
            ", hobbies=" + Arrays.toString(hobbies) + "}";
    }
}

public class JSONProcessingExample {
    public static void main(String[] args) {
        // This example requires the Jackson library
        ObjectMapper mapper = new ObjectMapper();

        try {
            // Creating a user object
            User user = new User("John Doe", 30,
                new String[]{"reading", "hiking", "coding"});

            // Writing to JSON file
            mapper.writeValue(new File("user.json"), user);
            System.out.println("User saved to JSON file");

            // Reading from JSON file
            User loadedUser = mapper.readValue(new File("user.json"), User.class);
            System.out.println("Loaded user: " + loadedUser);

            // Creating a list of users
            List<User> users = List.of(
                new User("Jane Smith", 25, new String[]{"swimming", "painting"}),
                new User("Mike Johnson", 40, new String[]{"chess", "cooking"})
            );

            // Writing array to JSON
            mapper.writeValue(new File("users.json"), users);
            System.out.println("Users saved to JSON file");

            // Reading array from JSON
            User[] loadedUsers = mapper.readValue(new File("users.json"),
User[].class);
            System.out.println("Loaded users: " + Arrays.toString(loadedUsers));
```

```
        } catch (IOException e) {
            System.err.println("Error processing JSON: " + e.getMessage());
        }
    }
}
```

8.6 Advanced File Operations

Working with ZIP Files

Java provides support for working with ZIP archives:

```java
import java.io.FileInputStream;
import java.io.FileOutputStream;
import java.io.IOException;
import java.nio.file.Files;
import java.nio.file.Path;
import java.util.zip.ZipEntry;
import java.util.zip.ZipInputStream;
import java.util.zip.ZipOutputStream;

public class ZipFileExample {
    public static void main(String[] args) {
        // Creating a ZIP file
        try      (ZipOutputStream      zos     =      new      ZipOutputStream(new
FileOutputStream("archive.zip"))) {
            // Add files to the ZIP
            addToZip(zos, "file1.txt", "This is the content of file 1");
            addToZip(zos, "file2.txt", "This is the content of file 2");
            addToZip(zos, "subfolder/file3.txt", "This is file 3 in a subfolder");

            System.out.println("ZIP file created successfully!");
        } catch (IOException e) {
            System.err.println("Error creating ZIP: " + e.getMessage());
        }

        // Reading a ZIP file
        try      (ZipInputStream      zis     =      new      ZipInputStream(new
FileInputStream("archive.zip"))) {
            ZipEntry entry;
            System.out.println("Contents of the ZIP file:");

            while ((entry = zis.getNextEntry()) != null) {
                System.out.println("- " + entry.getName() +
                                    (entry.isDirectory() ? " (directory)" : ""));

                // Read the content of the entry (if it's a file)
                if (!entry.isDirectory()) {
                    byte[] content = zis.readAllBytes();
                    System.out.println("  Content: " + new String(content));
                }
```

124

```java
                zis.closeEntry();
            }
        } catch (IOException e) {
            System.err.println("Error reading ZIP: " + e.getMessage());
        }
    }

    private static void addToZip(ZipOutputStream zos, String entryName, String
content)
            throws IOException {
        ZipEntry entry = new ZipEntry(entryName);
        zos.putNextEntry(entry);
        zos.write(content.getBytes());
        zos.closeEntry();
    }
}
```

Working with Properties Files

Properties files are commonly used for configuration:

```java
import java.io.FileInputStream;
import java.io.FileOutputStream;
import java.io.IOException;
import java.util.Properties;

public class PropertiesFileExample {
    public static void main(String[] args) {
        // Create and write properties
        Properties properties = new Properties();
        properties.setProperty("username", "admin");
        properties.setProperty("password", "secret");
        properties.setProperty("database.url", "jdbc:mysql://localhost:3306/mydb");
        properties.setProperty("max.connections", "10");

        try (FileOutputStream output = new FileOutputStream("config.properties")) {
            properties.store(output, "Application Configuration");
            System.out.println("Properties file saved!");
        } catch (IOException e) {
            System.err.println("Error saving properties: " + e.getMessage());
        }

        // Read properties
        Properties loadedProps = new Properties();
        try (FileInputStream input = new FileInputStream("config.properties")) {
            loadedProps.load(input);

            System.out.println("Loaded properties:");
            System.out.println("Username: " + loadedProps.getProperty("username"));
            System.out.println("Password: " + loadedProps.getProperty("password"));
```

```
            System.out.println("Database          URL:          "          +
loadedProps.getProperty("database.url"));
            System.out.println("Max             Connections:          "          +
loadedProps.getProperty("max.connections"));

            // Get with default value if property doesn't exist
            String timeout = loadedProps.getProperty("connection.timeout", "30");
            System.out.println("Connection Timeout: " + timeout);

        } catch (IOException e) {
            System.err.println("Error loading properties: " + e.getMessage());
        }
    }
}
```

8.7 Common Mistakes and Best Practices

Common Mistakes

1. **Not closing resources**: Forgetting to close streams can cause resource leaks.
2. **Ignoring exceptions**: Simply printing stack traces without proper handling.
3. **Using absolute paths**: Makes code less portable.
4. **Not handling character encoding**: Can cause issues with special characters.
5. **Inefficient reading/writing**: Reading or writing byte-by-byte is inefficient.

Best Practices

1. **Always use try-with-resources**: This ensures resources are closed properly.
2. **Use relative paths**: Makes applications more portable.
3. **Specify character encoding**: Use `StandardCharsets.UTF_8` explicitly.
4. **Use buffered streams**: Improves performance.
5. **Check file existence**: Before performing operations.
6. **Use NIO.2 for modern applications**: More features and better performance.
7. **Handle exceptions gracefully**: Provide meaningful error messages.

```
// Good practice example
import java.io.BufferedReader;
import java.io.BufferedWriter;
import java.io.IOException;
import java.nio.charset.StandardCharsets;
import java.nio.file.Files;
import java.nio.file.Path;
import java.nio.file.Paths;

public class BestPracticesExample {
    public static void main(String[] args) {
        Path inputPath = Paths.get("input.txt");
        Path outputPath = Paths.get("output.txt");

        // Check if input file exists
        if (!Files.exists(inputPath)) {
```

```java
                System.err.println("Input file does not exist!");
                return;
            }

            // Use try-with-resources for automatic resource management
            try (BufferedReader reader = Files.newBufferedReader(inputPath,
StandardCharsets.UTF_8);
                 BufferedWriter writer = Files.newBufferedWriter(outputPath,
StandardCharsets.UTF_8)) {

                String line;
                while ((line = reader.readLine()) != null) {
                    // Process line
                    String processed = line.toUpperCase();
                    writer.write(processed);
                    writer.newLine();
                }

                System.out.println("File processing completed successfully!");

            } catch (IOException e) {
                System.err.println("Error processing file: " + e.getMessage());
                // Log the exception or handle it appropriately
            }
        }
    }
}
```

8.8 Practical Exercise: Log File Analyzer

Let's build a practical application that analyzes a log file:

```java
import java.io.IOException;
import java.nio.file.Files;
import java.nio.file.Path;
import java.time.LocalDateTime;
import java.time.format.DateTimeFormatter;
import java.util.HashMap;
import java.util.List;
import java.util.Map;
import java.util.regex.Matcher;
import java.util.regex.Pattern;

public class LogFileAnalyzer {
    public static void main(String[] args) {
        // Sample log format: [2023-05-15 14:30:45] INFO - User logged in: john_doe
        Path logFile = Path.of("application.log");

        // Check if file exists
        if (!Files.exists(logFile)) {
            System.err.println("Log file not found!");
            return;
```

```
            }

        try {
            List<String> logLines = Files.readAllLines(logFile);
            System.out.println("Total log entries: " + logLines.size());

            // Statistics
            Map<String, Integer> logLevelCounts = new HashMap<>();
            Map<String, Integer> userActionCounts = new HashMap<>();
            int errorCount = 0;

            // Date range
            LocalDateTime earliest = null;
            LocalDateTime latest = null;
            DateTimeFormatter  formatter  =  DateTimeFormatter.ofPattern("yyyy-MM-dd
HH:mm:ss");

            // Regular expression for log entry parsing
            Pattern pattern = Pattern.compile("\\[(.*?)\\] (\\w+) - (.*)");

            for (String line : logLines) {
                Matcher matcher = pattern.matcher(line);
                if (matcher.find()) {
                    // Extract components
                    String timestamp = matcher.group(1);
                    String logLevel = matcher.group(2);
                    String message = matcher.group(3);

                    // Update log level counts
                    logLevelCounts.put(logLevel,
logLevelCounts.getOrDefault(logLevel, 0) + 1);

                    // Count errors
                    if (logLevel.equals("ERROR")) {
                        errorCount++;
                    }

                    // Extract user actions (if present)
                    if (message.contains("User")) {
                        String action = message.split(":")[0];
                        userActionCounts.put(action,
userActionCounts.getOrDefault(action, 0) + 1);
                    }

                    // Update timestamp range
                    try {
                        LocalDateTime  dateTime  =  LocalDateTime.parse(timestamp,
formatter);
                        if (earliest == null || dateTime.isBefore(earliest)) {
                            earliest = dateTime;
                        }
                        if (latest == null || dateTime.isAfter(latest)) {
```

```java
                    latest = dateTime;
                }
            } catch (Exception e) {
                System.err.println("Error parsing date: " + timestamp);
            }
        }
    }

    // Print results
    System.out.println("\nLog Analysis Results:");
    System.out.println("====================");

    System.out.println("\nLog Level Distribution:");
    for (Map.Entry<String, Integer> entry : logLevelCounts.entrySet()) {
        System.out.printf("%-10s: %d entries (%.1f%%)\n",
                        entry.getKey(),
                        entry.getValue(),
                        (entry.getValue() * 100.0 / logLines.size()));
    }

    System.out.println("\nUser Action Summary:");
    for (Map.Entry<String, Integer> entry : userActionCounts.entrySet()) {
        System.out.printf("%-20s:    %d    occurrences\n",    entry.getKey(),
entry.getValue());
    }

    System.out.println("\nError Summary:");
    System.out.println("Total errors: " + errorCount);

    System.out.println("\nTime Range:");
    if (earliest != null && latest != null) {
        System.out.println("Earliest           entry:            "            +
earliest.format(formatter));
        System.out.println("Latest entry: " + latest.format(formatter));
        System.out.println("Log duration: " +
                            java.time.Duration.between(earliest,
latest).toHours() +
                            " hours");
    }

} catch (IOException e) {
    System.err.println("Error reading log file: " + e.getMessage());
}
    }
}
```

 Quiz: Test Your Knowledge

1. **Which of the following is NOT a valid way to read a file in Java?**

a) Using `Files.readAllLines()` b) Using `Scanner` with a `File` object c) Using `FileReader` with `BufferedReader` d) Using `File.readContent()`

2. **What is the purpose of a BufferedReader?**

a) To read binary data b) To improve performance by reducing I/O operations c) To convert between different character encodings d) To compress data while reading

3. **Which method is used to read a line from a BufferedReader?**

a) `nextLine()` b) `readLine()` c) `getLine()` d) `fetchLine()`

4. **Which of the following correctly creates a file using Java NIO.2?**

a) `new File("example.txt").create()`
b) `Files.createFile(Path.of("example.txt"))`
c) `Path.of("example.txt").createFile()`
d) `File.create("example.txt")`

5. **When using the try-with-resources statement, what happens to resources?**

a) They are automatically closed when the try block exits b) They remain open until explicitly closed c) They are closed only if an exception occurs d) They are closed only if no exception occurs

 FAQ

Q: What's the difference between `java.io` and `java.nio.file`?

A: `java.io` is the original file I/O API in Java, while `java.nio.file` (NIO.2) was introduced in Java 7. NIO.2 provides more functionality, better performance, and a more intuitive API. It includes features like symbolic links, file attributes, and improved directory traversal.

Q: Why should I use buffered streams?

A: Buffered streams improve performance by reducing the number of I/O operations. Instead of reading or writing one byte/character at a time, buffered streams read or write chunks of data, which is much more efficient.

Q: How do I handle different character encodings?

130

A: Always specify the character encoding explicitly when reading or writing text files. Use the `StandardCharsets` class:

```
BufferedReader reader = Files.newBufferedReader(path, StandardCharsets.UTF_8);
```

Q: How can I read a large file without loading it all into memory?

A: Use streaming approaches like `BufferedReader` with `readLine()` or `Files.lines()` to process the file line by line:

```
try (Stream<String> lines = Files.lines(path, StandardCharsets.UTF_8)) {
    lines.forEach(line -> processLine(line));
}
```

Q: How do I traverse directories recursively?

A: Use `Files.walkFileTree()` or the simpler `Files.walk()` method:

```
try (Stream<Path> paths = Files.walk(rootPath)) {
    paths.filter(Files::isRegularFile)
         .forEach(System.out::println);
}
```

8.10 Summary

In this chapter, we covered:

- File I/O fundamentals and concepts
- Reading and writing files using modern Java NIO.2 API
- Working with byte and character streams
- Text processing techniques and regular expressions
- Processing structured data (CSV and JSON)
- Advanced file operations (ZIP files, properties files)
- Common mistakes and best practices
- A practical example of a log file analyzer

Working with files and processing text are essential skills for Java developers. The techniques covered in this chapter will help you build robust applications that can read, write, and manipulate data effectively.

8.11 Exercises

1. Create a program that counts the occurrences of each word in a text file.
2. Build a simple CSV parser that reads a CSV file and converts it to a list of objects.
3. Write a program that encrypts and decrypts a text file using a simple substitution cipher.

131

4. Implement a program that monitors a directory for file changes and logs them.
5. Create a configuration manager that reads settings from a properties file.
6. Build a simple text editor that can open, edit, and save text files.
7. Write a program that extracts all email addresses from a text file using regular expressions.

Chapter 9: Multithreading Basics

9.1 Introduction to Multithreading

In modern computing, the ability to perform multiple tasks simultaneously is essential for creating responsive and efficient applications. Java provides robust support for multithreading, allowing your programs to execute multiple paths of code in parallel.

What is a Thread?

A thread is the smallest unit of processing that can be scheduled by an operating system. Think of a thread as a single path of execution within your program.

Real-world analogy: Imagine a restaurant kitchen. A single chef (single thread) can only cook one dish at a time, working sequentially through each step. But with multiple chefs (multiple threads), several dishes can be prepared simultaneously, significantly increasing efficiency.

Why Use Multithreading?

1. **Improved Performance**: Utilize multiple CPU cores to execute operations in parallel
2. **Enhanced Responsiveness**: Keep UI responsive while performing background tasks
3. **Resource Efficiency**: Make better use of system resources by not leaving the CPU idle
4. **Simplified Program Design**: Handle multiple tasks without complex state management

Common Use Cases

- Web servers handling multiple client requests simultaneously
- GUI applications performing background operations while keeping the interface responsive
- Video games updating game state, rendering graphics, and processing input in parallel
- Data processing applications working on different data segments concurrently

9.2 Creating and Managing Threads

Creating Threads in Java

Java provides two main ways to create threads:

Method 1: Extending the Thread Class

```java
public class MyThread extends Thread {
    @Override
    public void run() {
```

```java
        // Code to be executed in the thread
        for (int i = 0; i < 5; i++) {
            System.out.println("Thread    running:    "   +   i   +   "   -   "   +
Thread.currentThread().getName());
            try {
                Thread.sleep(1000); // Sleep for 1 second
            } catch (InterruptedException e) {
                System.out.println("Thread interrupted");
            }
        }
    }

    public static void main(String[] args) {
        // Create and start the thread
        MyThread thread = new MyThread();
        thread.start(); // Don't call run() directly!

        // Main thread continues execution here
        System.out.println("Main thread continues...");
    }
}
```

COMMON MISTAKE: Calling `run()` instead of `start()`

```java
thread.run(); // WRONG! This will execute in the current thread, not a new one
thread.start(); // CORRECT! This creates a new thread and executes run()
```

Method 2: Implementing the Runnable Interface (Preferred)

```java
public class MyRunnable implements Runnable {
    @Override
    public void run() {
        // Code to be executed in the thread
        for (int i = 0; i < 5; i++) {
            System.out.println("Thread    running:    "   +   i   +   "   -   "   +
Thread.currentThread().getName());
            try {
                Thread.sleep(1000); // Sleep for 1 second
            } catch (InterruptedException e) {
                System.out.println("Thread interrupted");
            }
        }
    }

    public static void main(String[] args) {
        // Create a runnable instance
        Runnable runnable = new MyRunnable();

        // Create a thread with the runnable
        Thread thread = new Thread(runnable, "MyCustomThread");
        thread.start();

        // Main thread continues execution here
```

```
        System.out.println("Main thread continues...");
    }
}
```

Why Runnable is preferred:

- Java supports single inheritance, so extending Thread limits your class inheritance options
- Runnable separates the task from the execution mechanism (better design)
- Runnable is more compatible with executor frameworks and thread pools

Method 3: Using Lambda Expressions (Modern Approach)

```java
public class LambdaThread {
    public static void main(String[] args) {
        // Create a thread with a lambda expression
        Thread thread = new Thread(() -> {
            for (int i = 0; i < 5; i++) {
                System.out.println("Thread    running:    "   +   i   +   "   -   "   +
Thread.currentThread().getName());
                try {
                    Thread.sleep(1000);
                } catch (InterruptedException e) {
                    System.out.println("Thread interrupted");
                }
            }
        }, "LambdaThread");

        thread.start();
        System.out.println("Main thread continues...");
    }
}
```

Thread States and Lifecycle

Each thread in Java goes through various states during its lifecycle:

1. **NEW**: Thread is created but not yet started
2. **RUNNABLE**: Thread is executing or ready to execute
3. **BLOCKED**: Thread is waiting to acquire a lock
4. **WAITING**: Thread is waiting indefinitely for another thread
5. **TIMED_WAITING**: Thread is waiting for a specified period
6. **TERMINATED**: Thread has completed execution

```java
public class ThreadLifecycle {
    public static void main(String[] args) throws InterruptedException {
        Thread thread = new Thread(() -> {
            try {
                Thread.sleep(2000); // Thread will be in TIMED_WAITING state
            } catch (InterruptedException e) {
                e.printStackTrace();
            }
```

```java
    });

    // NEW state
    System.out.println("State after creation: " + thread.getState());

    thread.start();
    // RUNNABLE state
    System.out.println("State after starting: " + thread.getState());

    // Give time for thread to start sleeping
    Thread.sleep(1000);
    // TIMED_WAITING state
    System.out.println("State during sleep: " + thread.getState());

    // Wait for thread to finish
    thread.join();
    // TERMINATED state
    System.out.println("State after completion: " + thread.getState());
    }
}
```

Thread Control Methods

Java provides several methods to control thread execution:

Method	Description
start()	Begins thread execution
sleep(long millis)	Pauses thread for specified milliseconds
join()	Waits for thread to die
yield()	Temporarily pauses to allow other threads to execute
interrupt()	Interrupts a thread (sets interrupt flag)
isAlive()	Checks if thread is still running

Example of using join():

```java
public class JoinExample {
    public static void main(String[] args) throws InterruptedException {
        Thread backgroundThread = new Thread(() -> {
            for (int i = 0; i < 5; i++) {
                System.out.println("Background processing: " + i);
                try {
                    Thread.sleep(1000);
                } catch (InterruptedException e) {
                    e.printStackTrace();
                }
            }
            System.out.println("Background processing complete!");
```

```
    });

    backgroundThread.start();

    // Wait for background thread to complete before continuing
    System.out.println("Main    thread    waiting    for    background    thread    to
finish...");
    backgroundThread.join(); // Blocks until backgroundThread completes

    // This will only execute after the background thread is done
    System.out.println("Main thread continues after background thread");
    }
}
```

9.3 Thread Synchronization

When multiple threads access shared resources, synchronization becomes necessary to avoid data corruption and race conditions.

The Problem: Race Conditions

A race condition occurs when two or more threads access and modify the same data concurrently, leading to unexpected results.

Example of a race condition:

```
public class Counter {
    private int count = 0;

    // NOT thread-safe!
    public void increment() {
        count++;  // This is not an atomic operation!
    }

    public int getCount() {
        return count;
    }

    public static void main(String[] args) throws InterruptedException {
        Counter counter = new Counter();

        // Create two threads that increment the counter
        Thread thread1 = new Thread(() -> {
            for (int i = 0; i < 10000; i++) {
                counter.increment();
            }
        });

        Thread thread2 = new Thread(() -> {
            for (int i = 0; i < 10000; i++) {
```

```
                counter.increment();
            }
    });

        thread1.start();
        thread2.start();

        thread1.join();
        thread2.join();

        // Expected: 20000, but actual value may be less
        System.out.println("Final count: " + counter.getCount());
    }
}
```

Why this happens: The count++ operation is not atomic. It involves:

1. Reading the current value
2. Adding 1 to it
3. Storing the new value

If two threads execute this simultaneously, they might both read the same value, increment it separately, and store the same incremented value, effectively losing an increment.

Solution 1: Using the synchronized Keyword

The synchronized keyword creates a lock on an object, preventing multiple threads from executing the locked code simultaneously.

```
public class SynchronizedCounter {
    private int count = 0;

    // Thread-safe!
    public synchronized void increment() {
        count++;
    }

    public synchronized int getCount() {
        return count;
    }

    public static void main(String[] args) throws InterruptedException {
        SynchronizedCounter counter = new SynchronizedCounter();

        Thread thread1 = new Thread(() -> {
            for (int i = 0; i < 10000; i++) {
                counter.increment();
            }
    });
```

```java
        Thread thread2 = new Thread(() -> {
            for (int i = 0; i < 10000; i++) {
                counter.increment();
            }
        });

        thread1.start();
        thread2.start();

        thread1.join();
        thread2.join();

        // This will correctly show 20000
        System.out.println("Final count: " + counter.getCount());
    }
}
```

You can also synchronize blocks of code instead of entire methods:

```java
public void increment() {
    synchronized(this) {
        count++;
    }
    // Other non-synchronized code here
}
```

Solution 2: Using Atomic Classes

Java provides atomic classes in the `java.util.concurrent.atomic` package for common operations that need to be thread-safe.

```java
import java.util.concurrent.atomic.AtomicInteger;

public class AtomicCounter {
    // Thread-safe without explicit synchronization
    private AtomicInteger count = new AtomicInteger(0);

    public void increment() {
        count.incrementAndGet(); // Atomic operation
    }

    public int getCount() {
        return count.get();
    }

    public static void main(String[] args) throws InterruptedException {
        AtomicCounter counter = new AtomicCounter();

        Thread thread1 = new Thread(() -> {
            for (int i = 0; i < 10000; i++) {
```

```java
            counter.increment();
        }
    });

    Thread thread2 = new Thread(() -> {
        for (int i = 0; i < 10000; i++) {
            counter.increment();
        }
    });

    thread1.start();
    thread2.start();

    thread1.join();
    thread2.join();

    // Will correctly show 20000
    System.out.println("Final count: " + counter.getCount());
    }
}
```

9.4 Thread Communication

Threads often need to communicate with each other, especially when one thread's work depends on another's.

Using wait(), notify(), and notifyAll()

These methods are used to enable communication between threads:

- `wait()`: Causes the current thread to wait until another thread calls `notify()` or `notifyAll()`
- `notify()`: Wakes up a single thread that is waiting on this object
- `notifyAll()`: Wakes up all threads that are waiting on this object

Note: These methods must be called from within a synchronized context.

Example of a simple producer-consumer pattern:

```java
public class ProducerConsumer {
    private final java.util.Queue<Integer> buffer = new java.util.LinkedList<>();
    private final int CAPACITY = 5;

    public synchronized void produce(int value) throws InterruptedException {
        // Wait if the buffer is full
        while (buffer.size() == CAPACITY) {
            System.out.println("Buffer full, producer waiting...");
            wait();
        }
```

```java
        // Add value to the buffer
        buffer.add(value);
        System.out.println("Produced: " + value);

        // Notify consumers
        notifyAll();
    }

    public synchronized int consume() throws InterruptedException {
        // Wait if the buffer is empty
        while (buffer.isEmpty()) {
            System.out.println("Buffer empty, consumer waiting...");
            wait();
        }

        // Remove and return a value
        int value = buffer.poll();
        System.out.println("Consumed: " + value);

        // Notify producers
        notifyAll();
        return value;
    }

    public static void main(String[] args) {
        ProducerConsumer pc = new ProducerConsumer();

        // Producer thread
        Thread producer = new Thread(() -> {
            try {
                for (int i = 0; i < 10; i++) {
                    pc.produce(i);
                    Thread.sleep(500); // Simulate work
                }
            } catch (InterruptedException e) {
                e.printStackTrace();
            }
        });

        // Consumer thread
        Thread consumer = new Thread(() -> {
            try {
                for (int i = 0; i < 10; i++) {
                    pc.consume();
                    Thread.sleep(1000); // Consume slower than production
                }
            } catch (InterruptedException e) {
                e.printStackTrace();
            }
        });

        producer.start();
```

```
        consumer.start();
    }
}
```

9.5 Concurrency Utilities (java.util.concurrent)

Java provides a rich set of high-level concurrency utilities in the `java.util.concurrent` package, introduced in Java 5.

ExecutorService and Thread Pools

Thread pools manage a group of worker threads, reusing them to execute tasks, which is more efficient than creating new threads for each task.

```java
import java.util.concurrent.ExecutorService;
import java.util.concurrent.Executors;
import java.util.concurrent.TimeUnit;

public class ExecutorExample {
    public static void main(String[] args) {
        // Create a thread pool with 3 threads
        ExecutorService executor = Executors.newFixedThreadPool(3);

        // Submit 5 tasks
        for (int i = 1; i <= 5; i++) {
            final int taskId = i;
            executor.submit(() -> {
                System.out.println("Task " + taskId + " started by " +
                                Thread.currentThread().getName());
                try {
                    // Simulate work
                    Thread.sleep(1000);
                } catch (InterruptedException e) {
                    e.printStackTrace();
                }
                System.out.println("Task " + taskId + " completed");
                return taskId; // Return value if needed
            });
        }

        // Properly shutdown the executor
        executor.shutdown();
        try {
            // Wait for all tasks to complete or the timeout to occur
            if (!executor.awaitTermination(10, TimeUnit.SECONDS)) {
                executor.shutdownNow();
            }
        } catch (InterruptedException e) {
            executor.shutdownNow();
        }
```

```
        System.out.println("All tasks completed");
    }
}
```

COMMON MISTAKE: Forgetting to shut down the executor service. This can prevent your application from terminating as threads may remain active.

Future and CompletableFuture

The `Future` interface represents the result of an asynchronous computation. `CompletableFuture` (Java 8+) extends this with more advanced features for composing asynchronous operations.

```java
import java.util.concurrent.CompletableFuture;
import java.util.concurrent.ExecutionException;
import java.util.concurrent.TimeUnit;

public class CompletableFutureExample {
    public    static    void    main(String[]    args)    throws    ExecutionException,
InterruptedException {
        // Create and run a CompletableFuture
        CompletableFuture<String> future = CompletableFuture.supplyAsync(() -> {
            try {
                // Simulate a long-running task
                System.out.println("Processing       in       thread:       "       +
Thread.currentThread().getName());
                TimeUnit.SECONDS.sleep(2);
                return "Task completed";
            } catch (InterruptedException e) {
                return "Task interrupted";
            }
        });

        // Do other work while the future is running
        System.out.println("Main thread continues working...");

        // Chain operations
        CompletableFuture<String> transformedFuture = future
            .thenApply(result -> result + " and transformed")
            .thenApply(result -> result + " again");

        // Block and get the final result
        String result = transformedFuture.get();
        System.out.println("Final result: " + result);
    }
}
```

Other Concurrent Utilities

Java provides many other concurrent utilities:

143

- **BlockingQueue**: Thread-safe queues for producer-consumer patterns
- **CountDownLatch**: Allows threads to wait until a set of operations completes
- **CyclicBarrier**: Allows threads to wait at a predefined execution point
- **Semaphore**: Controls access to a resource by multiple threads
- **ConcurrentHashMap**: Thread-safe implementation of Map

Example of a CountDownLatch:

```java
import java.util.concurrent.CountDownLatch;

public class CountDownLatchExample {
    public static void main(String[] args) throws InterruptedException {
        // Create a CountDownLatch for 3 events
        CountDownLatch latch = new CountDownLatch(3);

        // Create and start three worker threads
        for (int i = 1; i <= 3; i++) {
            final int workerId = i;
            new Thread(() -> {
                try {
                    // Simulate different durations of work
                    Thread.sleep(workerId * 1000);
                    System.out.println("Worker " + workerId + " finished");

                    // Signal completion
                    latch.countDown();
                } catch (InterruptedException e) {
                    e.printStackTrace();
                }
            }).start();
        }

        // Main thread waits for all workers to complete
        System.out.println("Main thread waiting for workers...");
        latch.await();

        // This will only execute after all workers have called countDown()
        System.out.println("All workers have finished, main thread continues");
    }
}
```

9.6 Thread Safety Best Practices

1. **Minimize Shared Mutable State**: The fewer shared variables, the fewer synchronization issues.
2. **Use Immutable Objects**: Objects that can't be modified after creation are inherently thread-safe.

```java
// Immutable class example
public final class ImmutablePoint {
    private final int x;
    private final int y;
```

144

```java
public ImmutablePoint(int x, int y) {
    this.x = x;
    this.y = y;
}

public int getX() { return x; }
public int getY() { return y; }
}
```

3. **Prefer Concurrent Collections**: Use classes from `java.util.concurrent` instead of manually synchronizing regular collections.

```java
// Instead of:
Map<String, Integer> map = Collections.synchronizedMap(new HashMap<>());

// Prefer:
ConcurrentHashMap<String, Integer> map = new ConcurrentHashMap<>();
```

4. **Use Thread-Local Variables**: When each thread needs its own instance of a variable.

```java
public class ThreadLocalExample {
    // Each thread gets its own copy
    private        static        ThreadLocal<Integer>        threadLocalValue        =
ThreadLocal.withInitial(() -> 0);

    public static void main(String[] args) {
        for (int i = 1; i <= 3; i++) {
            final int threadId = i;
            new Thread(() -> {
                // Set a value specific to this thread
                threadLocalValue.set(threadId * 10);
                System.out.println("Thread " + threadId +
                                " set value: " + threadLocalValue.get());

                // Each thread sees its own value
                System.out.println("Thread " + threadId +
                                " gets value: " + threadLocalValue.get());
            }).start();
        }
    }
}
```

5. **Avoid Deadlocks**: Always acquire locks in a consistent order to prevent deadlocks.

```java
// Potential deadlock
public void transferMoney(Account from, Account to, double amount) {
    synchronized(from) {  // Lock the 'from' account
        synchronized(to) {  // Lock the 'to' account
            // Transfer money
        }
```

```
        }
    }
```

If another thread calls `transferMoney(to, from, amount)`, a deadlock can occur.

Solution: Acquire locks in a consistent order, e.g., based on account ID:

```java
public void transferMoney(Account from, Account to, double amount) {
    Account firstLock = from.getId() < to.getId() ? from : to;
    Account secondLock = from.getId() < to.getId() ? to : from;

    synchronized(firstLock) {
        synchronized(secondLock) {
            // Transfer money safely
        }
    }
}
```

9.7 Common Multithreading Pitfalls

1. **Race Conditions**: When code behavior depends on the relative timing of events.
   o Solution: Proper synchronization or atomic operations
2. **Deadlocks**: When two or more threads are blocked forever, waiting for each other.
   o Solution: Acquire locks in a consistent order, use timeout versions of lock acquisition
3. **Thread Starvation**: When a thread is unable to gain regular access to shared resources.
   o Solution: Use fair locks, avoid long-running tasks in synchronized blocks
4. **Livelock**: Similar to deadlock, but threads keep changing their state without making progress.
   o Solution: Add randomness to resource acquisition attempts
5. **Memory Visibility**: Changes made by one thread may not be visible to another.
   o Solution: Use proper synchronization or volatile variables
6. **Thread Leaks**: Threads that are created but never properly terminated.
   o Solution: Always close resources and manage thread lifecycles

9.8 Debugging Multithreaded Code

Debugging multithreaded code is challenging because:

- Issues can be intermittent and hard to reproduce
- The act of debugging can mask the problem (Heisenberg Uncertainty Principle of debugging)

Tips for Debugging Multithreaded Code:

1. **Add Detailed Logging**: Include thread names and timestamps

```java
System.out.println(Thread.currentThread().getName() + " at " +
            System.currentTimeMillis() + ": Variable value = " + value);
```

2. **Use Thread Dumps**: Analyze the state of all threads at a specific moment

```java
// In code, you can print a thread dump like this:
Map<Thread, StackTraceElement[]> allStackTraces = Thread.getAllStackTraces();
for (Map.Entry<Thread, StackTraceElement[]> entry : allStackTraces.entrySet()) {
    Thread thread = entry.getKey();
    StackTraceElement[] stackTrace = entry.getValue();

    System.out.println("Thread: " + thread.getName() + " (ID: " + thread.getId() +
")");
    System.out.println("State: " + thread.getState());
    for (StackTraceElement element : stackTrace) {
        System.out.println("\tat " + element);
    }
    System.out.println();
}
```

3. **Use Assertion Statements**: Add assertions to verify invariants

```java
assert count >= 0 : "Count should never be negative";
```

4. **Consider Thread Analysis Tools**: Tools like Java Flight Recorder, VisualVM, or commercial profilers

 Quiz: Test Your Understanding

1. **Question**: What happens when you call `run()` instead of `start()` on a Thread object?
   - A) The thread starts in a new thread
   - B) The code executes in the current thread, not a new one
   - C) A runtime exception is thrown
   - D) Nothing happens
2. **Question**: What is a race condition?
   - A) When two threads compete to finish first
   - B) When thread execution order affects the outcome
   - C) When threads race to acquire a lock
   - D) When the JVM decides which thread to run first
3. **Question**: Which statement about `volatile` variables is correct?
   - A) They are immune to race conditions
   - B) They guarantee thread safety for all operations
   - C) They guarantee visibility of changes across threads
   - D) They prevent other threads from accessing the variable
4. **Question**: What is the purpose of `wait()` and `notify()`?
   - A) To terminate threads
   - B) To synchronize thread execution times
   - C) To enable communication between threads

147

o D) To prevent deadlocks

5. **Question**: What will happen in the following code if two threads execute it concurrently?

```
public void transfer(Account from, Account to, double amount) {
    synchronized(from) {
        synchronized(to) {
            from.withdraw(amount);
            to.deposit(amount);
        }
    }
}
```

o A) It is thread-safe and will always work correctly
o B) It could cause a deadlock
o C) It will throw a ConcurrentModificationException
o D) It will always execute sequentially

Answers:

1. B) The code executes in the current thread, not a new one
2. B) When thread execution order affects the outcome
3. C) They guarantee visibility of changes across threads
4. C) To enable communication between threads
5. B) It could cause a deadlock

9.9 Practice Exercise: Build a Thread-Safe Bank Account System

Create a simple bank account system that can handle concurrent transactions safely. It should:

1. Allow transfers between accounts
2. Prevent overdrafts
3. Handle concurrent access safely

```
import java.util.concurrent.locks.Lock;
import java.util.concurrent.locks.ReentrantLock;

public class ThreadSafeBankingSystem {
    public static class Account {
        private final String id;
        private double balance;
        private final Lock lock = new ReentrantLock();

        public Account(String id, double initialBalance) {
            this.id = id;
            this.balance = initialBalance;
        }

        public String getId() {
            return id;
        }
```

```java
    public double getBalance() {
        lock.lock();
        try {
            return balance;
        } finally {
            lock.unlock();
        }
    }

    public boolean withdraw(double amount) {
        lock.lock();
        try {
            if (balance >= amount) {
                balance -= amount;
                return true;
            }
            return false;
        } finally {
            lock.unlock();
        }
    }

    public void deposit(double amount) {
        lock.lock();
        try {
            balance += amount;
        } finally {
            lock.unlock();
        }
    }
}

public static class Bank {
    public boolean transfer(Account from, Account to, double amount) {
        // Prevent deadlocks by always acquiring locks in the same order
        Account firstLock = from.getId().compareTo(to.getId()) < 0 ? from : to;
        Account secondLock = from.getId().compareTo(to.getId()) < 0 ? to : from;

        // Acquire first lock
        firstLock.lock.lock();
        try {
            // Acquire second lock
            secondLock.lock.lock();
            try {
                // Check if transfer is possible
                if (from.getBalance() >= amount) {
                    from.withdraw(amount);
                    to.deposit(amount);
                    return true;
                }
                return false;
            } finally {
```

```java
                    secondLock.lock.unlock();
                }
            } finally {
                firstLock.lock.unlock();
            }
        }
    }

    public static void main(String[] args) throws InterruptedException {
        // Create accounts
        Account accountA = new Account("A", 1000);
        Account accountB = new Account("B", 1000);
        Bank bank = new Bank();

        // Create threads that transfer money back and forth
        Thread thread1 = new Thread(() -> {
            for (int i = 0; i < 100; i++) {
                bank.transfer(accountA, accountB, 10);
                try {
                    Thread.sleep(5);
                } catch (InterruptedException e) {
                    e.printStackTrace();
                }
            }
        });

        Thread thread2 = new Thread(() -> {
            for (int i = 0; i < 100; i++) {
                bank.transfer(accountB, accountA, 5);
                try {
                    Thread.sleep(5);
                } catch (InterruptedException e) {
                    e.printStackTrace();
                }
            }
        });

        // Start threads
        thread1.start();
        thread2.start();

        // Wait for both to finish
        thread1.join();
        thread2.join();

        // Print final balances
        System.out.println("Final balance of Account A: $" + accountA.getBalance());
        System.out.println("Final balance of Account B: $" + accountB.getBalance());
        System.out.println("Total money in the system: $" +
                        (accountA.getBalance() + accountB.getBalance()));
    }
}
```

Here's a simplified example of how a web server might handle multiple client requests using threads:

```java
import java.io.*;
import java.net.*;
import java.util.concurrent.*;

public class SimpleWebServer {
    public static void main(String[] args) throws IOException {
        // Create a thread pool for handling client requests
        ExecutorService executor = Executors.newFixedThreadPool(10);

        // Create server socket
        ServerSocket serverSocket = new ServerSocket(8080);
        System.out.println("Server started on port 8080");

        try {
            while (true) {
                // Wait for a client connection
                Socket clientSocket = serverSocket.accept();
                System.out.println("Client          connected:          "          +
clientSocket.getInetAddress());

                // Submit client handling task to the thread pool
                executor.submit(() -> handleClient(clientSocket));
            }
        } finally {
            serverSocket.close();
            executor.shutdown();
        }
    }

    private static void handleClient(Socket clientSocket) {
        try (
            BufferedReader in = new BufferedReader(
                new InputStreamReader(clientSocket.getInputStream()));
            PrintWriter out = new PrintWriter(clientSocket.getOutputStream(), true)
        ) {
            // Read the request
            String request = in.readLine();
            System.out.println("Thread " + Thread.currentThread().getName() +
                            " handling request: " + request);

            // Simulate processing time
            Thread.sleep(500);

            // Send response
            out.println("HTTP/1.1 200 OK");
            out.println("Content-Type: text/html");
            out.println();
```

```
        out.println("<html><body>");
        out.println("<h1>Hello from Java Server</h1>");
        out.println("<p>Your request: " + request + "</p>");
        out.println("<p>Handled by thread: " + Thread.currentThread().getName()
+ "</p>");
        out.println("</body></html>");

        // Close the connection
        clientSocket.close();
        System.out.println("Response sent and connection closed");

    } catch (IOException | InterruptedException e) {
        System.out.println("Error handling client: " + e.getMessage());
    }
  }
}
```

 FAQ: Common Multithreading Questions

1. When should I use multithreading?

Multithreading is particularly useful when:

- Processing tasks that can be executed in parallel
- Handling multiple user requests simultaneously (servers)
- Performing background tasks while keeping the UI responsive
- Taking advantage of multi-core processors for computationally intensive tasks

However, multithreading adds complexity and should be used when the benefits outweigh the costs.

2. What's the difference between a process and a thread?

Process:

- An independent program in execution with its own memory space
- Processes are isolated from each other
- Communication between processes is relatively expensive

Thread:

- A lightweight execution unit within a process
- Threads share the memory space of their parent process
- Communication between threads is easier and faster

3. Why is thread synchronization necessary?

Thread synchronization is necessary to:

- Prevent race conditions when multiple threads access shared data
- Ensure that changes made by one thread are visible to other threads
- Coordinate thread execution when operations must happen in a specific order
- Prevent deadlocks, livelocks, and other threading issues

4. What's the difference between `volatile` and `synchronized`?

volatile:

- Ensures that variable reads and writes go directly to main memory (visibility guarantee)
- Does not provide atomicity for compound operations (like `i++`)
- Lighter weight than synchronized
- Cannot coordinate thread execution order

synchronized:

- Provides both visibility and atomicity guarantees
- Creates mutual exclusion (only one thread can execute a synchronized block/method at a time)
- Can be used for thread coordination
- Has more overhead than volatile

5. What are thread pools and why are they useful?

Thread pools are groups of reusable worker threads that:

- Reduce the overhead of thread creation/destruction
- Limit the number of concurrent threads to avoid resource exhaustion
- Provide a mechanism for managing task execution
- Separate task submission from execution mechanics

They are particularly useful in server applications where many short-lived tasks need to be executed.

6. How do I choose the right size for my thread pool?

The optimal thread pool size depends on:

- Nature of tasks (CPU-bound vs. I/O-bound)
- Available system resources (CPU cores, memory)
- Expected workload

For CPU-bound tasks, a good starting point is the number of available processors:

```
int nThreads = Runtime.getRuntime().availableProcessors();
```

153

For I/O-bound tasks, you might want more threads since they'll spend time waiting.

7. What are some alternatives to low-level thread management?

Modern Java offers higher-level concurrency tools:

- CompletableFuture for asynchronous programming
- Parallel Streams for data parallel operations
- Virtual threads (Project Loom in Java 21) for high-throughput concurrent applications
- Reactive programming models with libraries like Reactor or RxJava

8. What is a daemon thread?

A daemon thread is a background thread that does not prevent the JVM from exiting if all non-daemon threads have finished. They are typically used for service tasks like garbage collection.

```
Thread daemonThread = new Thread(() -> {
    while (true) {
        // Background task
        try {
            Thread.sleep(1000);
        } catch (InterruptedException e) {
            break;
        }
    }
});
daemonThread.setDaemon(true); // Set as daemon before starting
daemonThread.start();
```

9.11 Virtual Threads (Java 21 Preview Feature)

Java 21 introduced Virtual Threads, a lightweight alternative to platform threads that can significantly improve application throughput for I/O-bound workloads.

What are Virtual Threads?

Virtual threads are lightweight threads that:

- Are managed by the JVM rather than the operating system
- Have minimal memory footprint (compared to platform threads)
- Can be created in large numbers (millions)
- Use the same Thread API and programming model as platform threads

Using Virtual Threads

```
import java.util.concurrent.ExecutorService;
import java.util.concurrent.Executors;
```

```java
public class VirtualThreadsExample {
    public static void main(String[] args) throws Exception {
        // Create many virtual threads
        long start = System.currentTimeMillis();

        try                     (ExecutorService                    executor              =
Executors.newVirtualThreadPerTaskExecutor()) {
            for (int i = 0; i < 10_000; i++) {
                final int id = i;
                executor.submit(() -> {
                    // Simulate I/O operation
                    try {
                        Thread.sleep(100);
                        if (id % 1000 == 0) {
                            System.out.println("Task " + id + " completed");
                        }
                    } catch (InterruptedException e) {
                        e.printStackTrace();
                    }
                    return id;
                });
            }
            // The executor is auto-closed here, and we wait for all tasks to complete
        }

        long duration = System.currentTimeMillis() - start;
        System.out.println("Completed 10,000 tasks in " + duration + " ms");
    }
}
```

Creating Individual Virtual Threads

```java
// Create and start a virtual thread
Thread vThread = Thread.startVirtualThread(() -> {
    System.out.println("Running in a virtual thread");
    try {
        Thread.sleep(100);
    } catch (InterruptedException e) {
        e.printStackTrace();
    }
});

// Wait for the virtual thread to complete
vThread.join();
```

Benefits of Virtual Threads

- **Scalability**: Create millions of virtual threads without exhausting system resources
- **Simplified Code**: Write straightforward blocking code that still performs well
- **Improved Throughput**: Handle more concurrent connections with the same hardware
- **Familiar Model**: Use the same Thread API you're already familiar with

Virtual threads are particularly beneficial for:

- Server applications handling many concurrent connections
- I/O-bound applications (web clients, database operations)
- Applications that currently use asynchronous programming for scalability

They are less beneficial for:

- CPU-bound applications
- Applications that need real-time guarantees

9.12 Summary and Best Practices

Key Takeaways

1. **Threading Basics**:
   - Threads allow concurrent execution of code
   - Java provides multiple ways to create and manage threads
   - Thread lifecycle includes states like NEW, RUNNABLE, BLOCKED, etc.
2. **Synchronization**:
   - Proper synchronization is essential for thread safety
   - Tools include: synchronized keyword, locks, atomic variables
   - Avoid sharing mutable state when possible
3. **Concurrency Utilities**:
   - Thread pools manage thread creation and reuse
   - ExecutorService provides high-level task submission
   - Java includes many utilities for thread coordination and safety
4. **Thread Safety**:
   - Immutability is the simplest path to thread safety
   - Concurrent collections provide thread-safe data structures
   - Careful design can reduce synchronization needs
5. **Modern Java Concurrency**:
   - CompletableFuture for composing asynchronous operations
   - Virtual Threads for high-throughput concurrent applications

Best Practices

1. **Use high-level concurrency abstractions** when possible, like ExecutorService instead of raw threads.
2. **Prefer immutability** to simplify concurrent code.
3. **Minimize the scope of synchronization** to reduce contention.
4. **Always clean up thread resources** properly to avoid leaks.
5. **Use thread pools** instead of creating threads directly.
6. **Document threading expectations** in your API designs.

7. **Test thoroughly** with different thread interleaving scenarios.
8. **Use atomic variables** for simple counters and flags.
9. **Consider thread-local storage** for thread-specific data.
10. **Be aware of memory visibility issues** and use proper synchronization.

9.13 Challenge Exercise

Task: Create a program that simulates a simplified bank with multiple accounts. Multiple customers (threads) should be able to withdraw and deposit money concurrently while maintaining the integrity of account balances.

Requirements:

1. Create a Bank class with methods to create accounts, deposit, withdraw, and transfer money
2. Ensure all operations are thread-safe
3. Prevent overdrafts (withdrawals that would make the balance negative)
4. Add a transaction log that records all successful operations
5. Handle concurrent transfers between accounts without deadlocks

Here's a solution framework to get you started:

```java
import java.util.concurrent.*;
import java.util.concurrent.locks.*;
import java.util.*;
import java.time.LocalDateTime;
import java.time.format.DateTimeFormatter;

public class BankingSystem {
    public static class Transaction {
        private final String type;
        private final String accountId;
        private final String targetAccountId;  // For transfers
        private final double amount;
        private final LocalDateTime timestamp;

        public Transaction(String type, String accountId, String targetAccountId,
double amount) {
            this.type = type;
            this.accountId = accountId;
            this.targetAccountId = targetAccountId;
            this.amount = amount;
            this.timestamp = LocalDateTime.now();
        }

        @Override
        public String toString() {
            DateTimeFormatter formatter = DateTimeFormatter.ofPattern("yyyy-MM-dd
HH:mm:ss");
            String formattedTime = timestamp.format(formatter);
```

```java
            if ("TRANSFER".equals(type)) {
                return String.format("[%s] %s: $%.2f from %s to %s",
                                     formattedTime,   type,   amount,   accountId,
targetAccountId);
            } else {
                return String.format("[%s] %s: $%.2f in account %s",
                                     formattedTime, type, amount, accountId);
            }
        }
    }

    public static class Bank {
        private  final  ConcurrentHashMap<String,  Account>  accounts  =  new
ConcurrentHashMap<>();
        private final List<Transaction> transactionLog =
            Collections.synchronizedList(new ArrayList<>());

        public Account createAccount(String accountId, double initialBalance) {
            Account account = new Account(accountId, initialBalance);
            accounts.put(accountId, account);
            logTransaction("CREATE", accountId, null, initialBalance);
            return account;
        }

        public boolean deposit(String accountId, double amount) {
            Account account = accounts.get(accountId);
            if (account == null || amount <= 0) return false;

            account.lock.lock();
            try {
                account.balance += amount;
                logTransaction("DEPOSIT", accountId, null, amount);
                return true;
            } finally {
                account.lock.unlock();
            }
        }

        public boolean withdraw(String accountId, double amount) {
            Account account = accounts.get(accountId);
            if (account == null || amount <= 0) return false;

            account.lock.lock();
            try {
                if (account.balance >= amount) {
                    account.balance -= amount;
                    logTransaction("WITHDRAW", accountId, null, amount);
                    return true;
                }
                return false;
            } finally {
                account.lock.unlock();
```

```java
            }
        }

        public boolean transfer(String fromAccountId, String toAccountId, double
amount) {
            if (fromAccountId.equals(toAccountId) || amount <= 0) return false;

            Account fromAccount = accounts.get(fromAccountId);
            Account toAccount = accounts.get(toAccountId);

            if (fromAccount == null || toAccount == null) return false;

            // Prevent deadlocks by acquiring locks in a consistent order
            Account firstLock, secondLock;
            boolean fromFirst;

            if (fromAccountId.compareTo(toAccountId) < 0) {
                firstLock = fromAccount;
                secondLock = toAccount;
                fromFirst = true;
            } else {
                firstLock = toAccount;
                secondLock = fromAccount;
                fromFirst = false;
            }

            // Acquire first lock
            firstLock.lock.lock();
            try {
                // Acquire second lock
                secondLock.lock.lock();
                try {
                    // If we locked the "from" account first, check its balance first
                    if (fromFirst) {
                        if (fromAccount.balance >= amount) {
                            fromAccount.balance -= amount;
                            toAccount.balance += amount;
                            logTransaction("TRANSFER", fromAccountId, toAccountId,
amount);

                            return true;
                        }
                        return false;
                    }
                    // Otherwise, we locked the "to" account first
                    else {
                        if (fromAccount.balance >= amount) {
                            fromAccount.balance -= amount;
                            toAccount.balance += amount;
                            logTransaction("TRANSFER", fromAccountId, toAccountId,
amount);

                            return true;
                        }
```

```java
                    return false;
                }
            } finally {
                secondLock.lock.unlock();
            }
        } finally {
            firstLock.lock.unlock();
        }
    }


    public double getBalance(String accountId) {
        Account account = accounts.get(accountId);
        if (account == null) return -1;

        account.lock.lock();
        try {
            return account.balance;
        } finally {
            account.lock.unlock();
        }
    }


    public void printTransactionLog() {
        System.out.println("\n==== TRANSACTION LOG ====");
        synchronized(transactionLog) {
            for (Transaction tx : transactionLog) {
                System.out.println(tx);
            }
        }
        System.out.println("========================\n");
    }


    private    void    logTransaction(String    type,    String    accountId,    String
targetAccountId, double amount) {
        transactionLog.add(new    Transaction(type,    accountId,    targetAccountId,
amount));
    }
}


public static class Account {
    private final String id;
    private double balance;
    final Lock lock = new ReentrantLock();

    public Account(String id, double initialBalance) {
        this.id = id;
        this.balance = initialBalance;
    }

    public String getId() {
        return id;
    }
```

```java
    }

    public static void main(String[] args) throws InterruptedException {
        Bank bank = new Bank();

        // Create accounts
        bank.createAccount("A1", 1000);
        bank.createAccount("A2", 2000);
        bank.createAccount("A3", 1500);

        // Create customer threads performing random operations
        ExecutorService executor = Executors.newFixedThreadPool(10);
        CountDownLatch latch = new CountDownLatch(100); // 100 operations

        Random random = new Random();
        String[] accountIds = {"A1", "A2", "A3"};

        for (int i = 0; i < 100; i++) {
            executor.submit(() -> {
                try {
                    // Randomly select an operation
                    int operation = random.nextInt(3); // 0: deposit, 1: withdraw,
2: transfer

                    int accountIndex = random.nextInt(accountIds.length);
                    String accountId = accountIds[accountIndex];
                    double amount = 10 + random.nextInt(90); // $10-$100

                    boolean success = false;
                    switch (operation) {
                        case 0: // Deposit
                            success = bank.deposit(accountId, amount);
                            break;
                        case 1: // Withdraw
                            success = bank.withdraw(accountId, amount);
                            break;
                        case 2: // Transfer
                            // Select a different target account
                            int targetIndex;
                            do {
                                targetIndex = random.nextInt(accountIds.length);
                            } while (targetIndex == accountIndex);

                            String targetAccountId = accountIds[targetIndex];
                            success = bank.transfer(accountId, targetAccountId,
amount);

                            break;
                    }

                    // Small delay to simulate real-world timing
                    Thread.sleep(random.nextInt(100));

                } catch (Exception e) {
```

```
                    e.printStackTrace();
                } finally {
                    latch.countDown();
                }
            });
        }

        // Wait for all operations to complete
        latch.await();
        executor.shutdown();

        // Print final balances
        System.out.println("\n==== FINAL BALANCES ====");
        for (String accountId : accountIds) {
            System.out.printf("Account          %s:          $%.2f\n",          accountId,
bank.getBalance(accountId));
        }

        // Print transaction log
        bank.printTransactionLog();

        // Verify total money in the system is preserved
        double totalBalance = 0;
        for (String accountId : accountIds) {
            totalBalance += bank.getBalance(accountId);
        }
        System.out.printf("Total money in the system: $%.2f (Expected: $4500.00)\n",
totalBalance);
    }
}
```

When you run this code, you'll see a transaction log and final balances. The total money in the system should remain constant at $4500 (the sum of the initial balances), confirming that our concurrent operations are maintaining data integrity.

9.14 Further Learning Resources

1. **Documentation**:
   - Java Concurrency in Practice - Definitive book on Java concurrency
   - Oracle's Concurrency Tutorial
   - Virtual Threads Documentation
2. **Tools**:
   - Java Flight Recorder - Analyze thread behavior
   - VisualVM - Monitor thread activity visually
   - jconsole - Java monitoring and management console
3. **Advanced Topics**:
   - Lock-free algorithms
   - Actor model (with libraries like Akka)
   - Reactive programming (Project Reactor, RxJava)

- Software transactional memory

Remember, multithreading is a powerful tool, but also introduces complexity. Start simple, test thoroughly, and gradually adopt more advanced patterns as you gain experience. With practice, you'll develop the intuition needed for writing efficient and reliable concurrent code.

Chapter 10: Building a Complete Java Application

In this chapter, we'll bring together everything you've learned so far to build a complete Java application. We'll create a Command Line Interface (CLI) Task Manager that allows users to create, view, update, and delete tasks. This project will demonstrate how to apply Java concepts in a real-world scenario.

10.1 Design Patterns Overview

Design patterns are proven solutions to common problems in software design. They help you create more maintainable, flexible, and robust code. Let's explore some essential design patterns you'll use in your Java applications.

10.1.1 MVC (Model-View-Controller)

The MVC pattern separates an application into three main components:

- **Model**: Represents data and business logic
- **View**: Handles user interface and presentation
- **Controller**: Processes user input and manages interactions

```java
// Model class
public class Task {
    private int id;
    private String description;
    private boolean completed;
    private LocalDate dueDate;

    // Constructor, getters, setters, etc.
    public Task(int id, String description, LocalDate dueDate) {
        this.id = id;
        this.description = description;
        this.completed = false;
        this.dueDate = dueDate;
    }

    // Getters and setters
    public int getId() { return id; }

    public String getDescription() { return description; }
    public void setDescription(String description) { this.description = description;
}
```

```java
        public boolean isCompleted() { return completed; }
        public void setCompleted(boolean completed) { this.completed = completed; }

        public LocalDate getDueDate() { return dueDate; }
        public void setDueDate(LocalDate dueDate) { this.dueDate = dueDate; }

        @Override
        public String toString() {
            return String.format("[%d] %s (Due: %s) %s",
                                  id, description, dueDate, completed ? "[DONE]" :
"[PENDING]");
        }
    }
}
// View class
public class TaskView {
    public void displayTaskList(List<Task> tasks) {
        if (tasks.isEmpty()) {
            System.out.println("No tasks found!");
            return;
        }

        System.out.println("\n===== TASK LIST =====");
        for (Task task : tasks) {
            System.out.println(task);
        }
        System.out.println("=====================\n");
    }

    public void displayMessage(String message) {
        System.out.println(message);
    }

    // Other display methods
}
// Controller class
public class TaskController {
    private final TaskManager model;
    private final TaskView view;

    public TaskController(TaskManager model, TaskView view) {
        this.model = model;
        this.view = view;
    }

    public void showAllTasks() {
        List<Task> tasks = model.getAllTasks();
        view.displayTaskList(tasks);
    }

    public void addTask(String description, LocalDate dueDate) {
        Task newTask = model.createTask(description, dueDate);
        view.displayMessage("Task created: " + newTask);
```

```
    }

    // Other controller methods
}
```

10.1.2 Singleton Pattern

Singleton ensures a class has only one instance and provides a global point of access to it. This is useful for managing resources like database connections.

```
public class TaskDatabase {
    private static TaskDatabase instance;
    private List<Task> tasks;

    // Private constructor prevents direct instantiation
    private TaskDatabase() {
        tasks = new ArrayList<>();
    }

    // Global access point
    public static synchronized TaskDatabase getInstance() {
        if (instance == null) {
            instance = new TaskDatabase();
        }
        return instance;
    }

    public List<Task> getTasks() {
        return new ArrayList<>(tasks);  // Return a copy to prevent external
modification
    }

    public void addTask(Task task) {
        tasks.add(task);
    }

    // Other database operations
}
```

10.1.3 Repository Pattern

The repository pattern abstracts the data access layer, making your application more maintainable and testable.

```
// Repository interface
public interface TaskRepository {
    List<Task> findAll();
    Task findById(int id);
    Task save(Task task);
    boolean delete(int id);
```

```java
    List<Task> findByStatus(boolean completed);
}

// Implementation
public class InMemoryTaskRepository implements TaskRepository {
    private final Map<Integer, Task> taskMap = new HashMap<>();
    private int nextId = 1;

    @Override
    public List<Task> findAll() {
        return new ArrayList<>(taskMap.values());
    }

    @Override
    public Task findById(int id) {
        return taskMap.get(id);
    }

    @Override
    public Task save(Task task) {
        if (task.getId() == 0) {
            // New task
            Task newTask = new Task(nextId++, task.getDescription(),
task.getDueDate());
            newTask.setCompleted(task.isCompleted());
            taskMap.put(newTask.getId(), newTask);
            return newTask;
        } else {
            // Update existing task
            taskMap.put(task.getId(), task);
            return task;
        }
    }

    @Override
    public boolean delete(int id) {
        return taskMap.remove(id) != null;
    }

    @Override
    public List<Task> findByStatus(boolean completed) {
        return taskMap.values().stream()
                .filter(task -> task.isCompleted() == completed)
                .collect(Collectors.toList());
    }
}
```

10.2 Project Structure and Organization

A well-organized project structure makes your application easier to understand, maintain, and extend. Here's a common structure for Java applications:

167

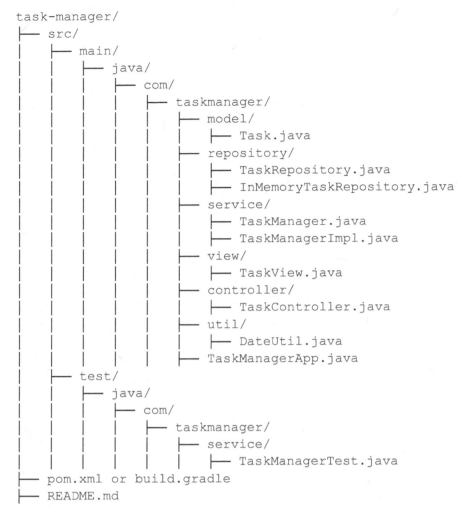

```
task-manager/
├── src/
│   ├── main/
│   │   ├── java/
│   │   │   ├── com/
│   │   │   │   ├── taskmanager/
│   │   │   │   │   ├── model/
│   │   │   │   │   │   ├── Task.java
│   │   │   │   │   ├── repository/
│   │   │   │   │   │   ├── TaskRepository.java
│   │   │   │   │   │   ├── InMemoryTaskRepository.java
│   │   │   │   │   ├── service/
│   │   │   │   │   │   ├── TaskManager.java
│   │   │   │   │   │   ├── TaskManagerImpl.java
│   │   │   │   │   ├── view/
│   │   │   │   │   │   ├── TaskView.java
│   │   │   │   │   ├── controller/
│   │   │   │   │   │   ├── TaskController.java
│   │   │   │   │   ├── util/
│   │   │   │   │   │   ├── DateUtil.java
│   │   │   │   │   ├── TaskManagerApp.java
│   │   ├── test/
│   │   │   ├── java/
│   │   │   │   ├── com/
│   │   │   │   │   ├── taskmanager/
│   │   │   │   │   │   ├── service/
│   │   │   │   │   │   │   ├── TaskManagerTest.java
├── pom.xml or build.gradle
├── README.md
```

10.2.1 Package Naming Conventions

Java uses a reverse domain name convention for package naming:

- Start with your organization's domain name in reverse (e.g., `com.example`)
- Add the project name (e.g., `com.example.taskmanager`)
- Organize subpackages by layer or feature

10.2.2 Service Layer

The service layer contains business logic and acts as a bridge between controllers and repositories:

```java
// Service interface
public interface TaskManager {
    List<Task> getAllTasks();
    List<Task> getPendingTasks();
    List<Task> getCompletedTasks();
    Task getTaskById(int id);
    Task createTask(String description, LocalDate dueDate);
    Task updateTask(int id, String description, LocalDate dueDate);
```

168

```java
    boolean markTaskAsCompleted(int id);
    boolean deleteTask(int id);
}


// Implementation
public class TaskManagerImpl implements TaskManager {
    private final TaskRepository repository;

    public TaskManagerImpl(TaskRepository repository) {
        this.repository = repository;
    }

    @Override
    public List<Task> getAllTasks() {
        return repository.findAll();
    }

    @Override
    public List<Task> getPendingTasks() {
        return repository.findByStatus(false);
    }

    @Override
    public List<Task> getCompletedTasks() {
        return repository.findByStatus(true);
    }

    @Override
    public Task getTaskById(int id) {
        Task task = repository.findById(id);
        if (task == null) {
            throw new IllegalArgumentException("Task not found with ID: " + id);
        }
        return task;
    }

    @Override
    public Task createTask(String description, LocalDate dueDate) {
        if (description == null || description.trim().isEmpty()) {
            throw new IllegalArgumentException("Task description cannot be empty");
        }

        Task newTask = new Task(0, description, dueDate);
        return repository.save(newTask);
    }

    @Override
    public Task updateTask(int id, String description, LocalDate dueDate) {
        Task existingTask = getTaskById(id);

        if (description != null && !description.trim().isEmpty()) {
            existingTask.setDescription(description);
```

```
        }

        if (dueDate != null) {
            existingTask.setDueDate(dueDate);
        }

        return repository.save(existingTask);
    }

    @Override
    public boolean markTaskAsCompleted(int id) {
        Task task = getTaskById(id);
        task.setCompleted(true);
        repository.save(task);
        return true;
    }

    @Override
    public boolean deleteTask(int id) {
        return repository.delete(id);
    }
}
```

10.3 Putting It All Together: CLI Task Manager

Now, let's create the main application class that brings all components together and provides a command-line interface:

```
import java.time.LocalDate;
import java.time.format.DateTimeFormatter;
import java.time.format.DateTimeParseException;
import java.util.Scanner;

public class TaskManagerApp {
    private      static    final    DateTimeFormatter    DATE_FORMATTER    =
DateTimeFormatter.ofPattern("yyyy-MM-dd");
    private static Scanner scanner = new Scanner(System.in);
    private static TaskController controller;

    public static void main(String[] args) {
        // Initialize components
        TaskRepository repository = new InMemoryTaskRepository();
        TaskManager taskManager = new TaskManagerImpl(repository);
        TaskView view = new TaskView();
        controller = new TaskController(taskManager, view);

        boolean running = true;

        // Welcome message
        System.out.println("===== Welcome to Task Manager =====");
```

```java
        // Add some sample tasks
        addSampleTasks();

        while (running) {
            displayMenu();
            int choice = getUserChoice();

            switch (choice) {
                case 1:
                    showAllTasks();
                    break;
                case 2:
                    showPendingTasks();
                    break;
                case 3:
                    showCompletedTasks();
                    break;
                case 4:
                    addNewTask();
                    break;
                case 5:
                    markTaskAsCompleted();
                    break;
                case 6:
                    deleteTask();
                    break;
                case 7:
                    running = false;
                    System.out.println("Thank    you    for    using    Task    Manager.
Goodbye!");
                    break;
                default:
                    System.out.println("Invalid choice! Please try again.");
            }
        }

        scanner.close();
    }

    private static void addSampleTasks() {
        controller.addTask("Complete            Java            assignment",
LocalDate.now().plusDays(7));
        controller.addTask("Buy groceries", LocalDate.now().plusDays(1));
        controller.addTask("Schedule            dentist            appointment",
LocalDate.now().plusDays(14));
    }

    private static void displayMenu() {
        System.out.println("\nPlease select an option:");
        System.out.println("1. Show all tasks");
        System.out.println("2. Show pending tasks");
        System.out.println("3. Show completed tasks");
```

```java
            System.out.println("4. Add new task");
            System.out.println("5. Mark task as completed");
            System.out.println("6. Delete task");
            System.out.println("7. Exit");
            System.out.print("Enter your choice (1-7): ");
        }

        private static int getUserChoice() {
            try {
                return Integer.parseInt(scanner.nextLine());
            } catch (NumberFormatException e) {
                return -1; // Invalid choice
            }
        }

        private static void showAllTasks() {
            controller.showAllTasks();
        }

        private static void showPendingTasks() {
            controller.showPendingTasks();
        }

        private static void showCompletedTasks() {
            controller.showCompletedTasks();
        }

        private static void addNewTask() {
            System.out.print("Enter task description: ");
            String description = scanner.nextLine();

            LocalDate dueDate = null;
            boolean validDate = false;

            while (!validDate) {
                System.out.print("Enter due date (yyyy-MM-dd): ");
                String dateStr = scanner.nextLine();

                try {
                    dueDate = LocalDate.parse(dateStr, DATE_FORMATTER);
                    validDate = true;
                } catch (DateTimeParseException e) {
                    System.out.println("Invalid date format! Please use yyyy-MM-dd
format.");
                }
            }

            controller.addTask(description, dueDate);
        }

        private static void markTaskAsCompleted() {
            System.out.print("Enter task ID to mark as completed: ");
```

172

```java
        try {
            int id = Integer.parseInt(scanner.nextLine());
            controller.completeTask(id);
        } catch (NumberFormatException e) {
            System.out.println("Invalid ID format!");
        } catch (IllegalArgumentException e) {
            System.out.println(e.getMessage());
        }
    }

    private static void deleteTask() {
        System.out.print("Enter task ID to delete: ");
        try {
            int id = Integer.parseInt(scanner.nextLine());
            controller.deleteTask(id);
        } catch (NumberFormatException e) {
            System.out.println("Invalid ID format!");
        } catch (IllegalArgumentException e) {
            System.out.println(e.getMessage());
        }
    }
}
```

10.4 Error Handling and Input Validation

Proper error handling and input validation are crucial for building robust applications:

```java
// Example of improved input validation in the TaskManagerApp
private static void addNewTask() {
    String description = "";

    // Validate description is not empty
    while (description.trim().isEmpty()) {
        System.out.print("Enter task description: ");
        description = scanner.nextLine();

        if (description.trim().isEmpty()) {
            System.out.println("Task description cannot be empty!");
        }
    }

    LocalDate dueDate = null;
    boolean validDate = false;

    while (!validDate) {
        System.out.print("Enter due date (yyyy-MM-dd) or press Enter for today: ");

        String dateStr = scanner.nextLine();

        try {
            if (dateStr.trim().isEmpty()) {
```

```
                    dueDate = LocalDate.now();
            } else {
                    dueDate = LocalDate.parse(dateStr, DATE_FORMATTER);
            }

            // Validate that the date is not in the past
            if (dueDate.isBefore(LocalDate.now())) {
                    System.out.println("Due date cannot be in the past!");
                    continue;
            }

            validDate = true;
        } catch (DateTimeParseException e) {
                System.out.println("Invalid   date   format!   Please   use   yyyy-MM-dd
format.");
            }
        }

        try {
            controller.addTask(description, dueDate);
        } catch (Exception e) {
            System.out.println("Error adding task: " + e.getMessage());
        }
    }
}
```

10.5 Testing the Application

Writing tests is essential for ensuring your application works correctly. Here's an example of a JUnit test for the TaskManager service:

```
import org.junit.jupiter.api.BeforeEach;
import org.junit.jupiter.api.Test;
import static org.junit.jupiter.api.Assertions.*;

import java.time.LocalDate;
import java.util.List;

public class TaskManagerTest {
    private TaskManager taskManager;
    private TaskRepository repository;

    @BeforeEach
    public void setUp() {
        repository = new InMemoryTaskRepository();
        taskManager = new TaskManagerImpl(repository);
    }

    @Test
    public void testCreateTask() {
        String description = "Test task";
        LocalDate dueDate = LocalDate.now().plusDays(1);
```

174

```java
        Task task = taskManager.createTask(description, dueDate);

        assertNotNull(task);
        assertEquals(description, task.getDescription());
        assertEquals(dueDate, task.getDueDate());
        assertFalse(task.isCompleted());
    }

    @Test
    public void testCreateTaskWithEmptyDescription() {
        assertThrows(IllegalArgumentException.class, () -> {
            taskManager.createTask("", LocalDate.now());
        });
    }

    @Test
    public void testMarkTaskAsCompleted() {
        Task task = taskManager.createTask("Test task", LocalDate.now());
        int taskId = task.getId();

        assertTrue(taskManager.markTaskAsCompleted(taskId));

        Task updatedTask = taskManager.getTaskById(taskId);
        assertTrue(updatedTask.isCompleted());
    }

    @Test
    public void testGetPendingTasks() {
        taskManager.createTask("Task 1", LocalDate.now());
        Task task2 = taskManager.createTask("Task 2", LocalDate.now());
        taskManager.markTaskAsCompleted(task2.getId());
        taskManager.createTask("Task 3", LocalDate.now());

        List<Task> pendingTasks = taskManager.getPendingTasks();

        assertEquals(2, pendingTasks.size());
        assertFalse(pendingTasks.get(0).isCompleted());
        assertFalse(pendingTasks.get(1).isCompleted());
    }

    @Test
    public void testDeleteTask() {
        Task task = taskManager.createTask("Task to delete", LocalDate.now());
        int taskId = task.getId();

        assertTrue(taskManager.deleteTask(taskId));

        assertThrows(IllegalArgumentException.class, () -> {
            taskManager.getTaskById(taskId);
        });
    }
```

```
}
```

10.6 Building and Running the Application

10.6.1 Using Maven

If you're using Maven for dependency management, your `pom.xml` might look like this:

```xml
<project xmlns="http://maven.apache.org/POM/4.0.0"
         xmlns:xsi="http://www.w3.org/2001/XMLSchema-instance"
         xsi:schemaLocation="http://maven.apache.org/POM/4.0.0
http://maven.apache.org/xsd/maven-4.0.0.xsd">
    <modelVersion>4.0.0</modelVersion>

    <groupId>com.example</groupId>
    <artifactId>task-manager</artifactId>
    <version>1.0-SNAPSHOT</version>

    <properties>
        <maven.compiler.source>21</maven.compiler.source>
        <maven.compiler.target>21</maven.compiler.target>
        <project.build.sourceEncoding>UTF-8</project.build.sourceEncoding>
    </properties>

    <dependencies>
        <dependency>
            <groupId>org.junit.jupiter</groupId>
            <artifactId>junit-jupiter</artifactId>
            <version>5.9.2</version>
            <scope>test</scope>
        </dependency>
    </dependencies>

    <build>
        <plugins>
            <plugin>
                <groupId>org.apache.maven.plugins</groupId>
                <artifactId>maven-compiler-plugin</artifactId>
                <version>3.11.0</version>
            </plugin>
            <plugin>
                <groupId>org.apache.maven.plugins</groupId>
                <artifactId>maven-surefire-plugin</artifactId>
                <version>3.1.2</version>
            </plugin>
            <plugin>
                <groupId>org.apache.maven.plugins</groupId>
                <artifactId>maven-jar-plugin</artifactId>
                <version>3.3.0</version>
                <configuration>
                    <archive>
```

```
                    <manifest>
                        <addClasspath>true</addClasspath>

<mainClass>com.example.taskmanager.TaskManagerApp</mainClass>
                    </manifest>
                </archive>
            </configuration>
        </plugin>
    </plugins>
  </build>
</project>
```

To build and run the application with Maven:

```
# Build the project
mvn clean package

# Run the application
java -jar target/task-manager-1.0-SNAPSHOT.jar
```

10.6.2 Using Gradle

If you prefer Gradle, your `build.gradle` might look like this:

```
plugins {
    id 'java'
    id 'application'
}

group = 'com.example'
version = '1.0-SNAPSHOT'

repositories {
    mavenCentral()
}

dependencies {
    testImplementation 'org.junit.jupiter:junit-jupiter:5.9.2'
}

java {
    sourceCompatibility = JavaVersion.VERSION_21
    targetCompatibility = JavaVersion.VERSION_21
}

application {
    mainClass = 'com.example.taskmanager.TaskManagerApp'
}

test {
    useJUnitPlatform()
}
```

```
jar {
    manifest {
        attributes 'Main-Class': 'com.example.taskmanager.TaskManagerApp'
    }
}
```

To build and run the application with Gradle:

```
# Build the project
./gradlew build

# Run the application
./gradlew run
```

 Quiz: Test Your Understanding

1. **Question**: What is the purpose of the MVC pattern in application design?

   a) To separate data from business logic
   b) To separate the user interface from the business logic and data
   c) To enable multiple controllers to work with a single model
   d) To eliminate the need for a repository layer

2. **Question**: In our Task Manager application, which pattern is used to ensure we only have one instance of TaskDatabase?

   a) Factory pattern
   b) Builder pattern
   c) Singleton pattern
   d) Adapter pattern

3. **Question**: What would happen if we tried to create a task with an empty description in our TaskManager implementation?

   a) The task would be created with an empty description
   b) The task would be created with a default description
   c) An IllegalArgumentException would be thrown
   d) Nothing would happen, but the task wouldn't be saved

4. **Question**: Looking at the code below, what is the output?

```
Task task = new Task(1, "Learn Java", LocalDate.of(2023, 5, 15));
task.setCompleted(true);
System.out.println(task);
```

178

a) [ ] Learn Java (Due: 2023-05-15) [PENDING]
b) [1] Learn Java (Due: 2023-05-15) [DONE]
c) Task@123abc
d) Task{id=1, description='Learn Java', completed=true, dueDate=2023-05-15:

5. **Question**: Which layer in our application is responsible for validating business rules like "task description cannot be empty"?

a) Controller layer
b) View layer
c) Repository layer
d) Service layer

Answers:

1. **b)** To separate the user interface from the business logic and data
2. **c)** Singleton pattern
3. **c)** An IllegalArgumentException would be thrown
4. **b)** [1] Learn Java (Due: 2023-05-15) [DONE]
5. **d)** Service layer

10.7 Common Mistakes and Best Practices

Common Mistakes

1. **Not Separating Concerns**: Mixing business logic, data access, and UI code makes your application hard to maintain and test.

```
// BAD: Mixing concerns
public void addTask() {
    System.out.print("Enter task description: ");
    String description = scanner.nextLine();

    // Direct database access from UI code
    Connection conn = DriverManager.getConnection("jdbc:mysql://localhost/tasks");
    PreparedStatement stmt = conn.prepareStatement("INSERT INTO tasks VALUES (?, ?)");
    stmt.setString(1, description);
    stmt.executeUpdate();
}
```

2. **Ignoring Error Handling**: Not handling exceptions properly can lead to application crashes and poor user experience.
3. **Hard-Coding Values**: Embedding configuration values directly in your code makes it difficult to change them later.

179

```
// BAD: Hard-coded connection string
Connection conn = DriverManager.getConnection("jdbc:mysql://localhost/tasks");

// GOOD: Use configuration
String connUrl = ConfigManager.getProperty("db.connection.url");
Connection conn = DriverManager.getConnection(connUrl);
```

4. **Not Testing Edge Cases**: Failing to test boundary conditions and error scenarios can lead to bugs in production.

Best Practices

1. **Follow SOLID Principles**:
   - **S**ingle Responsibility: Each class should have only one reason to change
   - **O**pen/Closed: Open for extension, closed for modification
   - **L**iskov Substitution: Subtypes must be substitutable for their base types
   - **I**nterface Segregation: Many client-specific interfaces are better than one general-purpose interface
   - **D**ependency Inversion: Depend on abstractions, not concretions
2. **Use Dependency Injection**: Pass dependencies to classes instead of creating them internally.

```
// BAD: Creating dependency internally
public class TaskService {
    private TaskRepository repository = new InMemoryTaskRepository();
}

// GOOD: Using dependency injection
public class TaskService {
    private final TaskRepository repository;

    public TaskService(TaskRepository repository) {
        this.repository = repository;
    }
}
```

3. **Write Clear, Self-Documenting Code**: Use meaningful names and comments to make your code easy to understand.
4. **Follow Java Naming Conventions**:
   - Classes: `PascalCase`
   - Methods/Variables: `camelCase`
   - Constants: `UPPER_SNAKE_CASE`
5. **Use Immutable Objects When Possible**: Immutable objects are thread-safe and easier to reason about.

```
// Using modern Java features for immutability
public record TaskDTO(int id, String description, boolean completed, LocalDate dueDate) {
    // Records automatically generate constructor, getters, equals, hashCode, and toString
```

180

}

10.8 Future Enhancements

Here are some ideas to extend your Task Manager application:

1. **Persistence**: Add database storage using JDBC or an ORM like Hibernate
2. **User Authentication**: Add user accounts and login functionality
3. **Web Interface**: Migrate to a web application using Spring Boot
4. **Task Categories**: Allow users to categorize tasks
5. **Notifications**: Implement reminders for upcoming tasks
6. **Search and Filter**: Add functionality to search and filter tasks
7. **Task Priorities**: Allow users to set task priorities

 FAQ

Q: Why did we use interfaces for our services and repositories?

A: Interfaces provide abstraction, making it easier to switch implementations (e.g., switching from in-memory storage to a database) without changing client code. They also facilitate testing through mocking.

Q: When should I use the Singleton pattern?

A: Use Singleton when you need exactly one instance of a class and want to provide a global point of access to it. Common examples include configuration managers and connection pools. However, use it sparingly as it can make testing more difficult.

Q: How do I improve performance for large data sets?

A: Consider implementing pagination for large lists, using efficient data structures, caching frequently accessed data, and optimizing database queries.

Q: What are some alternative project structures for larger applications?

A: For larger applications, you might organize by features instead of layers, use a hexagonal architecture (ports and adapters), or adopt a microservices approach.

Q: How can I handle concurrent modifications in a multi-user environment?

A: Use optimistic locking with version fields, pessimistic locking for critical operations, or implement conflict resolution strategies.

10.9 Summary

In this chapter, we've learned:

- How to apply design patterns like MVC, Singleton, and Repository to structure our application
- How to organize a Java project into packages and layers
- How to implement error handling and input validation
- How to build a complete CLI Task Manager application
- Best practices for writing maintainable Java code
- How to test a Java application using JUnit

You now have the skills to build complete Java applications from scratch! The Task Manager project demonstrates how to combine various Java concepts into a functional, well-structured application.

In the next chapter, we'll explore additional topics to further your Java journey, including more advanced APIs, libraries, and techniques for improving your applications.

Chapter 11: Next Steps in Your Java Journey

Now that you've built a complete Java application, you're ready to expand your knowledge and skills. This chapter will introduce you to more advanced Java topics, useful libraries, and professional development practices that will help you grow as a Java developer.

11.1 Java APIs and Libraries

Java has a rich ecosystem of built-in APIs and third-party libraries that can help you solve common programming challenges without reinventing the wheel.

11.1.1 Essential Java APIs

11.1.1.1 Java Stream API

The Stream API, introduced in Java 8, provides a powerful way to process collections of objects:

```java
// Without streams
List<String> longNames = new ArrayList<>();
for (String name : names) {
    if (name.length() > 5) {
        longNames.add(name.toUpperCase());
    }
}

// With streams
List<String> longNames = names.stream()
    .filter(name -> name.length() > 5)
    .map(String::toUpperCase)
    .collect(Collectors.toList());
```

Let's explore more stream operations:

```java
import java.util.*;
import java.util.stream.*;

public class StreamExample {
    public static void main(String[] args) {
        List<Task> tasks = List.of(
            new Task(1, "Learn Java", LocalDate.now().plusDays(7), false),
            new Task(2, "Buy groceries", LocalDate.now().plusDays(1), true),
```

```java
        new Task(3, "Fix bug in project", LocalDate.now(), false),
        new Task(4, "Read book", LocalDate.now().plusDays(14), false),
        new Task(5, "Call mom", LocalDate.now().minusDays(1), true)
    );

    // Filtering
    List<Task> pendingTasks = tasks.stream()
        .filter(task -> !task.isCompleted())
        .collect(Collectors.toList());
    System.out.println("Pending tasks: " + pendingTasks.size());

    // Mapping
    List<String> taskDescriptions = tasks.stream()
        .map(Task::getDescription)
        .collect(Collectors.toList());
    System.out.println("Descriptions: " + taskDescriptions);

    // Sorting
    List<Task> sortedByDueDate = tasks.stream()
        .sorted(Comparator.comparing(Task::getDueDate))
        .collect(Collectors.toList());
    System.out.println("First          due          task:          "          +
sortedByDueDate.get(0).getDescription());

    // Grouping
    Map<Boolean, List<Task>> tasksByStatus = tasks.stream()
        .collect(Collectors.groupingBy(Task::isCompleted));
    System.out.println("Completed tasks: " + tasksByStatus.get(true).size());

    // Statistics
    OptionalDouble averageDaysToComplete = tasks.stream()
        .filter(task -> !task.isCompleted())
        .mapToLong(task        ->        ChronoUnit.DAYS.between(LocalDate.now(),
task.getDueDate()))
        .average();
    System.out.println("Average days to complete: " +
                    averageDaysToComplete.orElse(0));

    // Reduce
    Optional<LocalDate> earliestDueDate = tasks.stream()
        .map(Task::getDueDate)
        .reduce((date1, date2) -> date1.isBefore(date2) ? date1 : date2);
    System.out.println("Earliest due date: " + earliestDueDate.orElse(null));
    }
}
```

11.1.1.2 Java Time API

The Java Time API (java.time package), introduced in Java 8, provides comprehensive date and time functionality:

```java
import java.time.*;
import java.time.format.*;
import java.time.temporal.*;

public class TimeExample {
    public static void main(String[] args) {
        // Current date and time
        LocalDate today = LocalDate.now();
        LocalTime now = LocalTime.now();
        LocalDateTime currentDateTime = LocalDateTime.now();
        ZonedDateTime currentZonedDateTime = ZonedDateTime.now();

        System.out.println("Today: " + today);
        System.out.println("Now: " + now);
        System.out.println("Current date and time: " + currentDateTime);
        System.out.println("Current zoned date and time: " + currentZonedDateTime);

        // Creating specific dates and times
        LocalDate date = LocalDate.of(2023, Month.MARCH, 15);
        LocalTime time = LocalTime.of(13, 45, 20);
        LocalDateTime dateTime = LocalDateTime.of(date, time);

        // Date manipulation
        LocalDate tomorrow = today.plusDays(1);
        LocalDate nextWeek = today.plusWeeks(1);
        LocalDate previousMonth = today.minusMonths(1);

        // Period and Duration
        Period period = Period.between(date, today);
        System.out.println("Period: " + period.getYears() + " years, " +
                        period.getMonths() + " months, " +
                        period.getDays() + " days");

        Duration duration = Duration.between(time, now);
        System.out.println("Duration: " + duration.toHours() + " hours, " +
                        duration.toMinutesPart() + " minutes");

        // Formatting
        DateTimeFormatter formatter = DateTimeFormatter.ofPattern("EEEE, MMMM d,
yyyy 'at' h:mm a");
        String formattedDateTime = currentDateTime.format(formatter);
        System.out.println("Formatted: " + formattedDateTime);

        // Parsing
        LocalDate parsedDate = LocalDate.parse("2023-03-15");
        LocalDateTime parsedDateTime = LocalDateTime.parse("2023-03-15T13:45:20");

        // Time zones
        ZoneId newYork = ZoneId.of("America/New_York");
        ZonedDateTime newYorkTime = ZonedDateTime.now(newYork);
        System.out.println("New York time: " + newYorkTime);
```

```java
        // Converting between time zones
        ZoneId tokyo = ZoneId.of("Asia/Tokyo");
        ZonedDateTime tokyoTime = newYorkTime.withZoneSameInstant(tokyo);
        System.out.println("Tokyo time: " + tokyoTime);
    }
}
```

11.1.1.3 Java NIO.2 (New I/O)

Java NIO.2 provides more powerful file operations:

```java
import java.nio.file.*;
import java.io.IOException;
import java.nio.charset.StandardCharsets;
import java.util.List;
import java.util.stream.Collectors;
import java.util.stream.Stream;

public class FileExample {
    public static void main(String[] args) {
        Path path = Paths.get("tasks.txt");

        // Writing to file
        try {
            List<String> lines = List.of(
                "1,Learn Java,2023-05-15,false",
                "2,Buy groceries,2023-05-10,true",
                "3,Fix bug in project,2023-05-09,false"
            );
            Files.write(path, lines, StandardCharsets.UTF_8);
            System.out.println("File written successfully");
        } catch (IOException e) {
            System.err.println("Error writing file: " + e.getMessage());
        }

        // Reading from file
        try {
            List<String> lines = Files.readAllLines(path, StandardCharsets.UTF_8);
            lines.forEach(System.out::println);
        } catch (IOException e) {
            System.err.println("Error reading file: " + e.getMessage());
        }

        // File operations
        try {
            // Check if file exists
            boolean exists = Files.exists(path);
            System.out.println("File exists: " + exists);

            // File attributes
            long size = Files.size(path);
```

186

```java
            System.out.println("File size: " + size + " bytes");

            // Copy file
            Path copyPath = Paths.get("tasks_backup.txt");
            Files.copy(path, copyPath, StandardCopyOption.REPLACE_EXISTING);

            // Move/rename file
            Path newPath = Paths.get("tasks_new.txt");
            Files.move(copyPath, newPath, StandardCopyOption.REPLACE_EXISTING);

            // Delete file
            Files.delete(newPath);

            // Directory operations
            Path dirPath = Paths.get("tasks_dir");
            Files.createDirectories(dirPath);

            // List directory contents
            try (Stream<Path> list = Files.list(dirPath)) {
                List<String> fileNames = list
                    .filter(Files::isRegularFile)
                    .map(p -> p.getFileName().toString())
                    .collect(Collectors.toList());
                System.out.println("Files in directory: " + fileNames);
            }

            // Walk directory tree
            try (Stream<Path> walk = Files.walk(dirPath, 2)) {
                List<String> allPaths = walk
                    .map(Path::toString)
                    .collect(Collectors.toList());
                System.out.println("All paths: " + allPaths);
            }
        } catch (IOException e) {
            System.err.println("File operation error: " + e.getMessage());
        }
    }
}
```

11.1.2 Popular Third-Party Libraries

Let's explore some widely used libraries that can enhance your Java applications:

11.1.2.1 Project Lombok

Lombok reduces boilerplate code with annotations:

```java
import lombok.Data;
import lombok.NoArgsConstructor;
import lombok.AllArgsConstructor;
```

```
import java.time.LocalDate;

@Data
@NoArgsConstructor
@AllArgsConstructor
public class Task {
    private int id;
    private String description;
    private LocalDate dueDate;
    private boolean completed;

    // No need to write getters, setters, equals, hashCode, toString - Lombok
generates them
}
```

To use Lombok, add this to your pom.xml:

```
<dependency>
    <groupId>org.projectlombok</groupId>
    <artifactId>lombok</artifactId>
    <version>1.18.26</version>
    <scope>provided</scope>
</dependency>
```

11.1.2.2 Apache Commons

Apache Commons provides reusable components:

```
// Commons Lang
import org.apache.commons.lang3.StringUtils;
import org.apache.commons.lang3.time.StopWatch;

public class CommonsExample {
    public static void main(String[] args) {
        // StringUtils
        String input = null;
        String safe = StringUtils.defaultString(input, "N/A");
        boolean isBlank = StringUtils.isBlank(input);
        String reversed = StringUtils.reverse("Hello");

        System.out.println("Safe: " + safe);
        System.out.println("Is blank: " + isBlank);
        System.out.println("Reversed: " + reversed);

        // StopWatch
        StopWatch watch = StopWatch.createStarted();
        // Some operation
        for (int i = 0; i < 1000000; i++) {
            Math.sqrt(i);
        }
        watch.stop();
```

```
        System.out.println("Time taken: " + watch.getTime() + " ms");
    }
}
```

To use Apache Commons Lang, add this to your pom.xml:

```
<dependency>
    <groupId>org.apache.commons</groupId>
    <artifactId>commons-lang3</artifactId>
    <version>3.12.0</version>
</dependency>
```

11.1.2.3 Google Guava

Guava provides utilities for collections, caching, concurrency, and more:

```
import com.google.common.collect.*;
import com.google.common.base.Joiner;
import com.google.common.cache.Cache;
import com.google.common.cache.CacheBuilder;

import java.util.concurrent.TimeUnit;
import java.util.concurrent.ExecutionException;

public class GuavaExample {
    public static void main(String[] args) {
        // Immutable collections
        ImmutableList<String> list = ImmutableList.of("a", "b", "c");
        ImmutableSet<String> set = ImmutableSet.of("x", "y", "z");
        ImmutableMap<String, Integer> map = ImmutableMap.of("one", 1, "two", 2);

        // Multimap (multiple values per key)
        Multimap<String, String> multimap = ArrayListMultimap.create();
        multimap.put("fruit", "apple");
        multimap.put("fruit", "banana");
        multimap.put("vegetable", "carrot");

        System.out.println("Fruits: " + multimap.get("fruit"));

        // BiMap (bidirectional map)
        BiMap<String, Integer> biMap = HashBiMap.create();
        biMap.put("one", 1);
        biMap.put("two", 2);

        // Get key by value
        String key = biMap.inverse().get(1);
        System.out.println("Key for value 1: " + key);

        // Joiner
        String joined = Joiner.on(", ")
            .skipNulls()
```

189

```java
            .join("Java", null, "is", "awesome");
        System.out.println("Joined: " + joined);

        // Cache
        Cache<String, String> cache = CacheBuilder.newBuilder()
            .maximumSize(100)
            .expireAfterWrite(10, TimeUnit.MINUTES)
            .build();

        try {
            String value = cache.get("key", () -> computeExpensiveValue("key"));
            System.out.println("Cache value: " + value);
        } catch (ExecutionException e) {
            System.err.println("Error computing value: " + e.getMessage());
        }
    }

    private static String computeExpensiveValue(String key) {
        // Simulate expensive computation
        return "Value for " + key;
    }
}
```

To use Guava, add this to your pom.xml:

```xml
<dependency>
    <groupId>com.google.guava</groupId>
    <artifactId>guava</artifactId>
    <version>31.1-jre</version>
</dependency>
```

11.2 Testing and Debugging

11.2.1 Advanced JUnit Testing

JUnit 5 offers powerful testing capabilities:

```java
import org.junit.jupiter.api.*;
import org.junit.jupiter.params.ParameterizedTest;
import org.junit.jupiter.params.provider.CsvSource;
import org.junit.jupiter.params.provider.ValueSource;
import org.mockito.Mockito;

import static org.junit.jupiter.api.Assertions.*;
import static org.mockito.Mockito.*;

public class AdvancedTestingExample {
    private TaskManager taskManager;
    private TaskRepository mockRepository;

    @BeforeEach
```

```java
    void setUp() {
        // Create a mock repository
        mockRepository = mock(TaskRepository.class);
        taskManager = new TaskManagerImpl(mockRepository);
    }

    @Test
    @DisplayName("Should create task with valid data")
    void testCreateTaskValid() {
        // Arrange
        String description = "Test Task";
        LocalDate dueDate = LocalDate.now().plusDays(1);
        Task expectedTask = new Task(1, description, dueDate);

        when(mockRepository.save(any(Task.class))).thenReturn(expectedTask);

        // Act
        Task result = taskManager.createTask(description, dueDate);

        // Assert
        assertNotNull(result);
        assertEquals(description, result.getDescription());
        assertEquals(dueDate, result.getDueDate());

        // Verify that repository.save() was called
        verify(mockRepository).save(any(Task.class));
    }

    @ParameterizedTest
    @CsvSource({
        "Task 1, 2023-05-15, false",
        "Task 2, 2023-06-20, true",
        "Task 3, 2023-07-10, false"
    })
    void testCreateTaskWithDifferentData(String description, String dateStr, boolean completed) {
        // Arrange
        LocalDate dueDate = LocalDate.parse(dateStr);
        Task expectedTask = new Task(1, description, dueDate);
        expectedTask.setCompleted(completed);

        when(mockRepository.save(any(Task.class))).thenReturn(expectedTask);

        // Act
        Task result = taskManager.createTask(description, dueDate);
        result.setCompleted(completed);

        // Assert
        assertEquals(description, result.getDescription());
        assertEquals(dueDate, result.getDueDate());
        assertEquals(completed, result.isCompleted());
    }
```

```java
@ParameterizedTest
@ValueSource(strings = {"", "   ", "\t"})
void testCreateTaskWithInvalidDescription(String description) {
    // Arrange
    LocalDate dueDate = LocalDate.now();

    // Act & Assert
    assertThrows(IllegalArgumentException.class, () -> {
        taskManager.createTask(description, dueDate);
    });

    // Verify that repository.save() was never called
    verify(mockRepository, never()).save(any(Task.class));
}

@Test
@Disabled("Demonstrate disabled test")
void disabledTest() {
    fail("This test should not run");
}

@Nested
@DisplayName("Task completion tests")
class TaskCompletionTests {
    @Test
    void testMarkAsCompleted() {
        // Arrange
        int taskId = 1;
        Task task = new Task(taskId, "Test", LocalDate.now());
        Task completedTask = new Task(taskId, "Test", LocalDate.now());
        completedTask.setCompleted(true);

        when(mockRepository.findById(taskId)).thenReturn(task);
        when(mockRepository.save(any(Task.class))).thenReturn(completedTask);

        // Act
        boolean result = taskManager.markTaskAsCompleted(taskId);

        // Assert
        assertTrue(result);
        verify(mockRepository).save(argThat(t -> t.isCompleted()));
    }

    @Test
    void testMarkNonExistentTaskAsCompleted() {
        // Arrange
        int taskId = 999;
        when(mockRepository.findById(taskId)).thenReturn(null);

        // Act & Assert
        assertThrows(IllegalArgumentException.class, () -> {
```

192

```
            taskManager.markTaskAsCompleted(taskId);
        });
    }
  }
}
```

Add Mockito to your pom.xml:

```xml
<dependency>
    <groupId>org.mockito</groupId>
    <artifactId>mockito-core</artifactId>
    <version>5.3.1</version>
    <scope>test</scope>
</dependency>
<dependency>
    <groupId>org.mockito</groupId>
    <artifactId>mockito-junit-jupiter</artifactId>
    <version>5.3.1</version>
    <scope>test</scope>
</dependency>
```

11.2.2 Debugging Techniques

Effective debugging is crucial for finding and fixing issues in your code:

1. **Using the Debugger**:
   o Set breakpoints to pause execution
   o Step through code line by line
   o Inspect variable values
   o Evaluate expressions
2. **Logging**:
   o Use SLF4J with Logback for structured logging:

```java
import org.slf4j.Logger;
import org.slf4j.LoggerFactory;

public class LoggingExample {
    private        static        final        Logger        logger        =
LoggerFactory.getLogger(LoggingExample.class);

    public void processTask(Task task) {
        logger.debug("Processing task with ID: {}", task.getId());

        try {
            // Process task
            if (task.isCompleted()) {
                logger.info("Task {} is already completed", task.getId());
                return;
            }

            // Perform some operation
```

193

```java
            logger.info("Task {} processed successfully", task.getId());
        } catch (Exception e) {
            logger.error("Error   processing   task   {}:   {}",   task.getId(),
e.getMessage(), e);
            throw e;
        }
    }
}
```

Add SLF4J and Logback to your pom.xml:

```xml
<dependency>
    <groupId>org.slf4j</groupId>
    <artifactId>slf4j-api</artifactId>
    <version>2.0.7</version>
</dependency>
<dependency>
    <groupId>ch.qos.logback</groupId>
    <artifactId>logback-classic</artifactId>
    <version>1.4.7</version>
</dependency>
```

Create a logback.xml configuration file in src/main/resources:

```xml
<configuration>
    <appender name="CONSOLE" class="ch.qos.logback.core.ConsoleAppender">
        <encoder>
            <pattern>%d{HH:mm:ss.SSS}    [%thread]    %-5level    %logger{36}    -
%msg%n</pattern>
        </encoder>
    </appender>

    <appender name="FILE" class="ch.qos.logback.core.FileAppender">
        <file>logs/application.log</file>
        <encoder>
            <pattern>%d{yyyy-MM-dd HH:mm:ss.SSS} [%thread] %-5level %logger{36} -
%msg%n</pattern>
        </encoder>
    </appender>

    <root level="info">
        <appender-ref ref="CONSOLE" />
        <appender-ref ref="FILE" />
    </root>
</configuration>
```

11.3 Database Integration

Most real-world applications need to store data persistently in a database.

JDBC provides a standard API for connecting to relational databases:

```java
import java.sql.*;
import java.time.LocalDate;
import java.util.ArrayList;
import java.util.List;

public class JdbcTaskRepository implements TaskRepository {
    private static final String URL = "jdbc:mysql://localhost:3306/taskmanager";
    private static final String USER = "root";
    private static final String PASSWORD = "password";

    // SQL statements
    private static final String SELECT_ALL = "SELECT * FROM tasks";
    private static final String SELECT_BY_ID = "SELECT * FROM tasks WHERE id = ?";
    private static final String INSERT = "INSERT INTO tasks (description, due_date, completed) VALUES (?, ?, ?)";
    private static final String UPDATE = "UPDATE tasks SET description = ?, due_date = ?, completed = ? WHERE id = ?";
    private static final String DELETE = "DELETE FROM tasks WHERE id = ?";

    static {
        try {
            // Load the JDBC driver
            Class.forName("com.mysql.cj.jdbc.Driver");
        } catch (ClassNotFoundException e) {
            throw new RuntimeException("Failed to load JDBC driver", e);
        }
    }

    @Override
    public List<Task> findAll() {
        List<Task> tasks = new ArrayList<>();

        try (Connection conn = getConnection();
             Statement stmt = conn.createStatement();
             ResultSet rs = stmt.executeQuery(SELECT_ALL)) {

            while (rs.next()) {
                Task task = mapResultSetToTask(rs);
                tasks.add(task);
            }

        } catch (SQLException e) {
            throw new RuntimeException("Error retrieving tasks", e);
        }

        return tasks;
    }
```

```java
    @Override
    public Task findById(int id) {
        try (Connection conn = getConnection();
             PreparedStatement stmt = conn.prepareStatement(SELECT_BY_ID)) {

            stmt.setInt(1, id);

            try (ResultSet rs = stmt.executeQuery()) {
                if (rs.next()) {
                    return mapResultSetToTask(rs);
                }
            }

        } catch (SQLException e) {
            throw new RuntimeException("Error retrieving task with ID: " + id, e);
        }

        return null;
    }

    @Override
    public Task save(Task task) {
        if (task.getId() == 0) {
            // Insert new task
            try (Connection conn = getConnection();
                 PreparedStatement    stmt    =    conn.prepareStatement(INSERT,
Statement.RETURN_GENERATED_KEYS)) {

                stmt.setString(1, task.getDescription());
                stmt.setDate(2, Date.valueOf(task.getDueDate()));
                stmt.setBoolean(3, task.isCompleted());

                int affectedRows = stmt.executeUpdate();

                if (affectedRows == 0) {
                    throw  new  SQLException("Creating  task  failed,  no  rows
affected.");
                }

                try (ResultSet generatedKeys = stmt.getGeneratedKeys()) {
                    if (generatedKeys.next()) {
                        Task    newTask    =    new    Task(generatedKeys.getInt(1),
task.getDescription(), task.getDueDate());
                        newTask.setCompleted(task.isCompleted());
                        return newTask;
                    } else {
                        throw  new  SQLException("Creating  task  failed,  no  ID
obtained.");
                    }
                }
```

```java
            } catch (SQLException e) {
                throw new RuntimeException("Error saving task", e);
            }
        } else {
            // Update existing task
            try (Connection conn = getConnection();
                 PreparedStatement stmt = conn.prepareStatement(UPDATE)) {

                stmt.setString(1, task.getDescription());
                stmt.setDate(2, Date.valueOf(task.getDueDate()));
                stmt.setBoolean(3, task.isCompleted());
                stmt.setInt(4, task.getId());

                int affectedRows = stmt.executeUpdate();

                if (affectedRows == 0) {
                    throw new SQLException("Updating task failed, no rows affected.");
                }

                return task;

            } catch (SQLException e) {
                throw new RuntimeException("Error updating task with ID: " + task.getId(), e);
            }
        }
    }

    @Override
    public boolean delete(int id) {
        try (Connection conn = getConnection();
             PreparedStatement stmt = conn.prepareStatement(DELETE)) {

            stmt.setInt(1, id);

            int affectedRows = stmt.executeUpdate();
            return affectedRows > 0;

        } catch (SQLException e) {
            throw new RuntimeException("Error deleting task with ID: " + id, e);
        }
    }

    @Override
    public List<Task> findByStatus(boolean completed) {
        List<Task> tasks = new ArrayList<>();

        try (Connection conn = getConnection();
             PreparedStatement stmt = conn.prepareStatement("SELECT * FROM tasks WHERE completed = ?")) {
```

197

```java
            stmt.setBoolean(1, completed);

            try (ResultSet rs = stmt.executeQuery()) {
                while (rs.next()) {
                    Task task = mapResultSetToTask(rs);
                    tasks.add(task);
                }
            }

        } catch (SQLException e) {
            throw new RuntimeException("Error retrieving tasks by status", e);
        }

        return tasks;
    }

    private Connection getConnection() throws SQLException {
        return DriverManager.getConnection(URL, USER, PASSWORD);
    }

    private Task mapResultSetToTask(ResultSet rs) throws SQLException {
        int id = rs.getInt("id");
        String description = rs.getString("description");
        LocalDate dueDate = rs.getDate("due_date").toLocalDate();
        boolean completed = rs.getBoolean("completed");

        Task task = new Task(id, description, dueDate);
        task.setCompleted(completed);
        return task;
    }
}
```

Add MySQL JDBC driver to your pom.xml:

```xml
<dependency>
    <groupId>mysql</groupId>
    <artifactId>mysql-connector-java</artifactId>
    <version>8.0.33</version>
</dependency>
```

SQL script to create the tasks table:

```sql
CREATE TABLE tasks (
    id INT AUTO_INCREMENT PRIMARY KEY,
    description VARCHAR(255) NOT NULL,
    due_date DATE NOT NULL,
    completed BOOLEAN DEFAULT FALSE
);
```

11.3.2 Connection Pooling with HikariCP

Connection pooling improves performance by reusing database connections:

```java
import com.zaxxer.hikari.HikariConfig;
import com.zaxxer.hikari.HikariDataSource;

import javax.sql.DataSource;
import java.sql.Connection;
import java.sql.SQLException;

public class DatabaseManager {
    private static HikariDataSource dataSource;

    static {
        HikariConfig config = new HikariConfig();
        config.setJdbcUrl("jdbc:mysql://localhost:3306/taskmanager");
        config.setUsername("root");
        config.setPassword("password");
        config.setMaximumPoolSize(10);
        config.setMinimumIdle(5);
        config.setIdleTimeout(300000); // 5 minutes
        config.setMaxLifetime(600000); // 10 minutes
        config.addDataSourceProperty("cachePrepStmts", "true");
        config.addDataSourceProperty("prepStmtCacheSize", "250");
        config.addDataSourceProperty("prepStmtCacheSqlLimit", "2048");

        dataSource = new HikariDataSource(config);
    }

    public static Connection getConnection() throws SQLException {
        return dataSource.getConnection();
    }

    public static DataSource getDataSource() {
        return dataSource;
    }

    public static void close() {
        if (dataSource != null) {
            dataSource.close();
        }
    }
}
```

Update the JdbcTaskRepository to use the connection pool:

```java
private Connection getConnection() throws SQLException {
    return DatabaseManager.getConnection();
}
```

Add HikariCP to your pom.xml:

199

```xml
<dependency>
    <groupId>com.zaxxer</groupId>
    <artifactId>HikariCP</artifactId>
    <version>5.0.1</version>
</dependency>
```

11.4 Build Tools and Dependency Management

11.4.1 Maven vs Gradle

Both Maven and Gradle are popular build tools for Java projects:

Maven Advantages:

- Declarative XML configuration
- Widely adopted and mature
- Consistent project structure
- Well-documented

Gradle Advantages:

- Groovy or Kotlin DSL
- More flexible and concise
- Better performance
- Better for multi-project builds

Maven Build Lifecycle

```
# Compile
mvn compile

# Run
```

Run tests

mvn test

Package

mvn package

Install to local repository

```
mvn install
```

Clean previous builds

```
mvn clean
```

Generate project site

```
mvn site
```

Deploy to repository

```
mvn deploy
```

Gradle Build Example

```gradle
plugins {
    id 'java'
    id 'application'
}

group = 'com.example'
version = '1.0-SNAPSHOT'
sourceCompatibility = '21'

repositories {
    mavenCentral()
}

dependencies {
    implementation 'org.apache.commons:commons-lang3:3.12.0'
    implementation 'com.google.guava:guava:31.1-jre'

    testImplementation 'org.junit.jupiter:junit-jupiter-api:5.9.2'
    testRuntimeOnly 'org.junit.jupiter:junit-jupiter-engine:5.9.2'
}

application {
    mainClass = 'com.example.Main'
}

test {
    useJUnitPlatform()
```

```
}

// Custom task
task createDocs(type: Exec) {
    commandLine 'javadoc', '-d', 'build/docs', '-sourcepath', 'src/main/java',
'com.example'
}
```

11.4.2 Dependency Management Best Practices

1. **Keep dependencies up-to-date**
   - Regularly check for updates to address security vulnerabilities
   - Use `mvn versions:display-dependency-updates` to see available updates
2. **Minimize transitive dependencies**
   - Be aware of what each dependency brings in
   - Use `mvn dependency:tree` to view the dependency tree
3. **Manage dependency scope**
   - Use appropriate scopes: `compile, runtime, test, provided`
   - Example:

```
<dependency>        <groupId>org.junit.jupiter</groupId>        <artifactId>junit-
jupiter</artifactId>    <version>5.9.2</version>    <scope>test</scope></dependency>
```

4. **Use Bill of Materials (BOM)**
   - Ensures compatible versions of related dependencies
   - Example:

```
<dependencyManagement>            <dependencies>                        <dependency>
<groupId>org.springframework.boot</groupId>                <artifactId>spring-boot-
dependencies</artifactId>                        <version>3.1.0</version>
<type>pom</type>                    <scope>import</scope>                </dependency>
</dependencies></dependencyManagement>
```

11.5 Modern Java Features

Since Java 8, many new features have been introduced to make Java more concise and powerful.

11.5.1 Lambda Expressions and Functional Interfaces

Lambda expressions provide a concise way to implement functional interfaces:

```
// Before Java 8
Button button = new Button();
button.setOnClickListener(new OnClickListener() {
    @Override
    public void onClick() {
        System.out.println("Button clicked");
    }
});
```

```java
// With lambda expressions
button.setOnClickListener(() -> System.out.println("Button clicked"));

// Functional interfaces in java.util.function
Consumer<String> printer = s -> System.out.println(s);
Predicate<Integer> isPositive = n -> n > 0;
Function<String, Integer> stringToLength = s -> s.length();
Supplier<LocalDate> currentDate = () -> LocalDate.now();
BiFunction<Integer, Integer, Integer> add = (a, b) -> a + b;

// Method references
Consumer<String> methodRefPrinter = System.out::println;
Function<String, Integer> methodRefLength = String::length;
```

11.5.2 Optional for Null Safety

The Optional class helps prevent NullPointerException:

```java
import java.util.Optional;

public class OptionalExample {
    public static void main(String[] args) {
        // Creating optionals
        Optional<String> empty = Optional.empty();
        Optional<String> present = Optional.of("Hello");
        Optional<String> nullable = Optional.ofNullable(getNameFromDatabase());

        // Using optional values
        if (nullable.isPresent()) {
            System.out.println("Value: " + nullable.get());
        }

        // Modern approach with methods
        nullable.ifPresent(value -> System.out.println("Value: " + value));

        // Default value if empty
        String result = nullable.orElse("Default Name");

        // Compute default value if empty
        String computed = nullable.orElseGet(() -> getDefaultName());

        // Throw exception if empty
        try {
            String value = nullable.orElseThrow(() -> new IllegalStateException("Name not found"));
        } catch (IllegalStateException e) {
            System.err.println("Error: " + e.getMessage());
        }

        // Transform value if present
        Optional<Integer> length = nullable.map(String::length);
```

```java
        // Chain operations
        Optional<String> upperCase = nullable
            .filter(s -> s.length() > 3)
            .map(String::toUpperCase);

        // FlatMap for operations returning Optional
        Optional<String> result2 = getOptionalUser()
            .flatMap(OptionalExample::getOptionalAddress)
            .flatMap(OptionalExample::getOptionalStreet);
    }

    private static String getNameFromDatabase() {
        // Simulated database call
        return Math.random() > 0.5 ? "John" : null;
    }

    private static String getDefaultName() {
        System.out.println("Computing default name...");
        return "Guest";
    }

    private static Optional<User> getOptionalUser() {
        return Optional.ofNullable(new User());
    }

    private static Optional<Address> getOptionalAddress(User user) {
        return Optional.ofNullable(user.getAddress());
    }

    private static Optional<String> getOptionalStreet(Address address) {
        return Optional.ofNullable(address.getStreet());
    }

    static class User {
        private Address address;

        public Address getAddress() {
            return address;
        }
    }

    static class Address {
        private String street;

        public String getStreet() {
            return street;
        }
    }
}
```

Records, introduced in Java 16, provide a concise way to define immutable data classes:

```java
// Before records
public class Point {
    private final int x;
    private final int y;

    public Point(int x, int y) {
        this.x = x;
        this.y = y;
    }

    public int getX() {
        return x;
    }

    public int getY() {
        return y;
    }

    @Override
    public boolean equals(Object o) {
        if (this == o) return true;
        if (o == null || getClass() != o.getClass()) return false;
        Point point = (Point) o;
        return x == point.x && y == point.y;
    }

    @Override
    public int hashCode() {
        return Objects.hash(x, y);
    }

    @Override
    public String toString() {
        return "Point{" +
                "x=" + x +
                ", y=" + y +
                '}';
    }
}

// With records
public record Point(int x, int y) {
    // All the boilerplate code above is automatically generated

    // You can add custom methods
    public double distance(Point other) {
        return Math.sqrt(
```

```java
            Math.pow(this.x - other.x, 2) +
            Math.pow(this.y - other.y, 2)
        );
    }

    // You can add validation in the canonical constructor
    public Point {
        if (x < 0 || y < 0) {
            throw new IllegalArgumentException("Coordinates cannot be negative");
        }
    }
}
```

11.5.4 Pattern Matching

Pattern matching improves code readability:

```java
// Enhanced instanceof (Java 16+)
Object obj = "Hello";

// Before
if (obj instanceof String) {
    String str = (String) obj;
    System.out.println(str.toUpperCase());
}

// With pattern matching
if (obj instanceof String str) {
    System.out.println(str.toUpperCase());
}

// Switch expressions (Java 17+)
DayOfWeek day = LocalDate.now().getDayOfWeek();

int numLetters = switch (day) {
    case MONDAY, FRIDAY, SUNDAY -> 6;
    case TUESDAY -> 7;
    case THURSDAY, SATURDAY -> 8;
    case WEDNESDAY -> 9;
    default -> throw new IllegalStateException("Invalid day: " + day);
};

// Pattern matching in switch (Java 21)
Object value = "Hello";

String result = switch (value) {
    case Integer i -> "Integer: " + i;
    case String s when s.length() > 5 -> "Long string: " + s;
    case String s -> "String: " + s;
    case null -> "Null value";
    default -> "Unknown type";
```

```
};
```

11.5.5 Text Blocks

Text blocks, introduced in Java 15, improve readability of multiline strings:

```java
// Before text blocks
String json = "{\n" +
              "  \"name\": \"John Doe\",\n" +
              "  \"age\": 30,\n" +
              "  \"address\": {\n" +
              "    \"street\": \"123 Main St\",\n" +
              "    \"city\": \"Anytown\"\n" +
              "  }\n" +
              "}";

// With text blocks
String json = """
              {
                "name": "John Doe",
                "age": 30,
                "address": {
                  "street": "123 Main St",
                  "city": "Anytown"
                }
              }
              """;

// HTML example
String html = """
              <!DOCTYPE html>
              <html>
                <head>
                  <title>Text Blocks Example</title>
                </head>
                <body>
                  <h1>Hello, World!</h1>
                  <p>This is a paragraph.</p>
                </body>
              </html>
              """;

// SQL example
String sql = """
             SELECT u.id, u.name, u.email, a.city
             FROM users u
             JOIN addresses a ON u.id = a.user_id
             WHERE u.active = true
             ORDER BY u.name
             """;
```

11.6.1 Online Resources

- **Official Documentation**
  - Java SE Documentation
  - Java Language Specification
  - Java API Documentation
- **Online Learning Platforms**
  - Baeldung - In-depth Java tutorials
  - JetBrains Academy - Project-based learning
  - Codecademy - Interactive Java course
  - Coursera - University-level Java courses
  - Udemy - Various Java courses
- **Coding Practice**
  - LeetCode - Coding challenges
  - HackerRank - Java practice problems
  - CodeGym - Java programming quests
  - Project Euler - Mathematical programming challenges

11.6.2 Books

- **For Beginners**
  - "Head First Java" by Kathy Sierra and Bert Bates
  - "Java: A Beginner's Guide" by Herbert Schildt
  - "Think Java" by Allen Downey and Chris Mayfield
- **For Intermediate Developers**
  - "Effective Java" by Joshua Bloch
  - "Java Concurrency in Practice" by Brian Goetz
  - "Modern Java in Action" by Raoul-Gabriel Urma, Mario Fusco, and Alan Mycroft
- **For Advanced Developers**
  - "Java Performance: The Definitive Guide" by Scott Oaks
  - "Java Performance Tuning" by Jack Shirazi
  - "Java: The Complete Reference" by Herbert Schildt

11.6.3 Community Resources

- **Forums and Communities**
  - Stack Overflow - Q&A for Java developers
  - Reddit's r/java - Java community discussions
  - JavaRanch - Friendly Java community
- **Conferences and Events**
  - JavaOne - Oracle's Java conference
  - Devoxx - Java community conference
  - JVM Language Summit - JVM technologies

- **Podcasts**
    - o <u>Java Pub House</u> - Java topics and news
    - o <u>Inside Java</u> - Official Java podcast
    - o <u>Java Off-Heap</u> - Java ecosystem news

11.7 Next Steps in Your Career

11.7.1 Career Path Options

Java opens doors to many career paths:

1. **Backend Developer**
    - o Build server-side applications using Spring Boot, Jakarta EE, or Quarkus
    - o Work with databases, APIs, and middleware services
2. **Android Developer**
    - o Create Android applications with Java and Android SDK
    - o Utilize Android Jetpack components and Material Design
3. **Enterprise Application Developer**
    - o Develop large-scale business applications
    - o Work with JMS, EJB, and transaction management
4. **DevOps Engineer**
    - o Automate build, test, and deployment processes
    - o Work with CI/CD tools like Jenkins, GitHub Actions, or GitLab CI
5. **Big Data Engineer**
    - o Process large datasets with Apache Hadoop, Spark, or Flink
    - o Build data pipelines and ETL processes

11.7.2 Building Your Portfolio

1. **Create Open Source Projects**
    - o Contribute to existing Java projects
    - o Start your own projects to demonstrate skills
2. **Build a Personal Website or Blog**
    - o Document your Java learning journey
    - o Share tutorials and code examples
3. **Participate in Coding Challenges**
    - o Solve algorithmic problems on platforms like LeetCode
    - o Join competitive programming contests
4. **Develop Real-World Applications**
    - o Build a complete web application with Spring Boot
    - o Create a mobile app with Java and Android
    - o Develop a desktop application with JavaFX

11.7.3 Specialization Areas

Consider specializing in one of these areas:

1. **Web Development**
   - Spring Framework ecosystem
   - Microservices architecture
   - RESTful API design
2. **Data Science and Analytics**
   - Machine learning libraries (DL4J, Weka)
   - Data processing frameworks (Spark, Flink)
   - Statistical analysis tools
3. **Cloud Computing**
   - AWS/Azure/GCP SDK for Java
   - Serverless applications
   - Cloud-native development
4. **Security**
   - Cryptography
   - Authentication and authorization frameworks
   - Security testing and analysis

11.8 Practice Project: Building a RESTful API

Let's apply what we've learned to build a simple RESTful API for our Task Manager application:

11.8.1 Setting up Spring Boot

Spring Boot makes it easy to create stand-alone, production-grade Spring applications.

First, create a new Maven project with these dependencies:

```
<parent>
    <groupId>org.springframework.boot</groupId>
    <artifactId>spring-boot-starter-parent</artifactId>
    <version>3.1.0</version>
    <relativePath/>
</parent>

<dependencies>
    <dependency>
        <groupId>org.springframework.boot</groupId>
        <artifactId>spring-boot-starter-web</artifactId>
    </dependency>
    <dependency>
        <groupId>org.springframework.boot</groupId>
        <artifactId>spring-boot-starter-data-jpa</artifactId>
    </dependency>
    <dependency>
        <groupId>org.springframework.boot</groupId>
```

```
            <artifactId>spring-boot-starter-validation</artifactId>
        </dependency>
        <dependency>
            <groupId>com.h2database</groupId>
            <artifactId>h2</artifactId>
            <scope>runtime</scope>
        </dependency>
        <dependency>
            <groupId>org.projectlombok</groupId>
            <artifactId>lombok</artifactId>
            <optional>true</optional>
        </dependency>
        <dependency>
            <groupId>org.springframework.boot</groupId>
            <artifactId>spring-boot-starter-test</artifactId>
            <scope>test</scope>
        </dependency>
    </dependencies>
```

11.8.2 Creating the Task Entity

```java
package com.example.taskmanager.model;

import jakarta.persistence.Entity;
import jakarta.persistence.GeneratedValue;
import jakarta.persistence.GenerationType;
import jakarta.persistence.Id;
import jakarta.validation.constraints.NotBlank;
import jakarta.validation.constraints.NotNull;
import lombok.AllArgsConstructor;
import lombok.Data;
import lombok.NoArgsConstructor;

import java.time.LocalDate;

@Entity
@Data
@NoArgsConstructor
@AllArgsConstructor
public class Task {
    @Id
    @GeneratedValue(strategy = GenerationType.IDENTITY)
    private Long id;

    @NotBlank(message = "Description is required")
    private String description;

    @NotNull(message = "Due date is required")
    private LocalDate dueDate;

    private boolean completed;
}
```

211

11.8.3 Creating the Repository

```java
package com.example.taskmanager.repository;

import com.example.taskmanager.model.Task;
import org.springframework.data.jpa.repository.JpaRepository;
import org.springframework.stereotype.Repository;

import java.util.List;

@Repository
public interface TaskRepository extends JpaRepository<Task, Long> {
    List<Task> findByCompleted(boolean completed);
}
```

11.8.4 Creating the Service

```java
package com.example.taskmanager.service;

import com.example.taskmanager.model.Task;
import com.example.taskmanager.repository.TaskRepository;
import jakarta.persistence.EntityNotFoundException;
import org.springframework.beans.factory.annotation.Autowired;
import org.springframework.stereotype.Service;

import java.util.List;

@Service
public class TaskService {
    private final TaskRepository taskRepository;

    @Autowired
    public TaskService(TaskRepository taskRepository) {
        this.taskRepository = taskRepository;
    }

    public List<Task> getAllTasks() {
        return taskRepository.findAll();
    }

    public Task getTaskById(Long id) {
        return taskRepository.findById(id)
            .orElseThrow(() -> new EntityNotFoundException("Task not found with id: " + id));
    }

    public List<Task> getTasksByStatus(boolean completed) {
        return taskRepository.findByCompleted(completed);
    }

    public Task createTask(Task task) {
        return taskRepository.save(task);
```

```java
    }

    public Task updateTask(Long id, Task taskDetails) {
        Task task = getTaskById(id);

        task.setDescription(taskDetails.getDescription());
        task.setDueDate(taskDetails.getDueDate());
        task.setCompleted(taskDetails.isCompleted());

        return taskRepository.save(task);
    }

    public void deleteTask(Long id) {
        Task task = getTaskById(id);
        taskRepository.delete(task);
    }

    public Task markTaskAsCompleted(Long id) {
        Task task = getTaskById(id);
        task.setCompleted(true);
        return taskRepository.save(task);
    }
}
```

11.8.5 Creating the Controller

```java
package com.example.taskmanager.controller;

import com.example.taskmanager.model.Task;
import com.example.taskmanager.service.TaskService;
import jakarta.validation.Valid;
import org.springframework.beans.factory.annotation.Autowired;
import org.springframework.http.HttpStatus;
import org.springframework.http.ResponseEntity;
import org.springframework.web.bind.annotation.*;

import java.util.List;

@RestController
@RequestMapping("/api/tasks")
public class TaskController {
    private final TaskService taskService;

    @Autowired
    public TaskController(TaskService taskService) {
        this.taskService = taskService;
    }


    @GetMapping
    public List<Task> getAllTasks() {
        return taskService.getAllTasks();
    }
```

213

```java
    @GetMapping("/{id}")
    public ResponseEntity<Task> getTaskById(@PathVariable Long id) {
        Task task = taskService.getTaskById(id);
        return ResponseEntity.ok(task);
    }

    @GetMapping("/status")
    public List<Task> getTasksByStatus(@RequestParam boolean completed) {
        return taskService.getTasksByStatus(completed);
    }

    @PostMapping
    @ResponseStatus(HttpStatus.CREATED)
    public Task createTask(@Valid @RequestBody Task task) {
        return taskService.createTask(task);
    }

    @PutMapping("/{id}")
    public Task updateTask(@PathVariable Long id, @Valid @RequestBody Task task) {
        return taskService.updateTask(id, task);
    }

    @DeleteMapping("/{id}")
    @ResponseStatus(HttpStatus.NO_CONTENT)
    public void deleteTask(@PathVariable Long id) {
        taskService.deleteTask(id);
    }

    @PatchMapping("/{id}/complete")
    public Task completeTask(@PathVariable Long id) {
        return taskService.markTaskAsCompleted(id);
    }
}
```

11.8.6 Exception Handling

```java
package com.example.taskmanager.exception;

import jakarta.persistence.EntityNotFoundException;
import jakarta.validation.ConstraintViolationException;
import org.springframework.http.HttpStatus;
import org.springframework.http.ResponseEntity;
import org.springframework.web.bind.MethodArgumentNotValidException;
import org.springframework.web.bind.annotation.ControllerAdvice;
import org.springframework.web.bind.annotation.ExceptionHandler;

import java.time.LocalDateTime;
import java.util.HashMap;
import java.util.Map;

@ControllerAdvice
```

```java
public class GlobalExceptionHandler {

    @ExceptionHandler(EntityNotFoundException.class)
    public                                          ResponseEntity<ErrorResponse>
handleEntityNotFound(EntityNotFoundException ex) {
        ErrorResponse error = new ErrorResponse(
            HttpStatus.NOT_FOUND.value(),
            ex.getMessage(),
            LocalDateTime.now()
        );
        return new ResponseEntity<>(error, HttpStatus.NOT_FOUND);
    }

    @ExceptionHandler(MethodArgumentNotValidException.class)
    public                  ResponseEntity<Map<String,            String>>
handleValidationExceptions(MethodArgumentNotValidException ex) {
        Map<String, String> errors = new HashMap<>();
        ex.getBindingResult().getFieldErrors().forEach(error ->
            errors.put(error.getField(), error.getDefaultMessage())
        );
        return new ResponseEntity<>(errors, HttpStatus.BAD_REQUEST);
    }

    @ExceptionHandler(ConstraintViolationException.class)
    public                  ResponseEntity<Map<String,            String>>
handleConstraintViolation(ConstraintViolationException ex) {
        Map<String, String> errors = new HashMap<>();
        ex.getConstraintViolations().forEach(violation ->
            errors.put(violation.getPropertyPath().toString(),
violation.getMessage())
        );
        return new ResponseEntity<>(errors, HttpStatus.BAD_REQUEST);
    }

    @ExceptionHandler(Exception.class)
    public ResponseEntity<ErrorResponse> handleGenericException(Exception ex) {
        ErrorResponse error = new ErrorResponse(
            HttpStatus.INTERNAL_SERVER_ERROR.value(),
            "An unexpected error occurred",
            LocalDateTime.now()
        );
        return new ResponseEntity<>(error, HttpStatus.INTERNAL_SERVER_ERROR);
    }

    static class ErrorResponse {
        private final int status;
        private final String message;
        private final LocalDateTime timestamp;

        public ErrorResponse(int status, String message, LocalDateTime timestamp) {
            this.status = status;
            this.message = message;
```

```
            this.timestamp = timestamp;
        }

        public int getStatus() {
            return status;
        }

        public String getMessage() {
            return message;
        }

        public LocalDateTime getTimestamp() {
            return timestamp;
        }
    }
}
```

11.8.7 Main Application Class

```
package com.example.taskmanager;

import org.springframework.boot.SpringApplication;
import org.springframework.boot.autoconfigure.SpringBootApplication;

@SpringBootApplication
public class TaskManagerApplication {
    public static void main(String[] args) {
        SpringApplication.run(TaskManagerApplication.class, args);
    }
}
```

11.8.8 Application Properties

Create a file named application.properties **in the** src/main/resources **directory:**

```
# H2 Database Configuration
spring.datasource.url=jdbc:h2:mem:taskdb
spring.datasource.driverClassName=org.h2.Driver
spring.datasource.username=sa
spring.datasource.password=password
spring.h2.console.enabled=true
spring.h2.console.path=/h2-console

# JPA Configuration
spring.jpa.database-platform=org.hibernate.dialect.H2Dialect
spring.jpa.hibernate.ddl-auto=update
spring.jpa.show-sql=true

# Server Configuration
server.port=8080
```

11.8.9 Testing the API

Create a test class:

```java
package com.example.taskmanager.controller;

import com.example.taskmanager.model.Task;
import com.example.taskmanager.service.TaskService;
import com.fasterxml.jackson.databind.ObjectMapper;
import org.junit.jupiter.api.Test;
import org.springframework.beans.factory.annotation.Autowired;
import org.springframework.boot.test.autoconfigure.web.servlet.WebMvcTest;
import org.springframework.boot.test.mock.mockito.MockBean;
import org.springframework.http.MediaType;
import org.springframework.test.web.servlet.MockMvc;

import java.time.LocalDate;
import java.util.Arrays;
import java.util.List;

import static org.hamcrest.Matchers.*;
import static org.mockito.ArgumentMatchers.any;
import static org.mockito.ArgumentMatchers.eq;
import static org.mockito.Mockito.when;
import static org.springframework.test.web.servlet.request.MockMvcRequestBuilders.*;
import static org.springframework.test.web.servlet.result.MockMvcResultMatchers.*;

@WebMvcTest(TaskController.class)
public class TaskControllerTest {

    @Autowired
    private MockMvc mockMvc;

    @MockBean
    private TaskService taskService;

    @Autowired
    private ObjectMapper objectMapper;

    @Test
    public void testGetAllTasks() throws Exception {
        Task task1 = new Task(1L, "Task 1", LocalDate.now(), false);
        Task task2 = new Task(2L, "Task 2", LocalDate.now().plusDays(1), true);
        List<Task> tasks = Arrays.asList(task1, task2);

        when(taskService.getAllTasks()).thenReturn(tasks);

        mockMvc.perform(get("/api/tasks"))
            .andExpect(status().isOk())
            .andExpect(jsonPath("$", hasSize(2)))
            .andExpect(jsonPath("$[0].id", is(1)))
```

```java
                .andExpect(jsonPath("$[0].description", is("Task 1")))
                .andExpect(jsonPath("$[1].id", is(2)))
                .andExpect(jsonPath("$[1].description", is("Task 2")));
    }

    @Test
    public void testCreateTask() throws Exception {
        Task task = new Task(null, "New Task", LocalDate.now().plusDays(3),
false);
        Task savedTask = new Task(1L, "New Task", LocalDate.now().plusDays(3),
false);

        when(taskService.createTask(any(Task.class))).thenReturn(savedTask);

        mockMvc.perform(post("/api/tasks")
            .contentType(MediaType.APPLICATION_JSON)
            .content(objectMapper.writeValueAsString(task)))
            .andExpect(status().isCreated())
            .andExpect(jsonPath("$.id", is(1)))
            .andExpect(jsonPath("$.description", is("New Task")))
            .andExpect(jsonPath("$.completed", is(false)));
    }

    @Test
    public void testUpdateTask() throws Exception {
        Task task = new Task(1L, "Updated Task", LocalDate.now().plusDays(5),
true);

        when(taskService.updateTask(eq(1L), any(Task.class))).thenReturn(task);

        mockMvc.perform(put("/api/tasks/1")
            .contentType(MediaType.APPLICATION_JSON)
            .content(objectMapper.writeValueAsString(task)))
            .andExpect(status().isOk())
            .andExpect(jsonPath("$.id", is(1)))
            .andExpect(jsonPath("$.description", is("Updated Task")))
            .andExpect(jsonPath("$.completed", is(true)));
    }

    @Test
    public void testCompleteTask() throws Exception {
        Task task = new Task(1L, "Task 1", LocalDate.now(), true);

        when(taskService.markTaskAsCompleted(1L)).thenReturn(task);

        mockMvc.perform(patch("/api/tasks/1/complete"))
            .andExpect(status().isOk())
            .andExpect(jsonPath("$.id", is(1)))
            .andExpect(jsonPath("$.completed", is(true)));
    }
}
```

1. **Which Java feature allows you to create immutable data classes with minimal boilerplate code?**
   - A) Lambda expressions
   - B) Streams
   - C) Records
   - D) Optional

2. **What is the primary purpose of the `Optional` class in Java?**
   - A) To make code more concise
   - B) To help prevent NullPointerExceptions
   - C) To improve performance
   - D) To enable functional programming

3. **Which build tool automatically handles dependency management for Java projects?**
   - A) JUnit
   - B) JVM
   - C) Maven
   - D) JavaFX

4. **What is the correct way to declare a lambda expression that takes two integers and returns their sum?**
   - A) `(int a, int b) -> a + b`
   - B) `(a, b) => a + b`
   - C) `function(a, b) { return a + b; }`
   - D) `a, b -> { a + b }`

5. **Which of the following is NOT a functional interface in the java.util.function package?**
   - A) Consumer
   - B) Provider
   - C) Supplier
   - D) Predicate

6. **What is the output of the following code?**

java
```
Optional<String> optional = Optional.ofNullable(null);
System.out.println(optional.orElse("Default"));
```

   - A) null
   - B) "Default"
   - C) Optional.empty
   - D) NullPointerException

7. **Which of the following is the correct way to use a text block in Java?**
   - A) `String text = """Hello World""";`
   - B) `String text = '''Hello World''';`
   - C) `String text = """ Hello World """;`

219

   o D) `String text = "Hello World";`

8. **What is the purpose of a BOM (Bill of Materials) in Maven?**
   o A) To list all the dependencies in a project
   o B) To ensure compatible versions of related dependencies
   o C) To document project requirements
   o D) To track project costs

9. **Which statement about pattern matching is correct?**
   o A) It allows you to assign a value when using instanceof
   o B) It's only available in Java 8 and above
   o C) It requires external libraries
   o D) It can only be used with primitive types

10. **What will the following code print?**

java
```java
record Point(int x, int y) {}
Point p1 = new Point(10, 20);
Point p2 = new Point(10, 20);
System.out.println(p1.equals(p2));
```

   o A) false
   o B) true
   o C) null
   o D) Runtime error

Answers:

1. C) Records
2. B) To help prevent NullPointerExceptions
3. C) Maven
4. A) `(int a, int b) -> a + b`
5. B) Provider
6. B) "Default"
7. C) `String text = """ Hello World """;`
8. B) To ensure compatible versions of related dependencies
9. A) It allows you to assign a value when using instanceof
10. B) true

 FAQ: Common Java Questions

General Questions

Q: Why is Java platform-independent?

A: Java achieves platform independence through its "Write Once, Run Anywhere" (WORA) approach. When you compile Java code, it creates bytecode (.class files) rather than machine code. This bytecode runs on the Java Virtual Machine (JVM), not directly on the hardware. Since JVMs are available for all major operating systems, the same bytecode can run on any platform with a compatible JVM installed.

Q: What's the difference between JDK, JRE, and JVM?

A:

- **JDK (Java Development Kit)**: Complete package for developers, including the JRE, compiler, debugger, and development tools.
- **JRE (Java Runtime Environment)**: Provides the runtime environment for running Java applications, including the JVM and standard libraries.
- **JVM (Java Virtual Machine)**: The virtual machine that executes Java bytecode on a specific platform.

Q: Is Java still relevant in 2025?

A: Yes, Java remains highly relevant. It's one of the most widely used programming languages, especially for enterprise applications, Android development, big data processing, and backend services. Java continues to evolve with regular updates adding modern features while maintaining backward compatibility. Its vast ecosystem, mature frameworks, and extensive community support ensure its continued relevance.

Language Features

Q: When should I use interfaces vs. abstract classes?

A: Use interfaces when:

- You want to define a contract that unrelated classes can implement
- Multiple inheritance is needed (a class can implement multiple interfaces)
- You're defining a capability rather than a type of object

Use abstract classes when:

- You want to share code among closely related classes
- You need to provide a default implementation for some methods
- You want to declare non-public members or non-final fields
- You need constructor parameters passed to subclasses

Q: What's the point of using `Optional` instead of just checking for null?

A: `Optional` offers several advantages over explicit null checks:

1. It makes the possibility of a missing value explicit in the method signature

2. It encourages a more functional programming style with methods like `map()`, `filter()`, and `flatMap()`
3. It reduces the risk of NullPointerExceptions by encouraging proper handling of absent values
4. It provides convenience methods for providing default values or actions

Q: When should I use records instead of regular classes?

A: Use records when:

- You need a simple data carrier class with immutable fields
- You don't need custom equality or hashCode implementations
- You don't need to enforce complex validation or invariants
- You want to minimize boilerplate code for getters, constructors, equals, hashCode, and toString

Regular classes are still better when you need mutable state, complex behavior beyond data access, or need to implement specific interfaces or extend other classes.

11.9 Practical Development

Q: Maven or Gradle: which one should I choose?

A: Both are excellent build tools with different strengths:

Choose Maven when:

- You prefer convention over configuration
- You want wide tool integration and support
- You need a stable, predictable build system
- Your project follows standard structure and practices

Choose Gradle when:

- You need more build customization
- You're working on complex, multi-project builds
- You want better performance for large projects
- You're developing Android applications (Android Studio uses Gradle)

Q: How do I handle exceptions properly in Java?

A: Best practices for exception handling include:

1. Only catch exceptions you can actually handle
2. Don't catch at too high a level (avoid catching `Exception` or `Throwable` without good reason)

222

3. Clean up resources in a `finally` block or use try-with-resources
4. Include meaningful information in exception messages
5. Consider creating custom exceptions for application-specific errors
6. Log exceptions with appropriate context
7. Don't use exceptions for flow control
8. Prefer unchecked exceptions for programming errors and checked exceptions for recoverable conditions

Q: What's the best way to learn design patterns in Java?

A: To learn design patterns effectively:

1. Start with understanding the problem each pattern solves
2. Study the classic "Gang of Four" patterns and their Java implementations
3. Examine real-world code in open-source projects
4. Practice implementing the patterns in small projects
5. Join communities like Stack Overflow or Java forums to discuss pattern applications
6. Read books like "Head First Design Patterns" for Java-specific examples
7. Remember that patterns are tools, not goals—use them when they solve real problems

11.10 Conclusion and Next Steps

Congratulations on reaching the end of our comprehensive Java guide! Throughout this journey, we've covered the essentials of Java programming, from basic syntax to advanced features, and built practical applications along the way.

11.10.1 What You've Learned

You've gained a solid foundation in Java programming, including:

- Java fundamentals: variables, control structures, methods
- Object-oriented programming concepts
- Modern Java features like records, pattern matching, and text blocks
- Working with collections and handling exceptions
- Building applications with frameworks like Spring Boot
- Testing and debugging techniques
- Best practices for structuring and organizing code

11.10.2 Your Learning Path Forward

As you continue your Java journey, consider these paths for further growth:

1. **Deepen Your Framework Knowledge**
   o Master Spring Boot for enterprise applications
   o Explore Jakarta EE for scalable server applications
   o Learn Hibernate for robust database integration

2. **Specialize in an Industry Domain**
   o Financial technology (FinTech)
   o Healthcare systems
   o E-commerce platforms
   o Enterprise resource planning (ERP)
3. **Explore Related Technologies**
   o Learn Kotlin as a modern alternative to Java on the JVM
   o Study DevOps practices for Java applications
   o Master containerization with Docker and Kubernetes
   o Develop microservices architectures
4. **Contribute to Open Source**
   o Find Java projects aligned with your interests
   o Start with documentation or small bugfixes
   o Gradually contribute larger features
   o Learn from code reviews and community feedback

11.10.3 Staying Current with Java

Java continues to evolve, with new releases every six months. To stay updated:

1. **Follow Official Sources**
   o OpenJDK mailing lists
   o Inside Java - Official blogs and podcasts
2. **Engage with the Community**
   o Attend Java conferences (in-person or virtual)
   o Join Java User Groups (JUGs)
   o Participate in forums and discussion boards
3. **Practice Continuously**
   o Challenge yourself with increasingly complex projects
   o Refactor old code using new Java features
   o Review and improve your existing applications

11.10.4 Final Thoughts

Remember that becoming a proficient Java developer is a journey, not a destination. The language and ecosystem will continue to evolve, and there will always be new things to learn. Embrace this continuous learning process, and you'll find Java programming to be a rewarding and valuable skill throughout your career.

Stay curious, keep coding, and enjoy your Java journey!

"The best way to predict the future is to implement it." - David Heinemeier Hansson

Java Project Structure Example

Below is an example of a well-organized Java project structure for the Task Manager API we built in the practice project. This structure follows Maven conventions and separates concerns appropriately.

```
task-manager/
├── src/
│   ├── main/
│   │   ├── java/
│   │   │   └── com/
│   │   │       └── example/
│   │   │           └── taskmanager/
│   │   │               ├── TaskManagerApplication.java   # Main application class
│   │   │               ├── controller/
│   │   │               │   └── TaskController.java        # REST endpoints
│   │   │               ├── model/
│   │   │               │   └── Task.java                  # Entity class
│   │   │               ├── repository/
│   │   │               │   └── TaskRepository.java        # Database access
│   │   │               ├── service/
│   │   │               │   └── TaskService.java           # Business logic
│   │   │               └── exception/
│   │   │                   └── GlobalExceptionHandler.java  # Error handling
│   │   └── resources/
│   │       ├── application.properties  # Configuration
│   │       ├── static/                 # Static resources (CSS, JS)
│   │       └── templates/              # HTML templates
│   └── test/
│       ├── java/
│       │   └── com/
│       │       └── example/
│       │           └── taskmanager/
│       │               ├── controller/
│       │               │   └── TaskControllerTest.java
│       │               ├── service/
│       │               │   └── TaskServiceTest.java
│       │               └── repository/
│       │                   └── TaskRepositoryTest.java
│       └── resources/
│           └── application-test.properties  # Test configuration
├── pom.xml              # Maven configuration
├── README.md            # Project documentation
├── .gitignore           # Git ignore file
└── mvnw, mvnw.cmd       # Maven wrapper
```

Key Components

Controller Layer

- Handles HTTP requests and responses
- Maps URLs to service methods
- Performs basic input validation
- Returns appropriate HTTP status codes

Service Layer

- Contains business logic
- Orchestrates operations across multiple repositories
- Handles transactions
- Enforces business rules and validation

Repository Layer

- Communicates with the database
- Implements data access operations
- Translates between entities and database tables

Model Layer

- Defines entity classes
- Represents business objects
- Contains validation annotations

Exception Handling

- Provides global exception handling
- Converts exceptions to appropriate HTTP responses
- Ensures consistent error reporting

Best Practices

1. **Separation of Concerns**
   - Each layer has a specific responsibility
   - Minimizes coupling between components
2. **Consistent Naming**
   - Classes are named according to their purpose
   - Packages organize related functionality
3. **Testability**
   - Tests are organized to mirror the main code structure
   - Each layer can be tested independently
4. **Configuration Management**
   - External configuration in properties files
   - Environment-specific settings separated
5. **Documentation**
   - README provides project overview
   - Code includes appropriate comments

This structure can be adapted for projects of different sizes, with additional packages for more complex applications.

Java Quick Reference Cheatsheet

Basic Syntax

Program Structure

```java
// Filename: MyClass.java
package com.example;  // Package declaration (optional)

import java.util.*;   // Import statement (optional)

public class MyClass {
    // Class body
    public static void main(String[] args) {
        // Main method - program execution starts here
        System.out.println("Hello, World!");
    }
}
```

Data Types

Type	Size	Range	Example
byte	8 bits	-128 to 127	byte b = 10;
short	16 bits	-32,768 to 32,767	short s = 1000;
int	32 bits	-2^31 to 2^31-1	int i = 100000;
long	64 bits	-2^63 to 2^63-1	long l = 100000L;
float	32 bits	~3.4E-38 to 3.4E+38	float f = 1.5f;
double	64 bits	~1.7E-308 to 1.7E+308	double d = 1.5;
char	16 bits	0 to 65,535	char c = 'A';
boolean	-	true or false	boolean b = true;

Variables and Constants

```java
// Variable declaration
int number;            // Declaration
number = 10;           // Initialization
int count = 20;        // Declaration and initialization

// Constants
final double PI = 3.14159;

// Multiple declarations
int a, b, c;
int x = 1, y = 2, z = 3;
```

Type Casting

```
// Widening (automatic)
int myInt = 9;
double myDouble = myInt;   // 9.0

// Narrowing (manual)
double myDouble = 9.78;
int myInt = (int) myDouble;   // 9

// String conversion
String str = Integer.toString(123);   // int to String
int num = Integer.parseInt("123");    // String to int
double d = Double.parseDouble("3.14");  // String to double
```

Operators

Arithmetic Operators

Operator	Description	Example
+	Addition	a + b
-	Subtraction	a - b
*	Multiplication	a * b
/	Division	a / b
%	Modulus	a % b
++	Increment	a++ or ++a
--	Decrement	a-- or --a

Comparison Operators

Operator	Description	Example
==	Equal to	a == b
!=	Not equal to	a != b
>	Greater than	a > b
<	Less than	a < b
>=	Greater than or equal to	a >= b
<=	Less than or equal to	a <= b

Logical Operators

Operator	Description	Example
&&	Logical AND	a && b
!	Logical NOT	!a

Bitwise Operators

Operator	Description	Example
&	Bitwise AND	a & b
|	Bitwise OR	a | b
^	Bitwise XOR	a ^ b
~	Bitwise NOT	~a
<<	Left shift	a << 2
>>	Right shift with sign	a >> 2
>>>	Right shift with zero	a >>> 2

Assignment Operators

Operator	Example	Equivalent to
=	a = b	a = b
+=	a += b	a = a + b
-=	a -= b	a = a - b
*=	a *= b	a = a * b
/=	a /= b	a = a / b
%=	a %= b	a = a % b

Control Flow

Conditional Statements

```
// if statement
if (condition) {
    // code
} else if (anotherCondition) {
    // code
} else {
    // code
}

// ternary operator
variable = (condition) ? expressionIfTrue : expressionIfFalse;

// switch statement
switch (variable) {
    case value1:
        // code
        break;
    case value2:
        // code
        break;
    default:
```

```
        // code
    }

    // Enhanced switch (Java 14+)
    switch (variable) {
        case value1 -> // code;
        case value2 -> // code;
        default -> // code;
    }
```

Loops

```
    // for loop
    for (int i = 0; i < 10; i++) {
        // code
    }

    // enhanced for loop (for-each)
    for (String item : collection) {
        // code
    }

    // while loop
    while (condition) {
        // code
    }

    // do-while loop
    do {
        // code
    } while (condition);

    // Loop control
    break;    // exit the loop
    continue; // skip to next iteration
```

Arrays

Declaration and Initialization

```
    // Declaration
    int[] numbers;
    String[] names;

    // Initialization
    numbers = new int[5];          // Creates array of size 5
    names = new String[3];         // Creates array of size 3

    // Declaration and initialization
    int[] scores = new int[5];     // [0, 0, 0, 0, 0]
    int[] values = {10, 20, 30};   // [10, 20, 30]

    // Multidimensional arrays
```

```
int[][] matrix = new int[3][4];
int[][] grid = {{1, 2}, {3, 4}, {5, 6}};
```

Array Operations

```
// Accessing elements
int firstNumber = numbers[0];  // First element
int lastNumber = numbers[numbers.length - 1];  // Last element

// Setting values
numbers[0] = 100;

// Array length
int size = numbers.length;

// Iterating
for (int i = 0; i < numbers.length; i++) {
    System.out.println(numbers[i]);
}

// For-each loop
for (int num : numbers) {
    System.out.println(num);
}

// Copying arrays
int[] copied = Arrays.copyOf(original, original.length);

// Sorting
Arrays.sort(numbers);

// Searching (on sorted arrays)
int index = Arrays.binarySearch(numbers, valueToFind);

// Filling
Arrays.fill(numbers, 0);  // Fill with zeros
```

Strings

Creation and Basic Operations

```
// Creating strings
String str1 = "Hello";
String str2 = new String("World");

// Concatenation
String result = str1 + " " + str2;  // "Hello World"
String built = str1.concat(" ").concat(str2);  // "Hello World"

// Length
int length = str1.length();  // 5

// Accessing characters
```

```
char firstChar = str1.charAt(0);  // 'H'

// Substring
String sub = str1.substring(1, 4);  // "ell"

// Case conversion
String upper = str1.toUpperCase();  // "HELLO"
String lower = str1.toLowerCase();  // "hello"
```

String Comparison and Searching

```
// Equality
boolean equals = str1.equals(str2);  // false
boolean equalsIgnoreCase = str1.equalsIgnoreCase("hello");  // true

// Comparison
int comparison = str1.compareTo(str2);  // negative if str1 < str2

// Contains, starts with, ends with
boolean contains = str1.contains("ell");  // true
boolean startsWith = str1.startsWith("He");  // true
boolean endsWith = str1.endsWith("lo");  // true

// Finding position
int index = str1.indexOf("l");  // 2 (first occurrence)
int lastIndex = str1.lastIndexOf("l");  // 3 (last occurrence)
```

String Manipulation

```
// Trimming whitespace
String trimmed = "  Hello  ".trim();  // "Hello"

// Replacing
String replaced = str1.replace('e', 'a');  // "Hallo"
String replacedAll = "Hello".replaceAll("l", "x");  // "Hexxo"

// Splitting
String[] parts = "Hello,World".split(",");  // ["Hello", "World"]

// Join (Java 8+)
String joined = String.join("-", "Hello", "World");  // "Hello-World"

// Format
String formatted = String.format("Name: %s, Age: %d", "John", 25);
```

StringBuilder

```
// Creating StringBuilder
StringBuilder sb = new StringBuilder();
StringBuilder sb2 = new StringBuilder("Hello");

// Appending
sb.append("Hello").append(" ").append("World");  // "Hello World"
```

```java
// Inserting
sb.insert(5, "!");   // "Hello! World"

// Deleting
sb.delete(5, 6);   // "Hello World"

// Replacing
sb.replace(6, 11, "Java");   // "Hello Java"

// Converting to String
String result = sb.toString();
```

Object-Oriented Programming

Classes and Objects

```java
// Class declaration
public class Person {
    // Instance variables (fields)
    private String name;
    private int age;

    // Constructor
    public Person(String name, int age) {
        this.name = name;
        this.age = age;
    }

    // Default constructor
    public Person() {
        this.name = "Unknown";
        this.age = 0;
    }

    // Getters and Setters
    public String getName() {
        return name;
    }

    public void setName(String name) {
        this.name = name;
    }

    public int getAge() {
        return age;
    }

    public void setAge(int age) {
        this.age = age;
    }
```

```java
    // Instance method
    public void introduce() {
        System.out.println("Hi, I'm " + name + " and I'm " + age + " years old.");
    }

    // Static method
    public static Person createAdult(String name) {
        return new Person(name, 18);
    }
}

// Creating objects
Person person1 = new Person("John", 25);
Person person2 = new Person();  // Using default constructor
Person adult = Person.createAdult("Alice");  // Using static method

// Accessing methods and properties
person1.introduce();
person1.setAge(26);
```

Inheritance

```java
// Base class (Superclass)
public class Animal {
    protected String name;

    public Animal(String name) {
        this.name = name;
    }

    public void eat() {
        System.out.println(name + " is eating.");
    }

    public void sleep() {
        System.out.println(name + " is sleeping.");
    }
}

// Derived class (Subclass)
public class Dog extends Animal {
    private String breed;

    public Dog(String name, String breed) {
        super(name);  // Call to superclass constructor
        this.breed = breed;
    }

    public void bark() {
        System.out.println(name + " is barking.");
    }
}
```

235

```java
    // Method overriding
    @Override
    public void eat() {
        System.out.println(name + " the " + breed + " is eating dog food.");
    }
}

// Using inheritance
Dog dog = new Dog("Max", "Labrador");
dog.eat();     // Uses Dog's implementation
dog.sleep();   // Uses Animal's implementation
dog.bark();    // Dog's own method
```

Interfaces

```java
// Interface declaration
public interface Drivable {
    void drive();   // Abstract method (implicitly public and abstract)

    // Default method (Java 8+)
    default void startEngine() {
        System.out.println("Engine started.");
    }

    // Static method (Java 8+)
    static boolean isLegal(int age) {
        return age >= 18;
    }
}

// Implementing an interface
public class Car implements Drivable {
    @Override
    public void drive() {
        System.out.println("Car is being driven.");
    }

    // Can override default methods
    @Override
    public void startEngine() {
        System.out.println("Car engine started with key.");
    }
}

// Using interfaces
Drivable vehicle = new Car();
vehicle.drive();
vehicle.startEngine();
boolean canDrive = Drivable.isLegal(20);   // true
```

Abstract Classes

```java
// Abstract class
```

```java
public abstract class Shape {
    protected String color;

    public Shape(String color) {
        this.color = color;
    }

    // Abstract method (must be implemented by subclasses)
    public abstract double calculateArea();

    // Concrete method
    public void display() {
        System.out.println("This shape is " + color);
    }
}

// Concrete subclass
public class Circle extends Shape {
    private double radius;

    public Circle(String color, double radius) {
        super(color);
        this.radius = radius;
    }

    @Override
    public double calculateArea() {
        return Math.PI * radius * radius;
    }
}

// Using abstract classes
Shape shape = new Circle("red", 5.0);
double area = shape.calculateArea();  // Uses Circle's implementation
shape.display();  // Uses Shape's implementation
```

Polymorphism

```java
// Base class
public class Animal {
    public void makeSound() {
        System.out.println("Animal makes a sound");
    }
}

// Derived classes
public class Dog extends Animal {
    @Override
    public void makeSound() {
        System.out.println("Dog barks");
    }
}
```

237

```java
public class Cat extends Animal {
    @Override
    public void makeSound() {
        System.out.println("Cat meows");
    }
}

// Polymorphic behavior
Animal myDog = new Dog();
Animal myCat = new Cat();

myDog.makeSound();   // "Dog barks"
myCat.makeSound();   // "Cat meows"

// Polymorphic collections and parameters
List<Animal> animals = new ArrayList<>();
animals.add(new Dog());
animals.add(new Cat());

for (Animal animal : animals) {
    animal.makeSound();   // Calls the right method based on actual type
}
```

Encapsulation

```java
public class BankAccount {
    // Private fields (data hiding)
    private String accountNumber;
    private double balance;

    // Constructor
    public BankAccount(String accountNumber, double initialBalance) {
        this.accountNumber = accountNumber;
        this.balance = initialBalance;
    }

    // Public methods provide controlled access
    public double getBalance() {
        return balance;
    }

    public void deposit(double amount) {
        if (amount > 0) {
            balance += amount;
        }
    }

    public boolean withdraw(double amount) {
        if (amount > 0 && balance >= amount) {
            balance -= amount;
            return true;
```

```
        }
        return false;
    }

    // Private helper method
    private void updateTransactionLog(String transaction) {
        // Implementation details hidden
    }
}
```

Exception Handling

Try-Catch-Finally

```
try {
    // Code that might throw an exception
    int result = 10 / 0;  // ArithmeticException

} catch (ArithmeticException e) {
    // Handle specific exception
    System.out.println("Cannot divide by zero: " + e.getMessage());

} catch (Exception e) {
    // Handle any other exception
    System.out.println("Error occurred: " + e.getMessage());

} finally {
    // Code that always executes, regardless of exception
    System.out.println("This will always execute");
}
```

Multiple Catch Blocks

```
try {
    int[] numbers = new int[5];
    numbers[10] = 50;  // ArrayIndexOutOfBoundsException

} catch (ArrayIndexOutOfBoundsException e) {
    System.out.println("Array index out of bounds");

} catch (ArithmeticException e) {
    System.out.println("Arithmetic error");

} catch (Exception e) {
    System.out.println("General error");
}
```

Try-with-Resources (Java 7+)

```
// Automatically closes resources that implement AutoCloseable
try (
    FileInputStream input = new FileInputStream("file.txt");
    BufferedReader reader = new BufferedReader(new InputStreamReader(input))
```

```java
) {
    String line = reader.readLine();
    // Process the file...

} catch (IOException e) {
    System.out.println("Error reading file: " + e.getMessage());
}
```

Throwing Exceptions

```java
public void validateAge(int age) {
    if (age < 0) {
        throw new IllegalArgumentException("Age cannot be negative");
    }

    if (age > 120) {
        throw new IllegalArgumentException("Age is too high");
    }
}

// Custom exceptions
public class InsufficientFundsException extends Exception {
    public InsufficientFundsException(String message) {
        super(message);
    }
}

// Using custom exceptions
public void withdraw(double amount) throws InsufficientFundsException {
    if (amount > balance) {
        throw new InsufficientFundsException("Not enough funds");
    }
    // Process withdrawal
}
```

Collections Framework

List Interface

```java
// ArrayList (dynamic array)
List<String> names = new ArrayList<>();
names.add("Alice");            // Add at the end
names.add(0, "Bob");           // Add at specific position
String name = names.get(0);    // Access by index
names.set(1, "Charlie");       // Modify
names.remove(0);               // Remove by index
names.remove("Charlie");       // Remove by value
boolean contains = names.contains("Alice");  // Check if exists
int size = names.size();       // Size of list

// LinkedList (doubly-linked list)
List<String> queue = new LinkedList<>();
queue.add("First");
```
240

```java
queue.addFirst("Zero");        // Add at beginning
queue.addLast("Last");         // Add at end
String first = queue.getFirst();
String last = queue.getLast();
queue.removeFirst();
queue.removeLast();
```

Set Interface

```java
// HashSet (unordered, no duplicates)
Set<Integer> numbers = new HashSet<>();
numbers.add(10);
numbers.add(20);
numbers.add(10);   // Ignored (duplicate)
boolean contains = numbers.contains(10);   // true
numbers.remove(10);

// TreeSet (ordered, no duplicates)
Set<String> sortedNames = new TreeSet<>();
sortedNames.add("Charlie");
sortedNames.add("Alice");
sortedNames.add("Bob");
// Will iterate in order: Alice, Bob, Charlie

// LinkedHashSet (preserves insertion order, no duplicates)
Set<String> orderedSet = new LinkedHashSet<>();
```

Map Interface

```java
// HashMap (key-value pairs, unordered)
Map<String, Integer> ages = new HashMap<>();
ages.put("Alice", 25);
ages.put("Bob", 30);
int bobAge = ages.get("Bob");           // 30
boolean hasKey = ages.containsKey("Charlie");   // false
boolean hasValue = ages.containsValue(25);       // true
ages.remove("Alice");

// Iterating through a Map
for (Map.Entry<String, Integer> entry : ages.entrySet()) {
    String key = entry.getKey();
    Integer value = entry.getValue();
    System.out.println(key + " is " + value + " years old");
}

// Just keys or values
for (String key : ages.keySet()) {
    System.out.println(key);
}

for (Integer value : ages.values()) {
    System.out.println(value);
}
```

241

```java
// TreeMap (sorted by keys)
Map<String, Integer> sortedMap = new TreeMap<>();

// LinkedHashMap (preserves insertion order)
Map<String, Integer> orderedMap = new LinkedHashMap<>();
```

Queue and Deque

```java
// Queue (FIFO)
Queue<String> queue = new LinkedList<>();
queue.add("First");        // Throws exception if full
queue.offer("Second");     // Returns false if full
String first = queue.peek();   // View the head (without removing)
String removed = queue.poll();   // Remove and return the head

// Deque (double-ended queue)
Deque<String> deque = new ArrayDeque<>();
deque.addFirst("First");
deque.addLast("Last");
String first = deque.getFirst();
String last = deque.getLast();
deque.removeFirst();
deque.removeLast();
```

File I/O

Reading Files

```java
// Using BufferedReader (line by line)
try (BufferedReader reader = new BufferedReader(new FileReader("file.txt"))) {
    String line;
    while ((line = reader.readLine()) != null) {
        System.out.println(line);
    }
} catch (IOException e) {
    e.printStackTrace();
}

// Using Files utility (Java 7+)
try {
    List<String> lines = Files.readAllLines(Paths.get("file.txt"));
    for (String line : lines) {
        System.out.println(line);
    }
} catch (IOException e) {
    e.printStackTrace();
}

// Reading as a single String
try {
    String content = new String(Files.readAllBytes(Paths.get("file.txt")));
    System.out.println(content);
```

```java
    } catch (IOException e) {
        e.printStackTrace();
    }
```

Writing Files

```java
// Using BufferedWriter
try (BufferedWriter writer = new BufferedWriter(new FileWriter("output.txt"))) {
    writer.write("Hello, World!");
    writer.newLine();
    writer.write("Another line");
} catch (IOException e) {
    e.printStackTrace();
}

// Using Files utility (Java 7+)
try {
    List<String> lines = Arrays.asList("First line", "Second line");
    Files.write(Paths.get("output.txt"), lines);
} catch (IOException e) {
    e.printStackTrace();
}

// Appending to a file
try (FileWriter fw = new FileWriter("output.txt", true);
     BufferedWriter writer = new BufferedWriter(fw)) {
    writer.write("Appended text");
} catch (IOException e) {
    e.printStackTrace();
}
```

File and Directory Operations

```java
// File info
File file = new File("example.txt");
boolean exists = file.exists();
boolean isFile = file.isFile();
boolean isDir = file.isDirectory();
long size = file.length();
boolean deleted = file.delete();

// Creating directories
File dir = new File("newDir");
boolean created = dir.mkdir();           // Single directory
boolean createdPath = dir.mkdirs();      // Including parent directories

// Listing directory contents
File folder = new File("myFolder");
File[] files = folder.listFiles();
for (File f : files) {
    System.out.println(f.getName());
}
```

243

```java
// Path operations (Java 7+)
Path path = Paths.get("dir", "subdir", "file.txt");
Files.createDirectories(path.getParent());  // Create parent dirs
Files.createFile(path);                      // Create file
Files.copy(source, target, StandardCopyOption.REPLACE_EXISTING);
Files.move(source, target, StandardCopyOption.REPLACE_EXISTING);
```

Generics

Generic Classes

```java
// Generic class with one type parameter
public class Box<T> {
    private T content;

    public Box(T content) {
        this.content = content;
    }

    public T getContent() {
        return content;
    }

    public void setContent(T content) {
        this.content = content;
    }
}

// Usage
Box<Integer> intBox = new Box<>(42);
int value = intBox.getContent();  // 42

Box<String> stringBox = new Box<>("Hello");
String message = stringBox.getContent();  // "Hello"
```

Generic Methods

```java
// Generic method
public <T> T findFirst(List<T> list) {
    if (list == null || list.isEmpty()) {
        return null;
    }
    return list.get(0);
}

// With multiple type parameters
public <K, V> void printPair(K key, V value) {
    System.out.println(key + ": " + value);
}

// Usage
String first = findFirst(Arrays.asList("a", "b", "c"));  // "a"
printPair("name", "John");  // "name: John"
```
244

Bounded Type Parameters

```java
// Upper bound (T must be Number or a subclass of Number)
public <T extends Number> double sum(List<T> numbers) {
    double total = 0;
    for (T number : numbers) {
        total += number.doubleValue();
    }
    return total;
}


// Multiple bounds (T must implement both interfaces)
public <T extends Comparable & Serializable> void process(T item) {
    // implementation
}


// Lower bound (accepts List<Integer> or any superclass)
public void addNumbers(List<? super Integer> list) {
    list.add(1);
    list.add(2);
}
```

Wildcards

```java
// Unknown type (read-only)
public void printList(List<?> list) {
    for (Object item : list) {
        System.out.println(item);
    }
}


// Upper bounded wildcard
public double sumOfNumbers(List<? extends Number> numbers) {
    double total = 0;
    for (Number number : numbers) {
        total += number.doubleValue();
    }
    return total;
}


// Lower bounded wildcard
public void addIntegers(List<? super Integer> list) {
    list.add(10);
    list.add(20);
}
```

Lambda Expressions and Functional Interfaces (Java 8+)

Functional Interfaces

```java
// Some common functional interfaces
Predicate<T>          // T -> boolean
Function<T, R>        // T -> R
```

```
Consumer<T>            // T -> void
Supplier<T>            // () -> T
BinaryOperator<T>      // (T, T) -> T
UnaryOperator<T>       // T -> T
```

Lambda Expressions

```
// Lambda syntax: (parameters) -> expression or statement block

// With Predicate
Predicate<String> isEmpty = s -> s.isEmpty();
boolean result = isEmpty.test("Hello");  // false

// With Function
Function<String, Integer> length = s -> s.length();
int len = length.apply("Hello");  // 5

// With Consumer
Consumer<String> printer = s -> System.out.println(s);
printer.accept("Hello");  // Prints "Hello"

// With Supplier
Supplier<Double> random = () -> Math.random();
double value = random.get();  // Random value between 0 and 1

// Multiple parameters
BinaryOperator<Integer> add = (a, b) -> a + b;
int sum = add.apply(5, 3);  // 8

// Block of code
Function<Integer, Integer> factorial = n -> {
    int result = 1;
    for (int i = 1; i <= n; i++) {
        result *= i;
    }
    return result;
};
```

Method References

```
// Types of method references:
// 1. Static method: ClassName::staticMethod
// 2. Instance method of a particular object: instance::method
// 3. Instance method of an arbitrary object of a particular type:
ClassName::instanceMethod
// 4. Constructor: ClassName::new

// Static method reference
Function<String, Integer> parseInt = Integer::parseInt;

// Instance method reference
String str = "Hello";
Supplier<Integer> length = str::length;
```

```java
// Instance method of arbitrary object
Function<String, String> toUpper = String::toUpperCase;

// Constructor reference
Supplier<List<String>> listCreator = ArrayList::new;
```

Stream API

```java
List<String> names = Arrays.asList("Alice", "Bob", "Charlie", "Dave");

// Creating streams
Stream<String> stream1 = names.stream();         // Sequential
Stream<String> stream2 = names.parallelStream(); // Parallel

// Common operations
// Filter
List<String> filtered = names.stream()
    .filter(name -> name.startsWith("A"))
    .collect(Collectors.toList());  // ["Alice"]

// Map
List<Integer> lengths = names.stream()
    .map(String::length)
    .collect(Collectors.toList());  // [5, 3, 7, 4]

// Sort
List<String> sorted = names.stream()
    .sorted()
    .collect(Collectors.toList());  // ["Alice", "Bob", "Charlie", "Dave"]

// ForEach
names.stream().forEach(System.out::println);

// Reduce
int totalLength = names.stream()
    .mapToInt(String::length)
    .sum();  // 19

// Find operations
Optional<String> first = names.stream()
    .filter(s -> s.length() > 5)
    .findFirst();  // Optional["Charlie"]

// Match operations
boolean anyMatch = names.stream().anyMatch(s -> s.length() > 5);     // true
boolean allMatch = names.stream().allMatch(s -> s.length() > 2);     // true
boolean noneMatch = names.stream().noneMatch(s -> s.isEmpty());      // true

// Collectors
// To list/set/map
List<String> list = names.stream().collect(Collectors.toList());
```

```java
Set<String> set = names.stream().collect(Collectors.toSet());
Map<String, Integer> map = names.stream()
    .collect(Collectors.toMap(s -> s, String::length));

// Joining
String joined = names.stream().collect(Collectors.joining(", "));
// "Alice, Bob, Charlie, Dave"

// Statistics
IntSummaryStatistics stats = names.stream()
    .mapToInt(String::length)
    .summaryStatistics();
//    stats.getAverage(),    stats.getMax(),    stats.getMin(),    stats.getSum(),
stats.getCount()
```

Concurrency and Multithreading

Creating and Running Threads

```java
// Extending Thread class
class MyThread extends Thread {
    @Override
    public void run() {
        System.out.println("Thread                running:                " +
Thread.currentThread().getName());
    }
}

// Using Runnable interface
class MyRunnable implements Runnable {
    @Override
    public void run() {
        System.out.println("Runnable                running:                " +
Thread.currentThread().getName());
    }
}

// Starting threads
MyThread thread1 = new MyThread();
thread1.start();  // Starts the thread

Thread thread2 = new Thread(new MyRunnable());
thread2.start();  // Starts the thread

// Using lambda expression (Java 8+)
Thread thread3 = new Thread(() -> {
    System.out.println("Lambda                thread                running:                " +
Thread.currentThread().getName());
});
thread3.start();
```

Thread Synchronization

248

```java
// Synchronized method
public synchronized void increment() {
    count++;
}

// Synchronized block
public void increment() {
    synchronized(this) {
        count++;
    }
}

// Lock objects
private final Object lock = new Object();

public void increment() {
    synchronized(lock) {
        count++;
    }
}
```

Thread Communication

```java
// wait, notify, and notifyAll
public synchronized void produce() throws InterruptedException {
    while (isFull()) {
        wait();  // Release lock and wait
    }
    // produce item
    notifyAll();  // Notify waiting threads
}

public synchronized void consume() throws InterruptedException {
    while (isEmpty()) {
        wait();  // Release lock and wait
    }
    // consume item
    notifyAll();  // Notify waiting threads
}
```

Thread Pools (ExecutorService)

```java
// Fixed thread pool
ExecutorService executor = Executors.newFixedThreadPool(5);

// Submit tasks
executor.submit(() -> {
    System.out.println("Task executed by " + Thread.currentThread().getName());
});

// Shutdown
executor.shutdown();
try {
```

```java
        if (!executor.awaitTermination(60, TimeUnit.SECONDS)) {
            executor.shutdownNow();
        }
    } catch (InterruptedException e) {
        executor.shutdownNow();
    }

    // Other thread pool types
    ExecutorService singleThreadExecutor = Executors.newSingleThreadExecutor();
    ExecutorService cachedThreadPool = Executors.newCachedThreadPool();
    ScheduledExecutorService                scheduledExecutor                =
Executors.newScheduledThreadPool(5);
```

Future and CompletableFuture

```java
    // Future for getting results from threads
    ExecutorService executor = Executors.newFixedThreadPool(1);

    // Submit callable task
    Future<Integer> future = executor.submit(() -> {
        Thread.sleep(1000);
        return 42;
    });

    // Get result (blocks until result is available)
    try {
        Integer result = future.get();   // 42
        Integer resultWithTimeout = future.get(2, TimeUnit.SECONDS);
    } catch (InterruptedException | ExecutionException | TimeoutException e) {
        e.printStackTrace();
    }

    // CompletableFuture (Java 8+)
    CompletableFuture<String> future = CompletableFuture.supplyAsync(() -> {
        try {
            Thread.sleep(500);
        } catch (InterruptedException e) {
            e.printStackTrace();
        }
        return "Result";
    });

    // Chain operations
    future
        .thenApply(s -> s + " processed")
        .thenAccept(System.out::println)
        .thenRun(() -> System.out.println("Done"));

    // Combine futures
    CompletableFuture<String> future1 = CompletableFuture.supplyAsync(() -> "Hello");
    CompletableFuture<String> future2 = CompletableFuture.supplyAsync(() -> "World");
```

250

```
CompletableFuture<String> combined = future1.thenCombine(future2,
    (s1, s2) -> s1 + " " + s2);   // "Hello World"
```

Concurrent Collections

```
// Thread-safe collections
List<String> syncList = Collections.synchronizedList(new ArrayList<>());
Map<String, Integer> concurrentMap = new ConcurrentHashMap<>();
Queue<String> concurrentQueue = new ConcurrentLinkedQueue<>();
BlockingQueue<String> blockingQueue = new LinkedBlockingQueue<>();

// CopyOnWriteArrayList (for read-heavy scenarios)
List<String> copyOnWriteList = new CopyOnWriteArrayList<>();

// Producer-Consumer with BlockingQueue
BlockingQueue<Integer> queue = new ArrayBlockingQueue<>(10);

// Producer
new Thread(() -> {
    try {
        for (int i = 0; i < 20; i++) {
            queue.put(i);   // Blocks if queue is full
        }
    } catch (InterruptedException e) {
        Thread.currentThread().interrupt();
    }
}).start();

// Consumer
new Thread(() -> {
    try {
        while (true) {
            Integer value = queue.take();   // Blocks if queue is empty
            System.out.println("Consumed: " + value);
        }
    } catch (InterruptedException e) {
        Thread.currentThread().interrupt();
    }
}).start();
```

Atomic Variables

```
// Thread-safe variables
AtomicInteger counter = new AtomicInteger(0);
AtomicLong longCounter = new AtomicLong(0);
AtomicBoolean flag = new AtomicBoolean(false);
AtomicReference<String> reference = new AtomicReference<>("initial");

// Operations
int value = counter.incrementAndGet();   // Atomic ++i
int prev = counter.getAndIncrement();    // Atomic i++
boolean success = counter.compareAndSet(5, 10);   // CAS operation
```

251

I/O Streams

```java
// Input streams
InputStream in = new FileInputStream("input.txt");
int byteData = in.read();  // Read one byte
byte[] buffer = new byte[1024];
int bytesRead = in.read(buffer);  // Read into buffer

// Output streams
OutputStream out = new FileOutputStream("output.txt");
out.write(65);  // Write one byte (ASCII 'A')
out.write(buffer, 0, bytesRead);  // Write from buffer

// Readers and Writers (character streams)
Reader reader = new FileReader("input.txt");
int charData = reader.read();  // Read one character
char[] cbuffer = new char[1024];
int charsRead = reader.read(cbuffer);  // Read into character buffer

Writer writer = new FileWriter("output.txt");
writer.write("Hello");  // Write string
writer.write(cbuffer, 0, charsRead);  // Write from buffer
```

NIO (New I/O)

```java
// Path
Path path = Paths.get("data", "input.txt");
Path absolute = path.toAbsolutePath();
Path parent = path.getParent();
Path fileName = path.getFileName();
Path normalized = path.normalize();

// Files
boolean exists = Files.exists(path);
boolean isRegularFile = Files.isRegularFile(path);
boolean isDirectory = Files.isDirectory(path);
long size = Files.size(path);
BasicFileAttributes        attrs       =        Files.readAttributes(path,
BasicFileAttributes.class);

// Reading/Writing
List<String> lines = Files.readAllLines(path);
byte[] bytes = Files.readAllBytes(path);

Files.write(path, lines);
Files.write(path, bytes);

// Directory operations
try (DirectoryStream<Path> stream = Files.newDirectoryStream(Paths.get("."))) {
    for (Path entry : stream) {
```

```java
        System.out.println(entry.getFileName());
    }
}

// Walking directory tree
Files.walkFileTree(Paths.get("."), new SimpleFileVisitor<Path>() {
    @Override
    public FileVisitResult visitFile(Path file, BasicFileAttributes attrs) {
        System.out.println("Visit file: " + file);
        return FileVisitResult.CONTINUE;
    }
});

// Watch Service (monitor directory for changes)
WatchService watchService = FileSystems.getDefault().newWatchService();
Path directory = Paths.get(".");
directory.register(watchService,
    StandardWatchEventKinds.ENTRY_CREATE,
    StandardWatchEventKinds.ENTRY_DELETE,
    StandardWatchEventKinds.ENTRY_MODIFY);

WatchKey key;
while ((key = watchService.take()) != null) {
    for (WatchEvent<?> event : key.pollEvents()) {
        System.out.println(event.kind() + ": " + event.context());
    }
    key.reset();
}
```

Serialization

```java
// Serializable class
public class Person implements Serializable {
    private static final long serialVersionUID = 1L;   // Recommended

    private String name;
    private int age;
    private transient String password;  // Won't be serialized

    // Constructor, getters, setters...
}

// Serializing object
try (ObjectOutputStream out = new ObjectOutputStream(
        new FileOutputStream("person.ser"))) {
    Person person = new Person("John", 30);
    out.writeObject(person);
} catch (IOException e) {
    e.printStackTrace();
}

// Deserializing object
```

253

```java
try (ObjectInputStream in = new ObjectInputStream(
        new FileInputStream("person.ser"))) {
    Person person = (Person) in.readObject();
} catch (IOException | ClassNotFoundException e) {
    e.printStackTrace();
}
```

Java Database Connectivity (JDBC)

Connection

```java
// Loading driver (not needed in newer JDBC versions)
Class.forName("com.mysql.cj.jdbc.Driver");

// Creating connection
String url = "jdbc:mysql://localhost:3306/mydb";
String user = "username";
String password = "password";
Connection conn = DriverManager.getConnection(url, user, password);

// Using try-with-resources
try (Connection connection = DriverManager.getConnection(url, user, password)) {
    // Use connection
} catch (SQLException e) {
    e.printStackTrace();
}
```

Statement and Query Execution

```java
// Statement for simple queries
try (Statement stmt = connection.createStatement()) {
    // Execute query
    ResultSet rs = stmt.executeQuery("SELECT * FROM users");

    // Process results
    while (rs.next()) {
        int id = rs.getInt("id");
        String name = rs.getString("name");
        System.out.println(id + ": " + name);
    }

    // Execute update
    int rowsAffected = stmt.executeUpdate(
        "UPDATE users SET active = true WHERE id = 1");
}

// PreparedStatement for parametrized queries
String sql = "SELECT * FROM users WHERE age > ? AND country = ?";
try (PreparedStatement pstmt = connection.prepareStatement(sql)) {
    // Set parameters
    pstmt.setInt(1, 18);
    pstmt.setString(2, "USA");
```

```java
        // Execute and process
        ResultSet rs = pstmt.executeQuery();
        while (rs.next()) {
            // Process results
        }
    }

    // Batch updates
    try (Statement stmt = connection.createStatement()) {
        stmt.addBatch("INSERT INTO users(name) VALUES('Alice')");
        stmt.addBatch("INSERT INTO users(name) VALUES('Bob')");
        stmt.addBatch("INSERT INTO users(name) VALUES('Charlie')");

        int[] results = stmt.executeBatch();
    }
```

Transcactions

```java
    // Manual transaction control
    Connection conn = DriverManager.getConnection(url, user, password);
    try {
        // Start transaction
        conn.setAutoCommit(false);

        // Perform multiple operations
        Statement stmt = conn.createStatement();
        stmt.executeUpdate("UPDATE accounts SET balance = balance - 100 WHERE id =
1");
        stmt.executeUpdate("UPDATE accounts SET balance = balance + 100 WHERE id =
2");

        // Commit if successful
        conn.commit();

    } catch (SQLException e) {
        // Rollback on error
        if (conn != null) {
            conn.rollback();
        }
        e.printStackTrace();
    } finally {
        // Restore auto-commit
        if (conn != null) {
            conn.setAutoCommit(true);
        }
    }
```

Date and Time API (Java 8+)

LocalDate, LocalTime, LocalDateTime

```java
    // Current date/time
    LocalDate today = LocalDate.now();
```

```java
LocalTime now = LocalTime.now();
LocalDateTime dateTime = LocalDateTime.now();

// Creating specific date/time
LocalDate date = LocalDate.of(2023, Month.APRIL, 15);
LocalTime time = LocalTime.of(13, 45, 20);
LocalDateTime dt = LocalDateTime.of(2023, Month.APRIL, 15, 13, 45, 20);

// Parsing from string
LocalDate parsedDate = LocalDate.parse("2023-04-15");
LocalTime parsedTime = LocalTime.parse("13:45:20");
LocalDateTime parsedDt = LocalDateTime.parse("2023-04-15T13:45:20");

// Getting components
int year = date.getYear();
Month month = date.getMonth();
int day = date.getDayOfMonth();
DayOfWeek dayOfWeek = date.getDayOfWeek();
int hour = time.getHour();
int minute = time.getMinute();

// Modifying
LocalDate tomorrow = today.plusDays(1);
LocalDate nextWeek = today.plusWeeks(1);
LocalDate prevMonth = today.minusMonths(1);
LocalDate withYear = today.withYear(2025);

LocalTime later = now.plusHours(2);
LocalTime earlier = now.minusMinutes(30);
LocalTime withHour = now.withHour(10);
```

ZonedDateTime and Timezones

```java
// Working with timezones
ZoneId zone = ZoneId.of("America/New_York");
ZonedDateTime zdt = ZonedDateTime.now(zone);
ZonedDateTime tokyoTime = ZonedDateTime.now(ZoneId.of("Asia/Tokyo"));

// Converting between zones
ZonedDateTime parisTime = tokyoTime.withZoneSameInstant(ZoneId.of("Europe/Paris"));

// Get all available zone IDs
Set<String> zones = ZoneId.getAvailableZoneIds();

// Convert to Instant (point in time)
Instant instant = zdt.toInstant();
```

Period and Duration

```java
// Period (date-based)
Period period = Period.between(LocalDate.of(2020, 1, 1), LocalDate.of(2023, 4, 15));
```

256

```java
int years = period.getYears();     // 3
int months = period.getMonths();   // 3
int days = period.getDays();       // 14

Period twoMonths = Period.ofMonths(2);
LocalDate futureDate = LocalDate.now().plus(twoMonths);

// Duration (time-based)
Duration duration = Duration.between(LocalTime.of(10, 0), LocalTime.of(12, 30));
long seconds = duration.getSeconds();   // 9000
long nanos = duration.getNano();

Duration threeHours = Duration.ofHours(3);
LocalTime laterTime = LocalTime.now().plus(threeHours);
```

Formatting and Parsing

```java
// Using predefined formatters
LocalDate date = LocalDate.now();
String basic = date.format(DateTimeFormatter.BASIC_ISO_DATE);        // 20230415
String iso = date.format(DateTimeFormatter.ISO_LOCAL_DATE);          // 2023-04-15
String pattern = date.format(DateTimeFormatter.ofPattern("dd/MM/yyyy"));   //
15/04/2023

// Creating custom formatters
DateTimeFormatter formatter = DateTimeFormatter.ofPattern("MMMM dd, yyyy");
String formatted = date.format(formatter);   // "April 15, 2023"

// Parsing
LocalDate parsedDate = LocalDate.parse("April 15, 2023", formatter);
```

Optional Class (Java 8+)

Creating Optionals

```java
// Empty Optional
Optional<String> empty = Optional.empty();

// From a non-null value
Optional<String> opt = Optional.of("Hello");

// From a potentially null value
Optional<String> nullable = Optional.ofNullable(mayBeNullString);
```

Using Optionals

```java
// Checking if value is present
if (opt.isPresent()) {
    // Use the value
    String value = opt.get();
} else {
    // Handle empty case
}
```

```java
// The modern way (Java 11+)
if (opt.isEmpty()) {
    // Handle empty case
}

// Conditional actions
opt.ifPresent(value -> System.out.println("Value: " + value));

// Default values
String result = opt.orElse("Default");
String computed = opt.orElseGet(() -> computeDefault());
String exceptionIfMissing = opt.orElseThrow(() ->
    new NoSuchElementException("Value not present"));

// Transforming values
Optional<Integer> length = opt.map(String::length);

// Chaining
Optional<String> transformed = opt
    .filter(s -> s.length() > 3)
    .map(String::toUpperCase);
```

Regular Expressions

Pattern and Matcher

```java
// Compiling a pattern
Pattern pattern = Pattern.compile("a.*b");

// Using a matcher
Matcher matcher = pattern.matcher("axxxb");
boolean matches = matcher.matches();  // true (entire string matches pattern)

// Finding occurrences
Pattern wordPattern = Pattern.compile("\\w+");
Matcher wordMatcher = wordPattern.matcher("This is a test");
while (wordMatcher.find()) {
    System.out.println(wordMatcher.group());  // Prints each word
    System.out.println(wordMatcher.start());  // Start index
    System.out.println(wordMatcher.end());    // End index
}

// Replacing
String result = wordMatcher.replaceAll("WORD");

// Quick methods
boolean isMatch = Pattern.matches("a.*b", "axxxb");  // true
String replaced = "This is a test".replaceAll("\\s+", "_");  // "This_is_a_test"
String[] parts = "This is a test".split("\\s+");  // ["This", "is", "a", "test"]
```

Common Regex Patterns

```
String emailRegex = "^[a-zA-Z0-9_+&*-]+(?:\\.[a-zA-Z0-9_+&*-]+)*@(?:[a-zA-Z0-9-
]+\\.)+[a-zA-Z]{2,7}$";
String phoneRegex = "^\\d{3}-\\d{3}-\\d{4}$";   // 123-456-7890
String dateRegex  = "^(0[1-9]|1[0-2])/(0[1-9]|[12][0-9]|3[01])/\\d{4}$";     //
MM/DD/YYYY
String urlRegex = "^(https?|ftp)://[^\\s/$.?#].[^\\s]*$";
String ipRegex = "^((25[0-5]|2[0-4][0-9]|[01]?[0-9][0-9]?)\\.){3}(25[0-5]|2[0-
4][0-9]|[01]?[0-9][0-9]?)$";
```

Reflection API

Class Information

```java
// Getting Class object
Class<?> clazz1 = String.class;
Class<?> clazz2 = obj.getClass();
Class<?> clazz3 = Class.forName("java.lang.String");

// Class information
String name = clazz1.getName();              // "java.lang.String"
String simpleName = clazz1.getSimpleName();  // "String"
Package pkg = clazz1.getPackage();           // java.lang
Class<?> superclass = clazz1.getSuperclass();   // Object.class

boolean isInterface = clazz1.isInterface();
boolean isArray = clazz1.isArray();
boolean isPrimitive = clazz1.isPrimitive();
```

Members and Metadata

```java
// Fields
Field[] allFields = clazz.getDeclaredFields();
Field[] publicFields = clazz.getFields();
Field field = clazz.getDeclaredField("fieldName");

// Making private field accessible
field.setAccessible(true);

// Getting/setting field values
Object value = field.get(obj);
field.set(obj, newValue);

// Methods
Method[] allMethods = clazz.getDeclaredMethods();
Method[] publicMethods = clazz.getMethods();
Method method = clazz.getDeclaredMethod("methodName", String.class, int.class);

// Invoking methods
method.setAccessible(true);
Object result = method.invoke(obj, "param1", 42);

// Constructors
Constructor<?>[] constructors = clazz.getDeclaredConstructors();
```

```java
Constructor<?> constructor = clazz.getDeclaredConstructor(String.class);

// Creating new instance
constructor.setAccessible(true);
Object newInstance = constructor.newInstance("parameter");

// Annotations
Annotation[] annotations = clazz.getAnnotations();
MyAnnotation annotation = clazz.getAnnotation(MyAnnotation.class);
boolean hasAnnotation = clazz.isAnnotationPresent(MyAnnotation.class);
```

Dynamic Instance Creation

```java
// Creating new instance
Object obj = clazz.newInstance();  // Deprecated in Java 9+

// Modern approach (Java 9+)
Object obj = clazz.getDeclaredConstructor().newInstance();

// With specific constructor
Constructor<?>   constructor   =   clazz.getDeclaredConstructor(String.class,
int.class);
Object obj = constructor.newInstance("Name", 42);
```

Networking

URL and HttpURLConnection

```java
// Working with URLs
URL url = new URL("https://www.example.com/page?param=value");
String protocol = url.getProtocol();  // "https"
String host = url.getHost();          // "www.example.com"
String path = url.getPath();          // "/page"
String query = url.getQuery();        // "param=value"

// HTTP connection (old way)
HttpURLConnection connection = (HttpURLConnection) url.openConnection();
connection.setRequestMethod("GET");
connection.setConnectTimeout(5000);
connection.setReadTimeout(5000);

int responseCode = connection.getResponseCode();
String responseMessage = connection.getResponseMessage();

// Reading response
try (BufferedReader reader = new BufferedReader(
        new InputStreamReader(connection.getInputStream()))) {
    String line;
    StringBuilder response = new StringBuilder();
    while ((line = reader.readLine()) != null) {
        response.append(line);
    }
    String content = response.toString();
```

```java
}

// POST request
HttpURLConnection connection = (HttpURLConnection) url.openConnection();
connection.setRequestMethod("POST");
connection.setDoOutput(true);
connection.setRequestProperty("Content-Type", "application/json");

String jsonPayload = "{\"name\":\"John\",\"age\":30}";
try (OutputStream os = connection.getOutputStream()) {
    os.write(jsonPayload.getBytes(StandardCharsets.UTF_8));
}

// Get response...
```

HttpClient (Java 11+)

```java
// Creating HttpClient
HttpClient client = HttpClient.newHttpClient();
// With custom settings
HttpClient customClient = HttpClient.newBuilder()
    .connectTimeout(Duration.ofSeconds(10))
    .followRedirects(HttpClient.Redirect.NORMAL)
    .build();

// GET request
HttpRequest request = HttpRequest.newBuilder()
    .uri(URI.create("https://www.example.com"))
    .GET()  // default
    .build();

// Sending synchronously
HttpResponse<String> response = client.send(request,
HttpResponse.BodyHandlers.ofString());
int statusCode = response.statusCode();
String body = response.body();

// Sending asynchronously
CompletableFuture<HttpResponse<String>> futureResponse =
    client.sendAsync(request, HttpResponse.BodyHandlers.ofString());

futureResponse.thenApply(HttpResponse::body)
            .thenAccept(System.out::println);

// POST request
HttpRequest postRequest = HttpRequest.newBuilder()
    .uri(URI.create("https://www.example.com/api"))
    .header("Content-Type", "application/json")

.POST(HttpRequest.BodyPublishers.ofString("{\"name\":\"John\",\"age\":30}"))
    .build();
```

```java
    // Different response body handlers
    HttpResponse<String> stringResponse =
        client.send(request, HttpResponse.BodyHandlers.ofString());
    HttpResponse<byte[]> bytesResponse =
        client.send(request, HttpResponse.BodyHandlers.ofByteArray());
    HttpResponse<Path> fileResponse =
        client.send(request,
HttpResponse.BodyHandlers.ofFile(Paths.get("response.txt")));
```

Sockets

```java
    // Server socket
    try (ServerSocket serverSocket = new ServerSocket(8080)) {
        System.out.println("Server listening on port 8080");

        while (true) {
            Socket clientSocket = serverSocket.accept();
            System.out.println("Client              connected:              " +
clientSocket.getInetAddress());

            // Handle client in new thread
            new Thread(() -> {
                try (
                    PrintWriter              out              =              new
PrintWriter(clientSocket.getOutputStream(), true);
                    BufferedReader in = new BufferedReader(
                        new InputStreamReader(clientSocket.getInputStream()))
                ) {
                    String inputLine;
                    while ((inputLine = in.readLine()) != null) {
                        System.out.println("Received: " + inputLine);
                        out.println("Echo: " + inputLine);
                    }
                } catch (IOException e) {
                    e.printStackTrace();
                }
            }).start();
        }
    }


    // Client socket
    try (
        Socket socket = new Socket("localhost", 8080);
        PrintWriter out = new PrintWriter(socket.getOutputStream(), true);
        BufferedReader in = new BufferedReader(
            new InputStreamReader(socket.getInputStream()));
        BufferedReader stdIn = new BufferedReader(
            new InputStreamReader(System.in))
    ) {
        String userInput;
        while ((userInput = stdIn.readLine()) != null) {
            out.println(userInput);
```

```
            System.out.println("Server response: " + in.readLine());
        }
    }
```

Annotations

Built-in Annotations

```java
// For classes, methods, or fields
@Deprecated  // Indicates element is deprecated
@SuppressWarnings("unchecked")  // Suppresses compiler warnings
@Override  // Indicates method overrides a superclass method
@FunctionalInterface  // Indicates interface is functional (one abstract method)

// For other annotations
@Retention(RetentionPolicy.RUNTIME)  // How long annotation should be retained
@Target(ElementType.METHOD)  // Where annotation can be applied
@Documented  // Include in Javadoc
@Inherited  // Subclasses inherit the annotation
@Repeatable  // Annotation can be applied multiple times to same element
```

Creating Custom Annotations

```java
// Simple marker annotation
public @interface Marker {
}

// Annotation with elements
@Retention(RetentionPolicy.RUNTIME)
@Target({ElementType.METHOD, ElementType.TYPE})
public @interface Author {
    String name();
    String date() default "Unknown";
    int revision() default 1;
}

// Using the annotation
@Author(name = "John Doe", date = "2023-04-15")
public class MyClass {
    @Author(name = "Jane Smith")
    public void myMethod() {
        // Code
    }
}

// Repeatable annotation
@Repeatable(Authors.class)
public @interface Author {
    String name();
}

public @interface Authors {
    Author[] value();
```

```java
}

// Using repeatable annotation
@Author(name = "John")
@Author(name = "Jane")
public class MyClass {
}
```

Processing Annotations

```java
// Check for annotation presence
boolean hasAnnotation = MyClass.class.isAnnotationPresent(Author.class);

// Get annotation
Author author = MyClass.class.getAnnotation(Author.class);
String name = author.name();
String date = author.date();

// Get all annotations
Annotation[] annotations = MyClass.class.getAnnotations();

// Get repeatable annotations
Author[] authors = MyClass.class.getAnnotationsByType(Author.class);

// Method annotations
Method method = MyClass.class.getMethod("myMethod");
Author methodAuthor = method.getAnnotation(Author.class);
```

Java 9+ Features

Module System (Java 9)

```java
// module-info.java
module com.myapp {
    requires java.sql;              // Dependency on another module
    requires transitive java.net;   // Dependency that's re-exported

    exports com.myapp.api;          // Exports package
    exports com.myapp.util to com.otherapp;  // Exports to specific module

    opens com.myapp.model;          // Open for reflection
    opens com.myapp.dto to java.json;  // Open to specific module

    provides com.myapp.spi.Service with com.myapp.impl.ServiceImpl;   // Service provider
    uses com.myapp.spi.Plugin;      // Service consumer
}
```

Records (Java 14 preview, 16 standard)

```java
// Compact class for data carriers
public record Person(String name, int age) {
    // Canonical constructor is generated automatically
```

264

```java
    // Compact constructor for validation
    public Person {
        if (age < 0) {
            throw new IllegalArgumentException("Age cannot be negative");
        }
    }

    // Additional constructor
    public Person(String name) {
        this(name, 0);
    }

    // Additional methods
    public boolean isAdult() {
        return age >= 18;
    }
}

// Using records
Person person = new Person("John", 30);
String name = person.name();   // Accessor
int age = person.age();        // Accessor
```

Pattern Matching (Java 14+ preview features)

```java
// Pattern matching for instanceof (Java 16+)
if (obj instanceof String s) {
    // Can use s directly here
    System.out.println(s.length());
}

// Switch expressions (Java 14+)
int value = switch (day) {
    case MONDAY, FRIDAY, SUNDAY -> 6;
    case TUESDAY -> 7;
    case THURSDAY, SATURDAY -> 8;
    case WEDNESDAY -> 9;
    default -> throw new IllegalStateException("Invalid day: " + day);
};

// Switch with pattern matching (Java 17 preview)
Object obj = "Hello";
String result = switch (obj) {
    case Integer i -> "Integer: " + i;
    case String s -> "String: " + s;
    case null -> "null";
    default -> "Unknown";
};
```

Text Blocks (Java 15)

```java
// Multi-line strings with preserved formatting
```
265

```java
String json = """
    {
        "name": "John Doe",
        "age": 30,
        "address": {
            "street": "123 Main St",
            "city": "Anytown"
        }
    }
    """;

// Avoiding line breaks at the end
String sql = """
    SELECT id, name, email \
    FROM users \
    WHERE active = true \
    ORDER BY name""";

// String formatting in text blocks
String name = "John";
String formatted = """
    Hello, %s!
    Welcome to our application.
    """.formatted(name);
```

Sealed Classes (Java 17)

```java
// Define a sealed class or interface
public sealed class Shape permits Circle, Rectangle, Square {
    // Common shape methods
}

// Permitted subclasses must use one of: final, sealed, or non-sealed
public final class Circle extends Shape {
    private final double radius;

    // Implementation
}

public final class Rectangle extends Shape {
    private final double width;
    private final double height;

    // Implementation
}

// Extend the sealed hierarchy
public sealed class Square extends Shape permits ColoredSquare {
    private final double side;

    // Implementation
}
```

```java
public final class ColoredSquare extends Square {
    private final String color;

    // Implementation
}

// Using non-sealed to allow any class to extend
public non-sealed class GenericShape extends Shape {
    // Implementation
}
```

Helpful NullPointerExceptions (Java 14)

```java
// Before Java 14
// person.getAddress().getCity() -> NullPointerException
// But which one was null? person? address?

// In Java 14+
// Exception message will point to exact null reference:
//   "Cannot invoke "Address.getCity()" because the return value of
"Person.getAddress()" is null"
```

Enhanced Switch (Java 14)

```java
// Switch expressions (returning a value)
int numLetters = switch (day) {
    case MONDAY, FRIDAY, SUNDAY -> 6;
    case TUESDAY -> 7;
    case THURSDAY, SATURDAY -> 8;
    case WEDNESDAY -> 9;
};

// With code blocks and yield
int result = switch (day) {
    case MONDAY, TUESDAY -> {
        System.out.println("It's the start of the week");
        yield 1;
    }
    case WEDNESDAY -> {
        System.out.println("It's the middle of the week");
        yield 2;
    }
    default -> {
        System.out.println("It's the end of the week");
        yield 3;
    }
};
```

Stream API Enhancements (Java 9+)

```java
// takeWhile and dropWhile (Java 9)
List<Integer> numbers = List.of(1, 2, 3, 4, 5, 2, 1);
```

```java
List<Integer> taken = numbers.stream()
    .takeWhile(n -> n < 4)   // [1, 2, 3]
    .collect(Collectors.toList());

List<Integer> dropped = numbers.stream()
    .dropWhile(n -> n < 4)   // [4, 5, 2, 1]
    .collect(Collectors.toList());

// ofNullable (Java 9)
Stream<String> stream = Stream.ofNullable(possiblyNullString);

// iterate with predicate (Java 9)
Stream<Integer> stream = Stream.iterate(1, n -> n < 100, n -> n * 2);
// [1, 2, 4, 8, 16, 32, 64]

// Collectors.teeing (Java 12)
double mean = Stream.of(1, 2, 3, 4, 5)
    .collect(Collectors.teeing(
        Collectors.summingDouble(i -> i),
        Collectors.counting(),
        (sum, count) -> sum / count));
```

File API Enhancements (Java 11+)

```java
// Reading a file to string (Java 11)
String content = Files.readString(Path.of("file.txt"));

// Writing string to file (Java 11)
Files.writeString(Path.of("output.txt"), "Hello, World!");

// Reading/writing with charset
String content = Files.readString(Path.of("file.txt"), StandardCharsets.UTF_8);
Files.writeString(Path.of("output.txt"),              "Hello,              World!",
StandardCharsets.UTF_8);

// File mismatch (Java 12)
long mismatchIndex = Files.mismatch(Path.of("file1.txt"), Path.of("file2.txt"));
// Returns -1 if files are identical, otherwise index of first mismatch
```

String API Enhancements (Java 11+)

```java
// isBlank (Java 11)
boolean empty = "   ".isBlank();  // true

// lines (Java 11)
Stream<String> lines = "line1\nline2\nline3".lines();

// strip, stripLeading, stripTrailing (Java 11)
String stripped = " hello ".strip();              // "hello"
String leadingStripped = " hello ".stripLeading();   // "hello "
String trailingStripped = " hello ".stripTrailing(); // " hello"

// repeat (Java 11)
```

```
String repeated = "abc".repeat(3);   // "abcabcabc"

// transform (Java 12)
String transformed = "hello".transform(s -> s + " world");

// formatted (Java 15)
String message = "Hello %s!".formatted("World");

// indent (Java 12)
String indented = "Hello\nWorld".indent(4);
// "    Hello\n    World\n"
```

Collections Factory Methods (Java 9)

```
// Immutable collections
List<String> list = List.of("a", "b", "c");
Set<Integer> set = Set.of(1, 2, 3);
Map<String, Integer> map = Map.of("a", 1, "b", 2, "c", 3);

// For more entries
Map<String, Integer> largeMap = Map.ofEntries(
    Map.entry("a", 1),
    Map.entry("b", 2),
    Map.entry("c", 3),
    Map.entry("d", 4)
);

// Characteristics:
// - Immutable (can't add/remove/change elements)
// - No null elements allowed
// - Implementation may be specialized for size
```

Optional Enhancements (Java 9+)

```
// or method (Java 9)
Optional<String> result = optional.or(() -> Optional.of("default"));

// ifPresentOrElse (Java 9)
optional.ifPresentOrElse(
    value -> System.out.println("Found: " + value),
    () -> System.out.println("Not found")
);

// stream (Java 9)
Stream<String> stream = optional.stream();  // Empty stream if optional is empty

// isEmpty (Java 11)
boolean isEmpty = optional.isEmpty();  // Opposite of isPresent()
```

Process API Enhancements (Java 9)

```
// Get current process
ProcessHandle current = ProcessHandle.current();
```

```java
        long pid = current.pid();

        // Information about process
        ProcessHandle.Info info = current.info();
        Optional<String> command = info.command();
        Optional<String[]> arguments = info.arguments();
        Optional<Instant> startTime = info.startInstant();
        Optional<Duration> cpuTime = info.totalCpuDuration();

        // List all processes
        ProcessHandle.allProcesses()
            .filter(process -> process.info().command().isPresent())
            .forEach(process -> {
                System.out.println("PID: " + process.pid() +
                                    ", Command: " + process.info().command().orElse(""));
            });

        // Wait for process completion
        boolean terminated = process.onExit().thenAccept(p -> {
            System.out.println("Process " + p.pid() + " terminated");
        }).isDone();

        // Destroy process
        process.destroy();              // Normal termination
        process.destroyForcibly();      // Force termination
```

HTTP Client (Standard in Java 11)

```java
        // Modern API for HTTP requests (shown previously)
        // See HttpClient examples in the Networking section above
```

Var Keyword (Java 10)

```java
        // Local variable type inference
        var name = "John";             // inferred as String
        var age = 30;                  // inferred as int
        var list = new ArrayList<String>();  // inferred as ArrayList<String>

        // In for loops
        for (var i = 0; i < 10; i++) {
            // i is inferred as int
        }

        for (var item : list) {
            // item is inferred as String
        }

        // Limitations:
        // - Only for local variables, not fields, method parameters, or return types
        // - Must be initialized
        // - Cannot be initialized with null
        // - Cannot be used with multiple variable declarations
        // - Not recommended for too complex right-hand-side expressions
```

Try-With-Resources Enhancements (Java 9)

```java
// Before Java 9
InputStream is = new FileInputStream("file.txt");
try (InputStream is2 = is) {
    // Use is2
}

// Java 9+ with effectively final variables
InputStream is = new FileInputStream("file.txt");
try (is) {   // No new variable needed
    // Use is directly
}
```

Private Interface Methods (Java 9)

```java
public interface MyInterface {
    // Public abstract method
    void abstractMethod();

    // Default method
    default void defaultMethod() {
        commonCode();
        System.out.println("Default implementation");
    }

    // Static method
    static void staticMethod() {
        commonStaticCode();
        System.out.println("Static implementation");
    }

    // Private method - can be used by default methods
    private void commonCode() {
        System.out.println("Common code");
    }

    // Private static method - can be used by both static and default methods
    private static void commonStaticCode() {
        System.out.println("Common static code");
    }
}
```

Reactive Streams (Java 9)

```java
// Core interfaces
// Publisher<T> - produces items consumed by Subscribers
// Subscriber<T> - consumes items from a Publisher
// Subscription - represents a subscription between Publisher and Subscriber
// Processor<T,R> - represents a processing stage, both Subscriber and Publisher

// Example implementation using Flow API
public class SimplePublisher implements Flow.Publisher<Integer> {
```

```java
    private final List<Integer> data = Arrays.asList(1, 2, 3, 4, 5);

    @Override
    public void subscribe(Flow.Subscriber<? super Integer> subscriber) {
        subscriber.onSubscribe(new Flow.Subscription() {
            private int index = 0;
            private boolean cancelled = false;

            @Override
            public void request(long n) {
                for (int i = 0; i < n && index < data.size() && !cancelled; i++)
{
                    subscriber.onNext(data.get(index++));
                }

                if (!cancelled && index >= data.size()) {
                    subscriber.onComplete();
                }
            }

            @Override
            public void cancel() {
                cancelled = true;
            }
        });
    }
}

// Example subscriber
public class SimpleSubscriber implements Flow.Subscriber<Integer> {
    private Flow.Subscription subscription;

    @Override
    public void onSubscribe(Flow.Subscription subscription) {
        this.subscription = subscription;
        subscription.request(1);   // Request one item
    }

    @Override
    public void onNext(Integer item) {
        System.out.println("Received: " + item);
        subscription.request(1);   // Request next item
    }

    @Override
    public void onError(Throwable throwable) {
        throwable.printStackTrace();
    }

    @Override
    public void onComplete() {
        System.out.println("Completed");
```

```java
    }
}

// Using the publisher and subscriber
SimplePublisher publisher = new SimplePublisher();
publisher.subscribe(new SimpleSubscriber());
```

Foreign Function & Memory API (Java 21)

```java
// Example using Foreign Function & Memory API to call C functions
// Note: This is Preview API in Java 21

// Import required packages
import java.lang.foreign.*;
import java.lang.invoke.MethodHandle;

// Access C's strlen function
void callStrlen() throws Throwable {
    // Get the linker for the current platform
    Linker linker = Linker.nativeLinker();

    // Get a handle to the C standard library
    SymbolLookup stdlib = linker.defaultLookup();

    // Look up the "strlen" function
    MethodHandle strlen = linker.downcallHandle(
        stdlib.find("strlen").orElseThrow(),
        FunctionDescriptor.of(ValueLayout.JAVA_LONG, ValueLayout.ADDRESS)
    );

    // Allocate memory for a string
    try (Arena arena = Arena.ofConfined()) {
        MemorySegment cString = arena.allocateUtf8String("Hello, World!");

        // Call the function
        long length = (long) strlen.invoke(cString);
        System.out.println("Length: " + length);  // Prints 13
    }
}
```

Vector API (Java 21)

```java
// Example using Vector API for SIMD operations
// Note: This is Preview API in Java 21

import jdk.incubator.vector.*;

void vectorExample() {
    // Define vector species
    VectorSpecies<Float> species = FloatVector.SPECIES_256;  // 256-bit vectors

    // Create input arrays
    float[] a = new float[1024];
```

273

```java
    float[] b = new float[1024];
    float[] c = new float[1024];

    // Fill arrays with data
    for (int i = 0; i < a.length; i++) {
        a[i] = i;
        b[i] = i * 2;
    }

    // Process vectors in chunks
    int i = 0;
    int upperBound = species.loopBound(a.length);

    for (; i < upperBound; i += species.length()) {
        // Load vectors
        FloatVector va = FloatVector.fromArray(species, a, i);
        FloatVector vb = FloatVector.fromArray(species, b, i);

        // Perform operation (a + b)
        FloatVector vc = va.add(vb);

        // Store result
        vc.intoArray(c, i);
    }

    // Handle remaining elements (tail)
    for (; i < a.length; i++) {
        c[i] = a[i] + b[i];
    }
}
```

Enhanced Pseudo-Random Number Generators (Java 17+)

```java
// New random number generators (Java 17+)
import java.util.random.RandomGenerator;
import java.util.random.RandomGeneratorFactory;

// Get default generator
RandomGenerator rng = RandomGenerator.getDefault();
int value = rng.nextInt(100);  // 0-99

// Choose specific algorithm
RandomGenerator xoroshiro = RandomGeneratorFactory.of("Xoroshiro128PlusPlus")
                                .create(42);  // With seed 42

// List available algorithms
RandomGeneratorFactory.all()
    .map(factory -> factory.name())
    .sorted()
    .forEach(System.out::println);
```

Pattern Matching for Switch (Java 21)

```java
// Advanced pattern matching in switch statements
Object obj = "Hello";

String formatted = switch (obj) {
    case null -> "It's null";
    case String s -> "String: " + s;
    case Integer i -> "Integer: " + i;
    case Long l -> "Long: " + l;
    case Number n -> "Number: " + n;
    case int[] ia -> "Int array of length " + ia.length;
    default -> "Something else: " + obj.getClass().getName();
};


// Pattern matching with guards
record Point(int x, int y) {}

String quadrant = switch (new Point(10, -5)) {
    case Point(var x, var y) when x > 0 && y > 0 -> "First quadrant";
    case Point(var x, var y) when x < 0 && y > 0 -> "Second quadrant";
    case Point(var x, var y) when x < 0 && y < 0 -> "Third quadrant";
    case Point(var x, var y) when x > 0 && y < 0 -> "Fourth quadrant";
    case Point(var x, var y) when x == 0 || y == 0 -> "On an axis";
};
```

Virtual Threads (Java 21)

```java
// Creating and starting a virtual thread
Thread vThread = Thread.startVirtualThread(() -> {
    System.out.println("Running in a virtual thread");
});

// Join the virtual thread
vThread.join();

// Using the builder
Thread vt = Thread.ofVirtual()
                .name("worker-1")
                .start(() -> {
                    System.out.println("Named virtual thread");
                });

// With ExecutorService
try (var executor = Executors.newVirtualThreadPerTaskExecutor()) {
    IntStream.range(0, 10_000).forEach(i -> {
        executor.submit(() -> {
            // Task code
            Thread.sleep(Duration.ofMillis(100));
            return i;
        });
    });
}  // Auto-close executor
```

```
// Characteristics:
// - Lightweight (thousands or millions of virtual threads)
// - Mounted on carrier threads (platform threads)
// - Transparent for blocking operations
// - Not bound to a particular OS thread
```

Structured Concurrency (Java 21)

```java
// Note: Preview API in Java 21
import jdk.incubator.concurrent.*;

// Using structured concurrency with a scope
try (var scope = StructuredTaskScope.ShutdownOnFailure()) {
    // Fork tasks
    Subtask<String> user = scope.fork(() -> fetchUser(userId));
    Subtask<List<Order>> orders = scope.fork(() -> fetchOrders(userId));

    // Wait for all tasks and handle exceptions
    scope.join();            // Wait for both tasks to complete
    scope.throwIfFailed();   // Propagate exceptions

    // Process results
    return new UserOrders(user.get(), orders.get());
}

// Using StructuredTaskScope.shutdownOnSuccess()
try (var scope = StructuredTaskScope.shutdownOnSuccess()) {
    // Fork multiple tasks that provide the same result
    scope.fork(() -> fetchFromPrimarySource());
    scope.fork(() -> fetchFromSecondarySource());
    scope.fork(() -> fetchFromTertiarySource());

    // Get first successful result
    return scope.join().result();
}
```

Time API Enhancements (Java 16+)

```java
// DateTimeFormatter with 'B' pattern (Java 16)
// For dayPeriod: "in the morning", "in the afternoon", etc.
DateTimeFormatter formatter = DateTimeFormatter.ofPattern("h B");
String period = formatter.format(LocalTime.of(10, 0));   // "10 in the morning"

// DateTimeFormatter with localized day periods
DateTimeFormatter jaFormatter = DateTimeFormatter
    .ofPattern("h B")
    .withLocale(Locale.JAPANESE);
String jaPeriod = jaFormatter.format(LocalTime.of(13, 0));
```

StringTemplate (Java 21)

```java
// Note: Preview API in Java 21
import static java.lang.StringTemplate.STR;
```

```java
// Basic string template
String name = "World";
String message = STR."Hello \{name}!";   // "Hello World!"

// Templates with expressions
int x = 10;
int y = 20;
String result = STR."\{x} + \{y} = \{x + y}";   // "10 + 20 = 30"

// Multiline templates
String html = STR."""
    <html>
        <body>
            <h1>Hello, \{name}!</h1>
            <p>The sum of \{x} and \{y} is \{x + y}.</p>
        </body>
    </html>
    """;
```

Collection Enhancements (Java 10+)

```java
// Collectors.toUnmodifiableList/Set/Map (Java 10)
List<String> immutableList = stream.collect(Collectors.toUnmodifiableList());
Set<String> immutableSet = stream.collect(Collectors.toUnmodifiableSet());
Map<String, Integer> immutableMap = stream.collect(
    Collectors.toUnmodifiableMap(String::toLowerCase, String::length)
);

// List.copyOf, Set.copyOf, Map.copyOf (Java 10)
List<String> copy = List.copyOf(originalList);   // Unmodifiable copy
Set<String> setCopy = Set.copyOf(originalSet);
Map<String, Integer> mapCopy = Map.copyOf(originalMap);

// Collection.toArray(IntFunction) (Java 11)
String[] array = list.toArray(String[]::new);

// Methods to generate a sequence of ints (Java 21)
// Generate 0, 1, 2, 3, 4
List<Integer> list = IntStream.range(0, 5).boxed().toList();
// Generate 0, 2, 4, 6, 8
List<Integer> evenList = IntStream.iterate(0, i -> i < 10, i -> i +
2).boxed().toList();

// SequencedCollection interface (Java 21)
// Methods: getFirst(), getLast(), addFirst(), addLast(), reversed()
String first = sequencedList.getFirst();
String last = sequencedList.getLast();
sequencedList.addFirst("start");
sequencedList.addLast("end");
List<String> reversed = sequencedList.reversed();
```

277

Primitive Wrapper (Java 21)

```java
// Instance creation directly from primitive
Integer i = 42;  // Autoboxing

// Converting to primitive
int j = i;  // Auto-unboxing

// Value manipulations in parallel streams
int sum = IntStream.range(0, 1000)
                   .parallel()
                   .sum();

// Method references for conversion
List<Integer> boxedInts = IntStream.range(0, 100)
                                   .boxed()
                                   .collect(Collectors.toList());

// Unboxing
int[] primitives = boxedInts.stream()
                            .mapToInt(Integer::intValue)
                            .toArray();
```

JVM Improvements (Recent Java Versions)

ZGC (Z Garbage Collector)

```java
// Enable ZGC
-XX:+UseZGC

// Key features:
// - Low latency (pauses <10ms)
// - Scales from small to very large heaps
// - Concurrent processing
// - Compact heap without long pauses
```

Shenandoah GC

```java
// Enable Shenandoah GC
-XX:+UseShenandoahGC

// Key features:
// - Low pause times
// - Concurrent processing
// - Works well with different heap sizes
```

G1GC (Default since Java 9)

```java
// Explicitly enable G1GC
-XX:+UseG1GC

// Performance tuning
-XX:MaxGCPauseMillis=200  // Target pause time
```

```
-XX:G1HeapRegionSize=16m  // Region size
```

Miscellaneous Features

Unicode Support in Identifiers (Java 9+)

```java
// Identifiers with Unicode characters
int π = 3;
int résumé = 10;
String 你好 = "hello";
```

Enhanced for-loop (Java 10+)

```java
// Old style
List<String> list = Arrays.asList("a", "b", "c");
for (String s : list) {
    System.out.println(s);
}

// With var
for (var s : list) {
    System.out.println(s);
}
```

Improved instanceof pattern matching (Java 16+)

```java
// Old style
if (obj instanceof String) {
    String s = (String) obj;
    // Use s
}

// Pattern matching
if (obj instanceof String s) {
    // Use s directly
}

// Combined with conditionals
if (obj instanceof String s && s.length() > 5) {
    // Use s when condition is met
}
```

Record Patterns (Java 21)

```java
// Record declarations
record Point(int x, int y) {}
record Rectangle(Point topLeft, Point bottomRight) {}

// Pattern matching with records
Object obj = new Rectangle(new Point(1, 2), new Point(5, 6));

if (obj instanceof Rectangle(Point(int x1, int y1), Point(int x2, int y2))) {
    int width = x2 - x1;
    int height = y2 - y1;
```

```java
    System.out.println("Area: " + (width * height));
}

// In switch expressions
int area = switch (obj) {
    case Rectangle(Point(var x1, var y1), Point(var x2, var y2)) ->
        (x2 - x1) * (y2 - y1);
    default -> 0;
};
```

Unnamed Patterns and Variables (Java 21)

```java
// Unnamed patterns with underscore
Object obj = new Point(10, 20);

if (obj instanceof Point(int x, _)) {
    // Only care about x coordinate
    System.out.println("X coordinate: " + x);
}

// Unnamed variables in lambda expressions
list.forEach(_ -> System.out.println("Element"));
```

Secure Random Generation (Java 17+)

```java
// Get a secure random instance
SecureRandom secureRandom = SecureRandom.getInstanceStrong();

// Generate random bytes
byte[] bytes = new byte[20];
secureRandom.nextBytes(bytes);

// Generate random integers, longs, etc.
int randomInt = secureRandom.nextInt(100);   // 0-99
```

Deprecated and Removed Features

Removed in Java 9+

```java
// Removed APIs
- java.util.logging.LogManager.addPropertyChangeListener
- java.util.logging.LogManager.removePropertyChangeListener
- java.util.jar.Pack200
- java.util.jar.Pack200.Packer
- java.util.jar.Pack200.Unpacker
- com.sun.awt.AWTUtilities

// Deprecated for removal
- java.applet package
- java.corba module
- java.transaction module
- java.xml.bind module
- java.xml.ws module
```

```
- java.xml.ws.annotation module
```

Removed in Java 11+

```
// Removed
- JavaFX (now a separate module)
- Java EE modules (now Jakarta EE)
- CORBA modules
- JMC (Java Mission Control, now separate download)
```

Removed in Java 17+

```
// Removed
- Applet API
- Security Manager (disabled by default)
- Experimental AOT and JIT compiler
```

Removed in Java 21+

```
// Removed
- Nashorn JavaScript engine
- Several legacy RMI activation methods
```

Packaging and Distribution

jlink (Java 9+)

```
# Create custom runtime image
jlink --module-path $JAVA_HOME/jmods:myjars/ \
      --add-modules java.base,java.sql,myapp \
      --output myruntime

# Run the application
myruntime/bin/java -m myapp/com.example.Main
```

jpackage (Java 14+)

```
# Create installable package (Windows .exe, Linux .deb, macOS .dmg)
jpackage --name MyApp \
         --module-path mods:$JAVA_HOME/jmods \
         --module myapp/com.example.Main \
         --runtime-image myruntime \
         --icon myicon.ico
```

Mult -Release JAR Files (Java 9+)

```
# JAR structure
jar-root/
  - META-INF/
    - MANIFEST.MF (with Multi-Release: true)
  - com/
    - example/
      - Main.class
      - Util.class
  - META-INF/
```

```
- versions/
  - 9/
    - com/
      - example/
        - Util.class  # Java 9 version
  - 17/
    - com/
      - example/
        - Util.class  # Java 17 version
```

A Humble Request from Our Small Team

If you enjoyed this book and found it helpful, we'd be incredibly grateful if you could take a moment to leave a kind review on Amazon. As a small publishing company, your feedback means the world to us—it helps new readers discover our work and allows us to keep creating quality guides.

Thank you for your support! Happy coding!

Re-Wise Publishers